WILDCAT

Also by John Boessenecker

Badge and Buckshot: Lawlessness in Old California

The Grey Fox: The True Story of Bill Miner, Last of the Old-Time Bandits (with Mark Dugan)

Lawman: The Life and Times of Harry Morse, 1835–1912

Against the Vigilantes: The Recollections of Dutch Charley Duane

Gold Dust and Gunsmoke: Tales of Gold Rush Outlaws, Gunfighters, Lawmen, and Vigilantes

Bandido: The Life and Times of Tiburcio Vasquez

When Law Was in the Holster: The Frontier Life of Bob Paul

Texas Ranger: The Epic Life of Frank Hamer, the Man Who Killed Bonnie and Clyde

Shotguns and Stagecoaches: The Brave Men Who Rode for Wells Fargo in the Wild West

Ride the Devil's Herd: Wyatt Earp's Epic Battle Against the West's Biggest Outlaw Gang

AUTHOR'S COLLECTION.

Pearl Hart in the Tucson jailyard, 1899, carrying a Winchester Model 1873 rifle and a holstered Colt Single Action Army revolver. A Colt Model 1877 Lightning revolver is tucked into her gun belt.

WILDCAT

THE UNTOLD STORY OF PEARL HART, THE WILD WEST'S MOST NOTORIOUS WOMAN BANDIT

JOHN BOESSENECKER

HANOVER
SQUARE
PRESS

Recycling programs for this product may not exist in your area.

ISBN-13: 978-1-335-47139-0

Wildcat: The Untold Story of Pearl Hart, the Wild West's Most Notorious Woman Bandit

This edition published by arrangement with Harlequin Books S.A.

Hanover Square Press
22 Adelaide St. West, 40th Floor
Toronto, Ontario M5H 4E3, Canada
HanoverSqPress.com
BookClubbish.com

Printed in U.S.A.

For Marta

"I shall never submit to be tried under the law that neither I nor my sex had a voice in making."

—Pearl Hart

Table of Contents

Introduction

Pearl Hart stroked her pet wildcat as she leaned back on the bunk in her cell in the courthouse in Tucson, Arizona Territory. It was 1899, and she was the most infamous woman in America. Pearl and her male companion had held up a stagecoach, disarmed the driver and passengers, and stolen their money and guns. They escaped on horseback, but were captured after a long manhunt in the remote high desert. Her story made newspaper headlines, for in an era when a woman's role was primarily domestic, Americans were simultaneously shocked and thrilled by the concept of a real woman bandit.

Journalists and cameramen flocked to the jail, seeking interviews and photographs. They found her a walking contradiction: a petite, attractive young woman who could alternately act like a street ruffian or a feminine ingenue. She dressed in rough cowboys' clothing and carried a pair of six-guns. Pearl Hart talked tough, smoked cigarettes, drank liquor, used morphine, and had sex with countless men. At the same time, they saw that she was extremely bright, well-spoken, and a voracious reader. She could knit, sew, and write poetry, yet also shoot straight with a heavy Colt's revolver. Americans had never seen or heard of anyone like her.

The public interest in Pearl Hart grew so intense that *Cosmopolitan* magazine sent two correspondents to seek an in-depth interview. Even in 1899, *Cosmopolitan* was the country's most popular women's publication. The journalists met a friendly, talkative woman in her late twenties, with her long brown hair tied up in a bun. She wore a man's dark-colored shirt, open at the neck, and trousers held up by suspenders. Pearl loved publicity, and despite the fact that she had been charged with stagecoach robbery and faced a long prison term, she had no qualms about telling her story.

"When I was but sixteen years old, and while still at boarding school, I fell in love with a man I met in the town in which the school was situated. I was easily impressed. I knew nothing of life. Marriage was to me but a name. It did not take him long to get my consent to an elopement. We ran away one night and were married. I was happy for a time, but not for long. My husband began to abuse me, and presently he drove me from him. Then I returned to my mother, in the village of Lindsay, Ontario, where I was born.

"Before long, my husband sent for me, and I went back to him. I loved him, and he promised to do better. I had not been with him two weeks before he began to abuse me again, and after bearing up under his blows as long as I could, I left him again. This was just as the World's Fair closed in Chicago, in the fall of 1893. Instead of going home to my mother again, as I should have done, I took the train for Trinidad, Colorado. I was only twenty-two years old. I was good-looking, desperate, discouraged, and ready for anything that might come."

Pearl continued on in detail, describing her adventures and misadventures on the Arizona frontier. The two correspondents, scribbling furiously, wrote it all down, oblivious to the fact that they were helping create one of the most enduring legends of the American frontier. For although Pearl Hart was the West's most notorious woman bandit, her true story has long been lost in the mists of the past. Her personal history is thoroughly obscured by legends, many of them created by Pearl herself. For the next century, newspaper reporters, magazine writers, and historians repeated, and even invented, countless wild tales about her: she was the West's first woman stage robber; she was the West's last stage robber; she was the daughter of a wealthy Canadian family; she was a virtuous schoolgirl in Phoenix; she performed with Buffalo Bill Cody's Wild West Show. Even her identity has been the subject of controversy: her real name was Mrs. Frank Hart, Pearl Bandman, Caroline Hartwell, Pearl Taylor, Mrs. E. P. Keele, Mrs. Earl Lighthawk, and Pearl Bywater. She was born in Canada, Ohio, and Kansas. Her husband was Brett Hart, Frederick Hart, Frank Hart, William Hart, James Taylor, Dick Baldwin, Harry Boardeman, Joe Boot, and Calvin Bywater.

But most of that is not true. The tales she spun in the Tucson jail have confounded authors, researchers, and historians for the last 120 years. Although Pearl Hart has been featured in hundreds of magazine articles and books, not one of them comes close to an accurate depiction of her life. But now, modern digital newspaper archives and genealogical data banks have provided the key to unraveling the mysteries of Pearl Hart's career. Her authentic story is alternately romantic, exciting, and disturbing. For the truth is far more fascinating—and instructive—than the myths spread by popular writers, casual researchers, and deliberate fictioneers.

Pearl Hart was a woman far ahead of her time. She was self-reliant, adventurous, unconstrained by convention, and sexually liberated. Those attributes were extremely rare for a woman in the nineteenth century. Then, few women worked outside the home. They dressed modestly, raised children, cooked, cleaned, and managed the household. In rural America, they helped tend the family farm and often labored next to their fathers or husbands in the fields. In urban areas, there were more opportunities for employment for women: as domestic workers in middle- and upper-class homes, as seamstresses in dress shops, and as mill girls in factories and textile mills. And despite such work obligations, women were still expected to marry, bear children, and be the bedrock for moral, religious, and familial stability.

In the American West, most pioneer women and girls came to the frontier with their fathers, brothers, and husbands. Yet in frontier boomtowns, the first female arrivals were often prostitutes. As the lyrics of a popular song of the 1849 California Gold Rush proclaimed:

> The miners came in forty-nine,
> The whores in fifty-one;
> And when they got together.
> They produced the native son.[1]

In that era, there were no welfare subsidies, no unemployment benefits, and no job security. For poor, uneducated, and unskilled women, prostitution often provided the only means of survival. Because of the huge gender imbalance on the frontier, prostitutes in the West were not held in the same disrepute as those in the East. Yet the life of a so-called fallen woman was brutal and debilitating. Many died of alcoholism, drug abuse, and violence. But many more left the profession, married, and led stable and respectable lives thereafter. Among the most notable examples are Josephine Marcus Earp and Allie Sullivan Earp, the wives, respectively, of Wyatt Earp and his brother Virgil. Both lived to old age, dying in the 1940s after leaving memoirs of their famous husbands. Modern research has revealed that both Josephine and Allie had been frontier prostitutes in the 1870s, and their husbands were fully aware of their pasts.[2]

Myths about women in the Old West abound, and Hollywood has been the leader in creating them. Beginning in the 1920s and '30s, a staple in Western films has been the cowgirl: a woman who rode and dressed like a man, wore blue jeans, boots, and a cowboy hat, and often sported a six-shooter hung low from a cartridge belt. That was a screenwriter's fantasy, for cowgirls did not exist in the Old West. The term first appeared in the 1880s and was used to describe female performers in Wild West shows. In that era, women on horseback wore skirts and rode sidesaddle. For a woman to ride like a man astride a horse was considered sexually suggestive and highly improper. Prior to 1900, women almost never wore men's trousers. In fact, most communities had laws against cross-dressing, and women who ventured out in male attire were subject to arrest. Split skirts first became popular for female bicyclists during the bicycle craze of the 1890s. But split skirts for horsewomen were virtually unknown before 1900, and such attire continued to be scandalous until the 1920s. That is why the American public was shocked by widely published photographs of Pearl Hart, wearing men's clothing and armed to the teeth with a Winchester rifle and a brace of revolvers.

Most Western filmmakers have been almost clueless about how women looked, dressed, and acted in the real West. Since the 1920s, any Western movie can be immediately dated by the hairstyles of its actresses. In Westerns made in the 1920s, the women wear 1920s hairdos; in Westerns made in the 1970s, the actresses sport 1970s hairstyles, and so on. Unlike depictions in fiction and film, American women in the late nineteenth century did not exhibit long hair draping over their shoulders. A woman was expected to keep her hair up or wrapped in a bun, for it was considered immodest for a woman to display her flowing locks. Only her husband or her family were allowed to see her with hair to her shoulders, and then only when she was at home or preparing for bed. Thus originated the expression *let your hair down*, meaning to relax and be oneself. And in the real West, women—even prostitutes—wore demure Victorian clothing, without the cleavage so often seen on screen.

Contrary to Hollywood films, there was not a single female gunfighter in the history of the Wild West. That is not to say that women did not participate in gunplay. Nineteenth-century newspapers are filled with accounts of women—from common prostitutes to upper-class matrons—shooting each other as well as men. Love triangles and domestic disputes were the most common cause of such female violence. Television and movie Westerns also frequently show supposed saloon girls drinking, gambling, and rubbing shoulders with men in bars. Such depictions are wildly inaccurate. Women in a saloon or gambling hall generally worked in a brothel situated upstairs. Respectable women were not allowed in saloons. If a woman stepped into a saloon or a card parlor, she would be immediately branded a prostitute and could never again show her face in polite society.

The vast majority of women in the nineteenth century did not have sexual relations outside of marriage. They did not smoke, and they certainly did not use opium and morphine. They did not wear men's clothing, ride astraddle, or carry six-shooters. Pearl Hart broke all these taboos and then some. She swore, smoked, drank, robbed, rode hard, broke jail, and used men with abandon. The Old West never saw another woman like her.

In order to understand Pearl Hart, one must know where she came from, how she grew up, and how her childhood affected her adult life. Her early years were extraordinarily traumatic, not only for her but also for her brothers and sisters. That childhood abuse created an inseparable bond between Pearl and her siblings, one that would last their entire lives. Like so many abused and neglected children today, they came to believe that they could only trust in each other. To understand her, one must know her family. Therefore, this book explores not only her reckless adventures but also those of her siblings.

Now, in the pages that follow, the true and untold story of Pearl Hart appears for the first time.

1

The Grass Widow's Daughter

A gentle, early-morning breeze ruffled the summer skirts of Alice Timms as she traipsed along a forest trail behind her father. When they reached the Midland Railway tracks, he headed to his farmwork in the fields to the west. Fourteen-year-old Alice bid him goodbye, and then, with her burly pet dog trotting beside her, she followed the railroad line one mile to a secluded meadow in the woods. There her dog ambled off to explore the surrounding countryside. Amid the scent of balsam fir and the sound of whistling and clicking of gray jays, Alice happily picked wild berries. For a young schoolgirl in the North Woods of Canada in 1877, it was a perfect, idyllic morning.

Then violence shattered the pastoral tranquility. A drunken ruffian, clutching a large knife in his right fist, burst out of the forest and lunged at Alice. The desperado seized the girl, threw her to the ground, and began to rip off her clothes. Young Alice, though terrified, fought like a wildcat, screaming for her father's help. But he was so far away he could not hear her cries. The man rammed his knife blade against Alice's throat and threatened to kill her if she did not stop her shrieking and crying. But she continued to fight, despite being beaten and battered. Then, as the man tried to rape her, a scene worthy of a Hollywood thriller suddenly unfolded. Alice's dog appeared at a dead run, hackles raised and teeth gnashing. The loyal animal slammed into the ruffian, growling and biting viciously, and the bloodied, knife-wielding attacker tore himself loose and fled. Alice was badly bruised, but she and her pet raced to her father and to safety.[1]

Canadian police soon arrested the would-be rapist. He was Albert Davy, the father of Pearl Hart. Her real name was Lillie Naomi Davy, and she was the daughter of a monster. As Lillie often said, "My father is a worthless wretch." She wasn't exaggerating about the man who was the most significant influence of her youth. Albert Davy's life was one of alcoholism, violence, abuse, and neglect. Lillie's father was born in 1841 to a family of settlers in the remote North Woods in Ontario, about a hundred and twenty miles north of Toronto. The area was later populated and surveyed and became known as Snowdon Township in Haliburton County. But in the 1840s, it was so isolated that there were no schools, and Albert Davy grew up uneducated and illiterate. He worked as a laborer and fisherman on the region's many rivers and lakes, and there he became a violent, brutal alcoholic. In that era heavy drinking was customary: adult males drank an average of half a pint of liquor a day. And in the rural areas of North America, there was very little in the way of entertainment or organized sports. For many young males like Albert Davy, drinking and brawling filled that void.[2]

During the mid-1860s, Davy drifted fifty miles south to Lindsay, located on the Scugog River at the southern tip of Sturgeon Lake. It was the principal town in an area that later became known as Kawartha Lakes, a chain of interconnected lakes in South Central Ontario. Lindsay was a prosperous lumbering and farming community of four thousand served by the Port Hope,

Lindsay and Beaverton Railway. Because Lindsay was a commercial center, it provided many opportunities for employment for a young man who was long on muscle and short on brains. There Albert met Anna Duval, a sweet and caring young woman who had been born in Lindsay in 1846. Her French-Canadian father was a farmer and carpenter who had sired twelve children. During Anna's childhood the village had only about three hundred residents, with no schools and little opportunity for a child's education. Like Albert, Anna was entirely illiterate and could not even sign her own name. The pair soon became romantically involved.[3]

Given Albert Davy's reputation as a lazy, drunken lout, it is a wonder that Anna would even consider a married life with him. She may have thought that he was little different than many rowdy—but hardworking—young men from the North Woods. But marry him she did. They tied the knot in 1864 and made their home in Lindsay. There Anna gave birth to their first child, Saphronia, born in 1867. Albert was of a roving disposition, and they soon moved ninety miles east to Belleville, near Lake Ontario. Anna's mother lived nearby. The Davys' first son, William Benjamin, whom they called Willie, was born in Belleville in 1869. But Albert's heavy drinking and belligerent nature made it difficult for him to hold down a job, and he and Anna moved back to Lindsay. There, on April 19, 1871, their third child, Lillie Naomi—destined to become the Wild West's most notorious woman bandit—was born.[4]

The responsibility of supporting a wife and three children had no sobering effect on Albert Davy. On February 17, 1872, when Lillie was ten months old, her father got drunk and raised a disturbance in Lindsay. He quickly found himself in court. The judge found Davy guilty of drunk and disorderly conduct and sentenced him to twenty-one days in the town jail. A year later, on March 3, 1873, he did it again. The mayor of Lindsay had Davy arrested for disorderly conduct, and he was sentenced to twenty days at hard labor. The jailer noted that he was "married, illiterate, intemperate." Three months after Albert's release, on June 16, 1873, Anna gave birth to their fourth child, Catherine Amelia, whom they called Katy. She and Lillie would have a very close relationship throughout their childhood and adult years. In fact they were almost inseparable, and Katy would have a wild career, rivaled only by that of her older sister and best friend.[5]

Family life was not easy in rural Canada. Husbands generally toiled in the fields or worked as hired hands and provided additional food by hunting and fishing. Wives cared for the children and performed the household chores, including making and mending all clothing. Children were expected to chip in at an early age: gathering firewood, feeding livestock, spinning wool, churning butter, collecting eggs, and picking vegetables. From their mothers, girls learned skills such as housekeeping, doing laundry, cooking, sewing, knitting, gardening, raising chickens, and caring for their younger siblings. The work was from dawn to dusk, day in and day out. An 1870 Canadian law required that children attend school four months a year. Yet that was often impossible, for in poor families, labor and survival took precedence over education. The Davy children did receive some minimal schooling, but given that their father was often too inebriated to put food on the table, their young lives were filled with hunger and privation.

Albert Davy became an itinerant farm laborer, unable to get steady employment due to his drunken and quarrelsome behavior. He took his family fifty miles north to his home township of Snowdon, where he and Anna had another daughter, Amy Nancy, in 1875. But they soon returned to Lindsay and moved into a ramshackle house on Water Street, next to the Scugog River that flowed through town. No doubt Albert Davy picked this location so he could partake in his two favorite pastimes: fishing and drinking. There, Anna gave birth to a sixth child, Henry Esau, in 1877. By this time an even darker side to Albert's character had begun to emerge, and he became well-known to the Lindsay police. As the town newspaper reported, "He is a bad character, having been in jail several times on serious charges."[6]

At dawn on August 1 of that year, when Lillie was six, Albert Davy attacked and attempted to rape young Alice Timms near the Midland Railway tracks west of Lindsay. Alice and her father immediately reported the assault to the Lindsay police, who soon identified Davy as the culprit and lodged him in jail. A month later, on September 14, 1877, the case came up for trial. Albert, hoping for leniency, agreed to be tried by a judge rather than a jury. After Alice Timms took the witness stand and bravely told her story, the judge promptly found Davy guilty. In Canada, a common punishment for this crime was imprisonment and flogging. The judge sentenced Lillie's father to a year in prison plus twelve lashes. By modern standards his prison term—for an attempted rape at knifepoint—was extraordinarily lenient.[7]

Albert Davy was taken to the Toronto Central Prison. Pursuant to Canadian law and the judge's order, he was "to be whipped once within the walls of the prison under the supervision of the medical officer of the prison, twelve strokes to be given with the cat-o'-nine tails." The cats, as they were commonly known, were made from nine pieces of rope with three knots on each length. The name derived both from the resemblance of its scars to the scratches of a cat and the myth that a cat had nine lives. Davy was stripped to the waist and strapped to the triangle, a wooden cross that spread the legs and arms outwards. As a doctor stood by, a prison officer delivered the twelve lashes "well laid on." An eyewitness to one such prison flogging recalled, "The cats were laid on the bare back; it made the whole back raw; brought blood at almost every stroke."[8]

Davy took his punishment and served out his one-year prison term. He then returned to his wife and family, unrepentant and meaner than ever. Since he was now a pariah in Lindsay, Davy moved Anna and the children back to Belleville. There they lived in poverty, and Anna gave birth to their seventh child, Anora Jane, whom they called Jennie, in 1880. Meanwhile their oldest son, Willie, had been incorrigible from an early age. Because the family often did not have enough to eat, he became a sneak thief. One day in the spring of that year, eleven-year-old Willie spotted a turkey hanging in the front door of a tannery. He quickly snatched it, then walked around to the back door of the tannery and sold it back to the unsuspecting owner. Willie's sister Lillie and the rest of their siblings, hungry and impoverished, soon followed his example. Despite the fact that they became petty thieves, the Davy children were bright and intelligent. They were also imaginative and creative—all of them loved music, poetry, and reading, something that would become particularly evident in adulthood.[9]

A year later, after Willie was again arrested for theft, the Davy family pulled up roots once more and in May 1881 moved to the village of Orillia, situated at the upper end of Lake Simcoe, fifty miles northwest of Lindsay. There Albert got occasional work as a teamster and managed to purchase a house on a small plot of land on Simcoe Street, a quarter mile outside of town. He became notorious, a newspaperman remarked, as "a drunken fellow, and of little service in supporting" his family. In Orillia, Lillie's mother had yet another child, Mary Alena, born in 1882. Anna Davy, with eight mouths to feed and a drunken, lazy, semiemployed husband, sent several of the eldest children, including Lillie and Willie, back to Belleville to live with her family.[10]

Belleville, a busy farming and lumbering town of nine thousand, provided plenty of opportunities for the wild Davy siblings to get into trouble. That year Lillie—just eleven—and thirteen-year-old Willie had their first serious brush with the law. They stole a cow from a farmer outside of Belleville, then drove it into town and sold it to a hotelkeeper for nine dollars. Then, in a repeat of the turkey-stealing incident, the pair sneaked into the hotel's barn, took away the cow, and sold it to another unsuspecting buyer for thirty dollars. A few days later, police officers collared Willie for stealing a watch. He and Lillie were quickly identified as the cow thieves. Lillie was released to her parents in Orillia, but Willie received three years in the Boys Reformatory of Upper Canada.[11]

Things only got worse for the Davy family. Albert continued his heavy drinking and abusive behavior. His history of brutality and attempted rape make it probable that he sexually abused Lillie and her elder sister, Saphronia. Both girls became sexualized at an early age. Decades later, Willie Davy recalled Lillie and her early teenage years. "She was of French descent and called herself Lillie de la Valle, meaning Lillie of the Valley," he said. "When she reached her teens she was very pretty and had a wonderful figure and voice; could imitate a croaking frog, an owl, and a hawk; could sing like a mockingbird, warble and trill like an oriole or a thrush. She was lithesome, blithe, and witty, gushing with fun and jollity; also a wonderful dancer and very attractive. And everybody admired her and was very proud of her acquaintance. But she possessed one detrimental fault which brought her many troubles. She was too amorous and accepted too many dates with handsome young men, which finally caused her undoing."[12]

In the summer of 1884 Albert Davy decided to sell the family home in Orillia. But there was a problem. At that time, Canadian law provided that married women had dower rights. This meant that he needed Anna's permission: she had to sign over her rights to the property so it could be sold. Anna was then several months pregnant with their ninth child, Acle, and did not want to lose her home. Despite the fact that she had been the repeated victim of domestic abuse, she bravely stood up to her husband and refused to cooperate. An enraged Albert threatened to beat her into submission, but still she refused. Then, according to a contemporary account, he declared that he would "make away with her if she did not comply." Anna's main concern was the safety of her offspring. Accordingly, in early September, she sent her older children to stay with a family friend in the little village of Campbellford, seventy miles east of Orillia. It would prove a fateful decision.

Because they had no money, the group, which included Lillie, Saphronia, and Katy, walked most of the way. Willie, who had been released from the reformatory, accompanied his sisters. As a local journalist reported, "On their arrival in Campbellford, they went from door to door asking for bread, and their wants were liberally supplied. They told the story that their father was a drunkard and treated their mother brutally." Willie, then fifteen, had become an accomplished thief, and he managed to beg—or steal—enough money to buy railroad fare so his mother and the rest of her brood could join them. Anna and the younger children soon arrived in Campbellford. The Davys first stayed with the family friend in a house near the railroad tracks on the east side of the village. Then they got permission to move into a shanty a mile and a half north of town, near the banks of the Trent River. The newspaper reporter described the place as "a pile of boards which may be called a house, up the river side." Not far away were a grist mill, a lime kiln, and the house of James Anderson, a kindly, forty-nine-year-old carpenter who had a wife and six children.[13]

Anderson worked at the lime kiln, where limestone was heated in a large outdoor oven to create quicklime that was used in making mortar and cement. He soon got to know the Davy family. Anna, thirty-seven, was worn down from her hard life and brutal beatings by her husband. She looked much older than her age. Although Anderson was twelve years Anna's senior, he referred to her as an "old woman." Word quickly spread that a grass widow lived alone in poverty with her children at the remote shanty. A *grass widow*, so-called because she had supposedly been seduced on a straw bed or taken a roll in the hay, was the common term for a wife who had been abandoned by her husband. This crude label branded and isolated many women of that era.

RENEE GALLAGHER COLLECTION.

Anna Davy in the late 1880s. She was worn down from her hard life and looked older than her age.

Lillie, then just thirteen, and Saphronia, seventeen, were attractive and flirtatious and may have had sexual relations with neighborhood men. Rumors soon spread that they were prostitutes. Given the want and hunger of their daily lives and their desperate need to survive, this may well have been true. Strict Victorian mores and the shame connected with prostitution meant little to women and girls who were starving. On one occasion Anderson witnessed a loud family quarrel at the Davys' tumbledown shack. As he recalled, "I have heard the people in the shanty talk of stealing and whoring; they accused the boy [Willie] of stealing and he accused them [Lillie and Saphronia] of whoring."[14]

On Friday night, October 3, 1884, not long after they moved into the board shack, Anna and her five younger children were asleep inside. Lillie, Saphronia, and Willie were not there and had apparently returned to Orillia. James Anderson finished his work at the lime kiln and was walking home when he encountered four young men. He knew three of them, sons of local farmers: William Keating, Narcisse Fauchier, and Alexander Armour. The fourth was a stranger, who turned out to be Philip Hearn, a ruffian from Napanee, a village on the shore of Lake Ontario. Each was about twenty years old, and one carried a bottle of liquor. They shared a drink with Anderson, then asked him about the Davy girls, whom they apparently believed were prostitutes. Anderson recalled, "They asked me if there were any girls in the shanty. I told them no, there was only a woman and some children. They said they were going over to have some fun. I told them not to bother the poor old woman."

Anderson then walked home. Not long after, the four young men crept up to the Davy shack and threw several rocks at the walls, probably hoping to rouse Lillie and Saphronia. But there was no response, and they left. At midnight all four returned and approached the door in the bright moonlight. As Anna remembered, "I heard a noise outside. I raised up the curtain and looked out. I saw four men outside, two of them came up to the door. One of them shoved the door open. The two went in. I tried to get out [and] got past them." She ran to Anderson's home and begged for help. Anderson rushed to the Davy cabin, where he confronted the four youths and demanded that they get out. Anderson took Narcisse Fauchier by the arm and walked him away from the house. Then Anderson, thinking that the other three would also leave, returned home and went to sleep. It was a terrible mistake.

Anna Davy walked back to her house and got into bed. A short time later Hearn, Keating, and Armour returned to the Davy shack and forced their way inside. Soon they were rejoined by Fauchier. While one of them guarded the children, the others seized Anna Davy and stripped off her nightclothes. Despite the facts that she was five months pregnant and her terrified children were present, they began sexually assaulting her. As Anna later explained, "They blew out the lamp, and one of them put something around my neck and choked me. I was trying to holler. I got my hand up at my neck and pulled off the cloth. I heard the little girl [four-year-old Jennie] making a noise. I searched around to find where she was. One of them had hold of her, shaking her. I begged him to let her go. After a little while he did and then got hold of me. Three of them then got hold of me and threw me on the bed. They held me down and kept me there. Two of them held me for the other. The whole four committed the rape. Two would hold me for the others."

Once the four had finished raping Anna, they stepped outside. She got up from the bed and tried to run for help, but they forced her back into the shack. Keating, clutching a whiskey bottle in one hand, threatened to beat her with it if she attempted to leave the shanty. Then the four walked off toward the nearby lime kiln. At that, eleven-year-old Katy and one of the other children slipped outside and raced to Anderson's house for help. While they were gone, the four rapists returned to the shack. "After a little while they came in again and slammed the door," Anna recalled. "Three of them again took hold of me and threw me on the bed. Two of them held me for the other." Then they began gang-raping Anna all over again.

Anderson was asleep when Katy banged frantically on his front door. "Two of her little children were at the door," he said later. "They told me four men were in the house. They had her Ma on the bed, killing her. I ran over. When I got to the lime kiln I picked up a stone. I went right to the house. Fauchier was standing at the door. Armour was sitting on the bed. Keating was on the woman. I told them to quit that kind of work. Armour got up and made as if he was going to strike me. I threw the stone at him and struck him with it. Fauchier jumped on my back. I went out with him on my back and threw him. He then got up and kicked at me. They swore at me and threatened what they would do." Then Anna, prostrate on the bed, leaped to her feet, grabbed a broom, and began striking two of her assailants with such force that the broom handle snapped in two.

This was too much for the rapists. One of them cursed and yelled, "Skin out of this!" Then all four fled into the night.[15]

Anderson took Anna and her five children to his house where they spent the night in safety. In the morning he and Anna went into Campbellford and reported the attack to the justice of the peace. Anderson identified Keating, Fauchier, and Armour, and the justice issued arrest warrants for them. Philip Hearn, who was unknown in Campbellford, managed to escape. Keating, Fauchier, and Armour were quickly picked up and lodged in jail in Cobourg, the county seat. Then, a few days later, two men appeared at Anna Davy's shanty. They were Terence McLean, the brother-in-law of William Keating, and John Fauchier, the uncle of Narcisse Fauchier. They offered Anna a hundred dollars "if she would leave the country and not appear at the trial against the prisoners." She refused, but they continued to visit the shack and pressure her into accepting the money. Finally they offered her two hundred dollars. For the impoverished Anna Davy, two hundred dollars was a fortune, and she agreed. She sent word to her husband that she was leaving him, and asked him to come from Orillia and pick up the children.

On October 16, McLean and Fauchier drove up to her shack in a buggy. They gave Katy ten dollars and warned her, "Say nothing about it." Then they bundled Anna into the buggy and took her a hundred and thirty miles east to Watertown, New York. There they kept her out of sight, hoping that the whole thing would blow over. Albert Davy arrived at the family's cabin just two hours after Anna had left with McLean and Fauchier. He gathered up the children and started back to Orillia. Albert was certain that his wife had finally left him, and the children kept the sexual assault a secret. The next day, Davy arrived in Orillia with his children, and a few hours later proceeded to get roaring drunk. He boasted that he was now "single and would be troubled no longer with a tartar of a wife."[16]

Anna's friends and family, distraught by her sudden disappearance, became convinced that Albert had killed her. Officials in Orillia quickly arrested him on a charge of murdering his wife. At that time, rural constables in Canada had no training, and most lacked the expertise and financial resources needed to investigate serious crimes. As a result, John Wilson Murray, a Canadian government detective, was assigned to the case. Murray was well on his way to becoming Canada's most famous sleuth. More than a hundred years later his career would inspire two popular television series, *The Great Detective* and *Murdoch Mysteries.* Murray, a native of Scotland, had emigrated to America as a boy. He enlisted in the US Navy in 1857 at age seventeen and served throughout the Civil War. In 1875, after seven years' service as a police and railroad detective, Murray became the first full-time government detective for the province of Ontario. He was a brilliant investigator and a pioneer in forensic techniques. His innate ability quickly became evident when he tackled the supposed murder of Anna Davy.

AUTHOR'S COLLECTION.

John Wilson Murray, the famed Canadian government detective who investigated the gang rape of Anna Davy in 1884.

Murray went to Orillia and began interviewing witnesses. It did not take him long to get the whole story from Katy Davy. He then proceeded to Campbellford where he interrogated Terence McLean and got him to confess that he had taken Anna to Watertown. McLean, to avoid prosecution for witness tampering, promised Murray that he would go to New York and bring Anna back to Canada. Then Detective Murray returned to Orillia and took the Davy children to Campbellford so they could be with their mother.

Either from McLean or the three jailed suspects, Murray discovered that the missing rapist was Philip Hearn. Murray later explained that Hearn "made his way to New York. He had a mother and sister living at that time in Napanee [Ontario]. His sister was ill. Hearn was very fond of her, and she worried over his fate. He communicated with her, saying he had escaped and telling her where he was. I intercepted the letter, and within an hour a telegram went to him saying that, if he wished to see his sister alive, he should come at once. I went to Napanee and watched the trains. Hearn was due on the night train twenty-four hours after the telegram was sent. The train arrived, but no Hearn alighted. I went to the house of his sister and found him. He had leaped from the train before it reached the station, and had made his way to the house by a roundabout route across the fields. I took him to Cobourg the next morning, in time for him to stand trial."[17]

The jury trial began in Cobourg on November 10, 1884, just five weeks after the assault. The prosecution witnesses were Anna Davy, her daughter Katy, and James Anderson. Anna, though dirt poor, was a respectable woman. In that era, the stain of rape was so severe that no married female would make such a charge unless it was true. And the gang rape of a pregnant mother was beyond the pale. The jury deliberated only minutes before they found the four men guilty of rape. The judge ordered them to stand and then intoned, "This is one of the most painful cases which it has ever been my duty to try. The jury could not have done otherwise than return the verdict they have, and you will pass the brightest years of your life in the provincial penitentiary for this terrible crime. Your counsel has said everything he could in your favor, but your defense was no defense." He then sentenced each of them to ten years at hard labor in the Ontario penitentiary.[18]

The friends of Philip Hearn later made a concerted effort to get him a pardon. They obtained an affidavit from a woman in his hometown of Napanee who claimed that "Mrs. Davy told her that she did not know Hearn, that she had never seen him until he had appeared in the dock of the Cobourg court house on trial, and that she would come to Napanee for $100 and clear him of the charge." Hearn's friends also obtained a statement from one of the other convicted rapists who claimed that Hearn "was not present when the offense was committed." Yet these declarations were belied by the impartial eyewitness testimony of James Anderson, who identified all four of the rapists in court. Hearn's attempts to obtain an early release failed.[19]

Anna Davy, like so many abused women before and after, went back to her brutal husband. She had eight children—with one more on the way—and no food, no job, no money, and no choice. On the other hand, Lillie and her sister Katy had no intention of returning to their violent father. Lillie, thirteen, and Katy, eleven, cut their hair short and donned their brother's clothes, then made their way south to Lake Ontario. They posed as boys because two young, unaccompanied girls would attract attention. The sisters stole aboard a lake steamer and ended up in the busy city of Buffalo, New York. They had no cash, but that was not a problem because it was an era of child labor, and there were plenty of jobs in Buffalo. The girls promptly got work in a factory. Two months later their mother managed to track them down and returned them to Canada. This was Lillie Davy's first attempt to break free and live life on her own terms.[20]

For the rest of their lives, Lillie and her siblings would stick together through thick and thin. Their extraordinarily abusive and traumatic upbringing created an unbreakable bond. They relied on each other and came to believe that they were the only ones whom they could trust. In January 1885 Anna gave birth to her ninth child, a boy. She named him Acle, but the children called him Ace. Later that year, Albert and Anna Davy moved their large brood across Lake Ontario to Rochester, New York. Anna hoped to start a new life for her family there, but fate would dictate otherwise. And for fourteen-year-old Lillie, her childhood of instability, privation, neglect, and mistreatment would continue to make its indelible mark.[21]

2

Runaways

Lillie Davy and her family found Rochester a far cry from rural Canada. It was a bustling, modern industrial city of one hundred thousand, served by five different railroads, and home to huge factories and flour mills. Rochester had seen a population explosion in the 1870s and '80s as laborers flooded in to work in garment and shoe manufactories, breweries, and tool-making plants. Among its most important businesses were the Bausch & Lomb Optical Company, one of the country's main makers of eyeglasses, and the new Eastman Kodak Company, which quickly became America's leading manufacturer of cameras and film. And Rochester boasted two of America's most important social reformers: civil-rights icon Frederick Douglass and women's-rights leader Susan B. Anthony, who also happened to be close friends.

The urban downtown was crammed with hundreds of multistory brick buildings. Its sprawling neighborhoods were connected by electric streetcars, and Albert Davy surely liked the fact that the city had no shortage of deadfalls, or cheap saloons.

The Davys moved into a small tenement house that they rented at 10 Glenwood Park, now called Glendale Park. This was the first of several homes they would occupy in Rochester. Located in the Edgerton neighborhood on Rochester's northwest side, it was a mile and a half north of downtown. The house faced the Genesee River, just a hundred feet away. There Albert Davy could spend his time drinking and fishing. Today, however, nothing is left of the family's home but a brush-filled empty lot. For Lillie, the city was an exciting place to live, but it presented far more temptations than did rural Canada.[1]

In Rochester, Lillie Davy turned fifteen—attractive, voluptuous, and worldly beyond her years. She soon met and became involved with a much older man. William A. Byers, a thirty-six-year-old Canadian carpenter, lived near the Davy home, and Lillie quickly became infatuated with him. Unknown to her, Byers was a bigamist. He was already married to a New York woman when, in 1879, he wed a wealthy, older lady from Minneapolis. She later sued for divorce, telling the judge that at first Byers "was all good, but in time became addicted to drunkenness, and when drunk was so violent that she alone could manage him. As time passed on he became gradually worse, until it became evident that even she could do nothing with him." She said that Byers, who had been comfortable financially, had lost all his money as a result of his alcoholism. When she finally left him in 1885, he moved to Rochester to work for his brother, an architect.[2]

For Lillie Davy, this Canadian carpenter seemed to offer excitement, romance, and a way out of poverty. Byers had no trouble seducing Lillie, and they began a sexual relationship. Lillie was under the age of consent, which was then sixteen in New York. On Saturday night, May 1, 1886, William Byers took Lillie out on the town. That must have been a real treat for her, and they spent the night together. Anna Davy was distraught when her daughter came home the next day. She managed to extract a confession from Lillie that Byers "had been immorally intimate with her at other times." Anna went immediately to the police station and demanded that an arrest warrant be issued for Byers for "abduction and seduction of her daughter." A police reporter described Lillie's mother as "a neatly dressed, respectable appearing woman" when she walked into the station. The officers told her to bring Lillie to police headquarters to make a statement.

The next day Anna returned with Lillie in tow. Lillie gave a detailed account of her affair with Byers, and the police-court judge issued a warrant for his arrest. Two detectives promptly collared Byers and lodged him in jail. At his preliminary hearing, Lillie took the stand and, according to a local journalist, "told a shocking story of depravity. The prisoner, she alleged, had enticed her away from home on two different nights, when she remained with him." The judge found that there was sufficient evidence to hold Byers in jail while the grand jury considered whether to charge him. In that era, indictments were commonly issued by grand juries, consisting of a panel of citizens who determined whether there was sufficient evidence to warrant felony charges. The judge also believed that Lillie might flee, so he ordered her jailed as a material witness. But Byers was lucky. As the reporter later said, "For some reason the grand jury failed to indict him and he was discharged. The girl was then released and taken home by her mother." New York's seduction law prohibited a man from obtaining a woman's consent to sexual intercourse by a false promise of marriage. Apparently there was insufficient evidence that Byers had promised to wed Lillie.[3]

A few days later Anna Davy brought Lillie back to the police station and complained that she "had been out nights considerably and had been absent from home." The officers took Lillie before the police-court judge who "gave the girl a lecture on the propriety of staying home nights and sent her back with her mother." The reporter remarked, "Lillie is only fifteen years old, but well developed for her age. She is a bright looking girl and by no means bad looking. Waywardness and disobedience have caused her ruin."[4]

Yet nothing said by Lillie's mother or the judge had any influence on her. Lillie later declared that she became engaged to marry Byers, and they decided to elope. "He came to my home for me," she explained, "and as the train was pulling out I dropped my kid glove and while I was obtaining it I missed the train. Mr. Byers was in the smoking car and did not miss me until he had gone some distance. I got on board the next train, but it was on the wrong road, and I was farther away than ever." Lillie said that she got off the passenger cars in Hamilton, Ontario, and took another train back to Rochester. Byers continued on to Calgary, then part of Canada's North-West Territories, where he opened a restaurant.

"Shortly afterward I was forwarded $30 by Byers for my transportation, but mother would not let me go alone," Lillie recalled. "She took the money away from me. My father is a worthless wretch, and I concluded that if I married Byers I could provide a home for mother and the rest of the family." Lillie later gave more details about her affair with Byers: "I heard, after I started from home, that he had two or three wives, and concluded that I wouldn't go. He sent me $30 to come on, and my mother got the check and put a mark on it, and told them at the bank it was my mark and got the money. That made me mad, and I took my sister and started anyhow. She goes wherever I do."[5]

That is not exactly what happened. In June 1886, a month after Byers went to Calgary, Lillie and Katy again ran away from home. They beat their way by train to Hamilton, a bustling Canadian port city of forty thousand, situated at the western tip of Lake Ontario, a hundred and forty miles from Rochester. There they had an encounter with Alexander D. Stewart, the highly capable and college-educated police chief of Hamilton. The girls got work in a grocery and candy store run by an Italian, Frank Perras, and his brother. Lillie recalled that they worked in the Perras store for a short time during June and July. "We wanted to leave but they wouldn't let us," she said. "There were two brothers of them. They locked up our clothes in their trunks, and when they went down to the stand in the market—they had a stand in the market too—and left us two girls tending the store. I said, 'Katy, I am goin' to get my clothes and leave.' We tried to unlock the trunks with a button-hook, but we couldn't, so we broke upon one of the trunks and they were there, and we took our clothes and went away and stayed a week. Saturday night we went to the Salvation Army—we used to go there to have fun—and they were there and saw us, and the next time we went there he put a cop on our track."

AUTHOR'S COLLECTION.

Alexander D. Stewart, the highly capable and college-educated police chief of Hamilton, Ontario. He knew the Davy family well.

It turned out that the Perras brothers had reported that the girls had broken into the trunk and stolen property from their store. As Lillie explained, "The cop said, 'I want to speak with you.' I said, 'Come up to the corner and speak with me,' for I didn't want anybody to see us. He came up to the corner and asked me about it, and then he says, 'Come down to the police station.' We went down to the station and [Chief] Stewart was not there, and the policeman could not understand the Italian Perras was speaking. They would ask us what the Italian said and we would tell them it was something else, and the Italian got disgusted and he said, 'Letta she go,' he didn't want to make an arrest."

Lillie said that the officers released her and Katy, but their freedom was short-lived. "We was out on the market selling some things, and Stewart come around and says, 'I want you.' They took us in the patrol wagon to the police station at city hall on James Street, and they put us in the lockup for about half an hour. Stewart said he was going to send us to the House of Refuge for six months for breaking open the trunk." When the sisters explained that they had only taken their own clothing, the surprised chief exclaimed, "You ought to get a mob and break open the Italian store and kill him." Or so Lillie claimed. Stewart then ordered the two girls released.[6]

Chief Stewart gave the sisters railroad fare, and they promptly returned to Rochester. Lillie could not have been too heartbroken over the loss of William Byers, for within a few days she met twenty-one-year-old Charles Dean. During the day he worked as a streetcar brakeman, but at night he burglarized homes. Despite the fact that Dean had already been wed twice before, Lillie fell hard for him. On about the first of August 1886, he proposed that they elope and get married in Tonawanda, New York, a popular place for weddings, located just downriver from Niagara Falls. Lillie agreed, as long as Katy could come along. The three boarded a train, but Dean took them to Hamilton instead of Tonawanda. Chief Stewart quickly spotted the trio. He later said that he was surprised "to see the girl [Lillie] accompanied by a sister, Katy, back on the streets of Hamilton. With them was the man [Dean]."

Within days a daring burglary took place, and Chief Stewart suspected that Charles Dean was the culprit. Dean quickly fled Hamilton and left the girls behind. Lillie was distraught. On the night of August 13, as she walked down King Street, she suffered an anxiety attack, and bystanders brought her to the police station. There she tearfully told how Dean had brought her to Hamilton. Lillie claimed that she had rejected his advances, and he had then left her without a cent. Policemen brought her to the city hospital and sent word to her parents in Rochester. Then the officers picked up Katy and took both sisters to the police station where they questioned them about the burglary. Lillie quickly invented a cover story to protect her lover. As a journalist later wrote, "Lillie Davy said she might have committed the burglary dressed in male attire. She said that she had often thought of this, and believed she might easily appear as a man. Both girls said considerable upon this subject, but the police never believed for a moment that they were speaking seriously."[7]

The Davy sisters returned to Rochester, and Lillie later said that they got jobs there in a cigarette factory, while their mother labored as a washerwoman. Lillie and Katy probably worked for the huge Kimball Tobacco Company, rolling and packing cigarettes. It employed girls who were paid at piece rate, a fixed price for each pack. "We earned about eight dollars apiece a week in the cigarette factory," recalled Lillie. That amount was about two hundred and forty dollars in modern currency. "Our father is worthless and mother, who washes, has a big family, and we always give her seven dollars a week. We did not live at home. We rented a room and lived by ourselves, because that way there was less quarreling."[8]

Lillie seems to have picked up the tobacco habit in Rochester.

In that era, smoking by women was considered taboo. Cigarettes were a fairly new commodity. During the nineteenth century, men primarily smoked cigars and pipes. Prior to 1880, cigarette users had to roll their own, but the following year the first cigarette-rolling machine was invented. Ready-made smokes became available in commercial packs, like those made by the Davy girls. Hand-rolled cigarettes had long been popular in Mexico, and Texas cowboys were among the earliest Americans to adopt the custom. Many US servicemen first smoked cigarettes in Cuba or the Philippines during the Spanish–American War and brought the habit home with them. Nonetheless, by 1900, smokers of cigars and pipes still made up ninety-eight percent of the American tobacco market. Though cigarettes gradually gained popularity, respectable women would not smoke them until the 1920s.[9]

In Rochester, Lillie reconnected with Charles Dean. Chief Stewart suspected that Lillie and Katy, dressed in male attire, assisted Dean in a number of burglaries. Newspapers later reported that Dean was a member of an organized gang of housebreakers that operated out of Rochester. The band included Chester W. Green, an ex-convict, who had been recently released from the New York state prison in Auburn. Green was an oil-well driller from Pennsylvania. A journalist who saw Green described him as "about thirty-two years of age, well dressed, and fine looking." He became friends with Lillie and Katy and was exactly the kind of man Lillie was attracted to: older and tough, with money in his wallet. Whether Lillie had a romantic relationship with Green is unclear, but he carried in his pocket a tintype photograph of himself with Lillie and Katy. Despite Lillie's friendship with Chester Green, she simultaneously pursued her romantic affair with Charles Dean.[10]

Meanwhile her oldest sister, Saphronia, had her own troubles with the law. She had obtained work as a maid in a hotel in Buffalo, New York. In August 1886 Saphronia stole some clothes from the hotel and decamped for Rochester. A police detective soon found her and returned her to Buffalo to face charges of larceny. Saphronia could not have been punished too harshly, for she was soon back home in Rochester. There she became involved with Andrew Wahl, who worked with Charles Dean as a brakeman. Lillie and Saphronia thought that they had each found true love. On January 29, 1887, in a double wedding in Rochester, Lillie, sixteen, married Charles Dean, and Saphronia, nineteen, married Andrew Wahl. No doubt Lillie saw this union as a way out of her impoverished and out-of-control life.[11]

But Lillie's marital bliss was short-lived. Less than two weeks later a family brawl broke out, with Andrew Wahl on one side and Charles Dean and his older brother, William, on the other. Apparently Lillie and Saphronia did not take part. Wahl went to the police station and swore out a warrant for the arrest of the Dean brothers. The officers soon lodged the Deans in jail. The police-court judge offered Charles Dean the choice of a ten-dollar fine or ten days behind bars and released his brother. The cause of the fracas is unknown, but Lillie had married Dean in order to escape her brutal father, and she now recognized that her new spouse had the same violent traits. Lillie decided to leave her husband and go with thirteen-year-old Katy to Calgary in search of her former lover, William Byers. As Lillie recalled, "Before we left we cut our hair and dressed in male attire in order, as we thought, to insure safety to our persons when traveling. We did not have much money, so we concluded that we must endure more or less hardship." Wearing boys' clothing was their way of avoiding attention as well as unwanted sexual advances and even rape.[12]

On about February 25, 1887, the girls slipped aboard a train in Rochester and made their way west toward Chicago. They sneaked into freight cars or rode on the blind baggage, a car that was coupled behind the coal tender. In that era, railroad brakemen patrolled the cars, always ready to throw tramps from the train. During the next few days, in freezing weather, the sisters were put off three different trains. Each time they begged for food or got a little money doing odd jobs before boarding another westbound train. On one occasion the girls entered a passenger car and encountered what was called a peanut butcher, a train boy who sold snacks and newspapers. While one sister struck up a conversation with him, the other pilfered a bag of nuts from his supply. Finally they arrived in Chicago. A massive winter storm had closed the rail lines west through Minnesota, so the girls found themselves stranded in the Windy City. One of the Davy sisters managed to borrow a shoe-shining outfit from a bootblack, while the other peddled newspapers.

According to a journalist who interviewed Lillie years afterward, "They worked first in the south end of the business district, and later, as they became acquainted with the other bootblacks, roamed all over the downtown district, seeking refuge when night fell in the boxcars out along State Street, in Wabash Avenue livery barns, in lofts, or wherever they could sneak in unnoticed." A Chicago journalist, who also later interviewed the Davy girls, reported, "For a week the girls worked here, lived with newsboys, strutted on the streets at night smoking cigarettes, and in other ways displaying themselves as regular toughs. But Chicago proved too tame for them, and they resolved to go West. They had no money, their earnings being squandered in riotous living. They went by freight, taking fortune as it came, and living for days with tramps and stranded theatrical companies."[13]

Once the heavy snow was plowed from the rail lines, Lillie and Katy continued west on a freight train. Finally they got off—or, more likely, were put off—in Windom, a village on the Chicago, St. Paul, Minneapolis and Omaha Railway, located in southwestern Minnesota. It was late Saturday night, March 12, and a friendly newspaperman found them loitering around the station, cold, hungry, and exhausted. When a band of young ruffians began tormenting the two urchins, Katy broke into tears. The journalist scooped her into his arms and, with Lillie following, walked to a nearby hotel, the Clark House. There the girls told him that their names were Charley and Bertie Byers. They said that they were penniless and were on their way to Calgary to visit their brother, W. A. Byers. The hotelkeeper, a kindly man named Julian Kendall, gave them room and board in exchange for doing chores around the hotel. He got them new boys' clothes to replace their ragged garments.

The next day Kendall and his wife took the sisters with them to church. As a journalist later wrote, "Both 'boys' asked to be furnished with a Bible, and during the service paid such strict attention to the sermon and prayed so fervently that the hotelman was astonished to see so much religious character in boys of their tender age. After that he watched them closely, and finding their deportment modest and generally correct, began to suspect the truth." As Katy recalled, "We were most too pious. That's all that was wrong with us. In church we sat still and didn't stick pins into each other, an' the people guessed we couldn't be boys."

Some villagers noticed that "their hands were remarkably soft and white and their feet remarkably small for boys." That evening they sang for Mrs. Kendall, who thought that "their voices were remarkably feminine." Her fourteen-year-old son Walter heard this talk and became curious. On Monday night, before bed, the sisters asked him for a needle and thread so they could sew a patch on a pair of trousers. Walter brought it to their room, but lollygagged there until they had partially undressed for bed. Then, staring at Lillie, he suddenly blurted out, "You're a girl. I know you are!"

Lillie soon admitted the truth, and Mrs. Kendall notified Sheriff William Barlow. He arrived at the hotel, listened to their story, and decided not to arrest them. Lillie admitted that Byers was her lover, not her brother, and that their home was in Rochester. The villagers took pity on the waifs and provided them with dresses and blouses to wear. Sheriff Barlow took the girls to a local photograph gallery and had their images taken, one showing them together in their boys' attire, the second with them wearing girls' clothing. In the photograph in which they posed as boys, they stood next to each other, their hair cut short and caps in hand, with Lillie clutching a Bible in her left fist. Barlow gave the girls a copy of each photo.[14]

AUTHOR'S COLLECTION.

The runaways Lillie and Katy Davy dressed like boys. This is a wood engraving of the photograph taken in Windom, Minnesota, in 1887.

The story of the Davy sisters was published widely in the newspapers. Runaway girls dressed as boys was something highly unusual in that era, for laws prohibited women from wearing men's clothing and vice versa. As scandalous as such cross-dressing behavior was, their fleeing from home, traveling halfway across the country, stealing rides on trains, and sleeping with tramps in boxcars and hobo encampments was beyond the pale. When the sensational story hit the wire services, it was eagerly followed by journalists and their readers. Typical Midwestern headlines read, "Two Young Girls in Pantaloons," "Masquerading in Boys' Attire," "Plucky Girls," "Adventurous Maidens," and "Two Tough Girls."[15]

Meanwhile charitable townsfolk in Windom raised a purse of almost two hundred dollars to pay for new wardrobes and railroad fare back to Rochester. Lillie and Katy felt guilty about the villagers' generosity, for they soon admitted that they had stolen various items from the Clark House. Lillie showed a tear in the lining of her dress where she had concealed hidden photographs of prominent citizens of Windom. The girls confessed that they had pilfered the pictures from the photograph gallery. As a result, Sheriff Barlow returned the two hundred dollars to the townsfolk, and Lillie and Katy again found themselves penniless. On March 24, twelve days after the girls had landed in Windom, Barlow took them by train to Saint Paul.

The Windom newspaper declared that the pair "behaved like ingrates and abused the hand that befriended them. They have left for the good of the village and the morals of the children." Sheriff Barlow delivered the sisters to Morgan L. Hutchins, head of the Society for the Relief of the Poor. Hutchins in turn promptly placed them with a respectable family in Hamline, at that time a suburb of Saint Paul. In that era of low taxes and minimal government, the care of poor or neglected children was left to public charities. Just like in Canada, juvenile courts, departments of social services, and child protective services were then unknown.[16]

For the next two weeks Lillie and Katy worked dutifully—and without drama—for the family in Hamline. Hutchins believed that there "they would be free from the contaminating influence of 'bad reporters'." He was referring to so-called yellow journalists who worked for sensationalist, quasitruthful newspapers. The girls received a little money, which was turned over to Hutchins to pay for their railroad fare home. Hutchins sent a telegraph message to William Byers in Calgary, advising, as a journalist reported, "if he wished to marry Lillie that now is the accepted time and Saint Paul the place, and [Hutchins] hopes to bring about the wedding in the near future. Newspaper men will be invited to the ceremony, and if nothing goes wrong, the little romance will be crowned with a happy ending." Hutchins also wired the Calgary police chief and learned that Byers was a bigamist. He then wrote to Anna Davy in Rochester. She replied that Byers "was 'all right,' in spite of the fact that he was already twice married." Anna added that Lillie had her permission to proceed to Calgary but asked that Katy be sent home. When William Byers failed to respond to Hutchins's invitation, Lillie declared that she "didn't care whether she married Byers or not now."[17]

While the girls were in Minnesota, Lillie's friend Chester Green busily pursued his profession as a burglar in Upstate New York. Nighttime house burglaries were common in that era. Today, thieves generally commit residential burglaries in the daytime, when residents are at work, children are in school, and no witnesses are at home. However, in the nineteenth century, few women worked outside the family residence. That meant that housewives and their children were often at their abodes during the day, and that was enough to scare off most sneak thieves. As a result, residential burglars operated at night, when families were asleep. They often carried an array of burglars' tools, keys, folding ladders, ropes, and sacks to carry away their booty. Instead of noisily breaking windows or doors, they picked locks or quietly slipped inside through open windows and made off with loot without waking anyone in the household.

Chester Green and several accomplices made their way to Jamestown, New York, a hundred and forty miles southwest of

Rochester. Jamestown was then undergoing a crime wave. The city of sixteen thousand people had only one police officer on duty in the daytime and two at night. Today, American towns and cities average about two full-time officers per thousand residents. Under that formula a town like Jamestown would have thirty-two police. But in 1887, no community that size had a tax base large enough to pay for thirty-two police officers. As a result, reported one newspaper, "During the past few months a dozen gambling rooms have been in operation, and several hundred gamblers, crooks, and blacklegs have congregated there." Among the blacklegs, or career criminals, were Chester Green and his gang.

In early April they broke into a number of Jamestown homes. Then, at three in the morning of April 9, Green tried to enter the house of Ashbill R. Catlin, a prominent merchant who, as a young man, had spent time on the Western frontier. Catlin was asleep upstairs, but a noise from his dining room window on the first floor awakened him. He looked out in time to see a shadowy figure running away. Catlin was unafraid and seized his single-shot Marlin-Ballard rifle, a powerful longarm used for hunting and target shooting. As the *New York Times* reported, Catlin's "nerve and skill with the rifle were gained in the California gold and Colorado silver mines." He crept downstairs, and finding that the window had been forced open, sat in a chair with his rifle ready. After an agonizingly long wait of thirty minutes, a man's head reappeared in the window. Then the prowler began pulling himself through it. Catlin took dead aim and squeezed the trigger. The heavy slug slammed into the man's neck, ripped through the carotid artery, then tore through his upper torso, lodging behind one shoulder. The prowler dropped to the ground, staggered off a hundred feet, then fell on his face, dead.

The lifeless burglar was taken to the city morgue and hundreds of gawkers lined up to view his corpse. He was quickly identified as Chester W. Green. In his pockets were half a dozen letters addressed to him by his niece, a set of burglary tools, and items stolen in four other Jamestown burglaries. In a small journal, he had made the following notation: "Katy and Lillie Davy have gone to Windom, Minn." He also carried a tintype photo of himself with two pretty girls, who were soon recognized as the Davy sisters. Chief Stewart of Hamilton, Ontario, visited the morgue in Jamestown and correctly identified the girls in the photograph as Lillie and Katy Davy. But he mistakenly reported that Green was the burglar whom he had seen with the girls in Hamilton a year before. In fact their companion in Hamilton had been Charles Dean. Wire-service reports claimed that hours before he was killed, Green hired a livery rig in Jamestown, picked up two young women from a tenement house, and drove off with them. Newspapers speculated that the women were Lillie and Katy Davy and that, dressed as boys, they had helped him commit burglaries. That was impossible, for the girls were in Minnesota when Green died. The partially incorrect story of Green's death and his connection with the Davy sisters was quickly published in newspapers throughout the East and the Midwest.[18]

A Saint Paul journalist brought the news to the girls, telling them that the deceased burglar had their photo in his pocket. Lillie immediately assumed that the dead man was Charles Dean rather than Chester Green. She burst into tears and cried, "Charlie Dean, my husband, is dead." The reporter wrote, "Recovering her equanimity, she refused to talk for a time, but on being urged by her sister to tell all, she cleared up considerable of the mystery surrounding them. She said she had married Charles Dean, a Rochester street car driver, in January, when she was but fifteen. She said he did not work very regularly at his business, but was often away from home, when she understood he went by the name of Green." Declared the newspaperman, "The evidence seems conclusive that the dead burglar is the husband of Lillie Davy."[19]

The next day, April 12, a reporter for the *Saint Paul Daily*

Globe paid the Davy sisters a visit to try to find out the truth. He provided a pen picture of the pair: "Both these girls are bright and quick, but possessed of no education. Lillie, as the eldest, takes the lead, but in conversation always relies on her sister to help her out. Their features are plain—almost homely. Their black hair is shortly cropped behind, and their general makeup is even boyish." The newspaperman asked them whether they had helped Chester Green commit burglaries in Hamilton, Ontario, while they were dressed as boys. He wrote that in response, "both girls repeatedly contradicted themselves," and added, "When interrogated as to whether they were ever in Hamilton or not, they refused to answer, but finally Lillie admitted that they were, but refused to account for their presence there, or whether there was anyone with them."

The journalist then asked Lillie, "Do you know Chief Stewart?"

"Well, I should smile," she replied sarcastically.

"Did he ever accuse you of being accomplices to a burglary there?"

"No."

"Did he ever have you brought to the station and question you about your business and who the man was with you?"

"There wasn't any man with us."

"Are you sure?"

"Well, if you know all about it, why do you ask me?"

"Oh, go on and tell him what we was up for," interjected Katy. At that, Lillie explained how they had been falsely accused of theft by the Perras brothers in Hamilton and then released by Chief Stewart. The reporter concluded, "They have told a great many conflicting stories since coming to Saint Paul, and there is little dependence to be placed in what either, especially Katy, has to say."[20]

The *Daily Globe* ran the story with a front-page—but slightly erroneous—headline: "Those Davy Girls: Mysterious Relations between the Waifs in Male Attire and a Burglar Shot in Rochester." And the *New York Herald* declared, "Two girls not yet out of their teens have created the biggest sensation Minnesota has experienced for many a day." Morgan Hutchins soon reported that the family in Hamline that had taken in the sisters "have been so much annoyed over the publicity that they do not want to keep them any longer." A week later Hutchins sent Lillie and Katy to the House of the Good Shepherd, a home for unwed mothers, prostitutes, and incorrigible girls, run by Catholic nuns in Saint Paul.[21]

Their stay in the House of the Good Shepherd was a brief one. On April 25 the girls were put aboard an eastbound passenger train, and they arrived in Chicago early the next morning. A wire had been sent ahead, and a police officer awaited them at the Chicago depot. He took them to the Harrison Street police station, and when word spread, journalists swarmed inside. One of them paid Lillie a dollar for her copy of the photo of them in boys' clothing. She thought that she had only loaned it to him, and when he failed to return the photograph, Lillie became furious. She was still mad when a *Chicago Daily News* reporter showed up the next morning to interview the sisters.

The writer found Lillie and Katy sitting in a jail cell. "One result of their escapade," he wrote, "was the laying in of an unabridged vocabulary of street slang that the younger one uses with startling freedom and vigor. Their closely cropped heads and somewhat coarse features give them a boyish look, and they are about as tough as any of the street gamins they have been running with for the last two months." Then the newspaperman asked Lillie if she was willing to return to Rochester.

"I won't go until they give me back my picture," she responded. "There was about 'steen hundred reporters down here last night and one of 'em gimme a dollar for our picture to stick in his paper, and I want it back or I won't budge a step."

Katy then pulled out her copy of the photo and pointed a

grimy finger at her sister's image. "'Pipe' [look at] the bible in her hand," she laughed. "We was workin' some goody-goodies for a soft mark and we played de pious racket."

Then the reporter, without mentioning the death of Chester Green, asked Lillie if she had ever been in Jamestown, New York. "I don't know anything about that burglary," she snapped.

"What burglary?" the journalist inquired.

"Why, that burglary where Chester Green got killed."

"Who said his name was Chester?"

"Why, I saw it in the papers. They tried to make out in Saint Paul that we were the girls, but they couldn't do it." Referring to Morgan Hutchins, she declared, "When that happened we were working for a man who is an inspector, or something, near Saint Paul."

"How did Green come to have your pictures in his pocket when he was killed?"

"Why, I suppose he bought them," Lillie lied. "When we were arrested in Windom the sheriff had our pictures taken in boys' clothes and then in girls' clothes, and when he brought us to Saint Paul he sold any number of them on the train at twenty-five cents apiece."

"Did he give you the money?"

"No, he didn't. But he was a fool to sell them for a quarter. He might as well have had half a dollar."

"Will you go home now?"

"I'll go if they send me, or if they don't we will do the best we can."

As the interview took place, Katy sat next to her sister, sewing a white apron. "It is for my little sister," she said proudly. Katy then told the reporter that she "had traveled one season with Coup's circus in the east." To prove it, she jumped to her feet, then bent over backward and touched her head on the stone floor of the cell. "I am pretty nimble myself." Katy smiled, forgetting to use her street slang. "I can kick higher than my head without any trouble and turn a handspring." Coup's circus was real enough—William C. Coup had been a partner of P. T. Barnum and ran a popular traveling show in the 1880s. But there is no evidence that Katy ever performed for him.[22]

Reporters who visited the sisters in Saint Paul and Chicago gave varying descriptions of their appearance. A Saint Paul journalist remarked, "Indeed their features are quite masculine." But another called them "two handsome young girls," and a *Chicago Times* writer declared, "The young misses are intelligent and very pretty." The reporter for the *Chicago Inter Ocean* concurred: "Lillie is a pretty, big-blue-eyed lassie, with red lips and well-developed figure, that would contradict her statement that she was only sixteen years of age, did not her thirteen-year-old sister Katy testify to the truth of the story."[23]

Officials in Chicago telegraphed the police chief of Rochester, asking for money to buy the girls' train fare home. The chief sent a telegram back, insisting that "Chicago would confer a favor on Rochester by keeping the girls." When a newspaperman asked Lillie if it was true that she had deserted her husband, Charles Dean, she admitted it but snapped, "I don't know what business it is of your'n, anyway." The two were then taken into police court and charged with disorderly conduct. As a journalist explained, "This was done in order to detain them until arrangements can be made for sending them back to Rochester." The judge ordered that they be held in the Erring Women's Refuge, a home for prostitutes and wayward girls.

The reporter described what happened next: "When the sentence was pronounced in court, Lillie broke into tears and protested, between sobs and wild gesticulations, that she and her sister had done nothing for which they should be so severely punished." Katy's reaction was different. As they were led by a police matron from the courtroom, a male officer smiled at them. The journalist said that "she landed a masculine right hander on the officer's face, supplementing it with a vigorous shove. The policeman fell backward into a seat as the adolescent vixen reproved him."

"Damn you," Katy yelled at the officer. "Don't you laugh at me!"

The newspaperman concluded, "The twain were taken downstairs again when the matron tried to soothe them, but to no avail. Lillie kept up her sobbing and Katy her denunciation of the world in general and Chicagoans in particular, characterizing the good people as 'sneaks' and insisting that she and her sister were old enough to take care of themselves without the assistance of the police." Then the girls were taken to the Erring Women's Refuge, a four-story brownstone building in Chicago's South Side.[24]

AUTHOR'S COLLECTION.

The Erring Women's Refuge in Chicago. Lillie and Katy Davy escaped through a third-floor window.

The Erring Women's Refuge—so named because it was supposed to reform those who had erred in their ways—held about sixty girls and young women. A woman journalist, who visited in disguise, later wrote, "Out of all sixty I did not see half a dozen who had attained twenty years." The home had been established in the 1860s to educate and train girls who had been abandoned by their families, rescued from brothels, or were lawbreakers or unwed mothers. The top two floors held large and crowded dormitory rooms with a nursery that was home to thirteen babies belonging to inmates of the home. The girls spent their days alternating between school classes, doing washing, cooking, and cleaning, and learning dressmaking. The woman writer explained, "For lack of room they were all together—the corrigible with the incorrigible—the redeemable with the unredeemable, the recoverable with the reprobate. The hardened in crime was free to instill the poison of her mind into the ear of the poor girl who had fallen rather from ignorance than desire. The only isolation possible under the circumstances was to lock a particularly violent inmate up in her bedroom until she were inclined to become docile. This was seldom resorted to, and could only be continued a brief time at the most."[25]

The Davy girls had no love for the Erring Women's Refuge nor for the opportunities it afforded to acquire job skills or education. Less than a month later they began planning an escape. Shortly before midnight on May 19 the sisters quietly arose from their beds on the third floor. They fastened two sheets and a nightgown into a long rope, then tied the nightgown sleeve to a bed. The girls opened a window and dropped the line to the ground, more than twenty feet below. Because Katy was the smallest and lightest, she descended first. Then it was Lillie's turn. Halfway to the ground, as she shimmied down the makeshift rope, the nightgown sleeve ripped in two, and she plunged to the earth, stunned but not injured.

The sisters walked north to Chicago's downtown and spent the day looking for a job. They had no success, and that night a policeman spotted the pair wandering the streets. He brought them to the station house, where a police reporter described the two: "With little quaint blue dresses and extremely old fashioned straw hats, the girls look fresh and pretty, but they have in no degree abandoned their rough and tough manners, and still wear their skirts rather like a man."[26]

In the morning the police-court judge sent them back to the Erring Women's Refuge for a brief stay while arrangements were made to send them home. Within a few days they were on board a passenger train, headed back to Rochester. For Lillie and Katy Davy, it was the beginning of an even wilder chapter of their tumultuous young lives.[27]

3

The Notorious Davy Girls

The headline in the Rochester newspaper was an eye-grabber: "On the Warpath. The Notorious Davy Girls Make Trouble for the Police." Its writer declared, "There is probably no family in this city that has, in the past two years, gained as much undesirable distinction as has the Davy family. They have lived in all parts of the city, and their stay in any neighborhood, if short, is the only pleasing trait they are known to possess." He added, "To the police, this family has been a source of endless trouble, and officers say that it would be hard to name one of the children who since infancy has not been arrested on various occasions."

Lillie and Katy Davy had arrived back in Rochester in late May 1887. Soon they were again in the news. At five o'clock in the morning of June 6, a policeman spotted Lillie "acting in a disorderly manner on State Street" and arrested her on a charge of "being a streetwalker." Whether she was soliciting for prostitution or merely associating with street ruffians is unclear. The officer took Lillie into police court where the judge sentenced her to three months in the State Industrial School in Rochester, which held juveniles under the age of sixteen. The next day two policemen went to the family home on South Washington Street, where neighbors had complained that the Davys were disturbing the peace. The officers arrested Saphronia, twenty, and Willie, eighteen, for disorderly conduct. A reporter met Saphronia at the police station. "She is a tall, slim girl," he wrote, "with a rather pale face, and snapping black eyes and hair."

As a detective led her into a jail cell, Saphronia gave the journalist "a withering look of scorn" and told the officer, "Tell all you know." The detective was happy to oblige. "Saphronia has been arrested before. I arrested her once for larceny and she was taken to Buffalo, but she is just as bad as ever, and her little brother [Henry] is the most accomplished liar that ever breathed. He used to play the role of being lost, and every few nights it would be reported that a lost boy was at some place. He used to tell that his mother had run away with a man, and that his father put him in a farmer's wagon and sent him into the country, and that he had just got back, and had no home or place to go. He is almost as much of a terror as the girls, and they have no equal." The police-court judge who heard their defense in court the next day was unimpressed. Because Saphronia and Willie were adults, he gave them twenty days each in jail.[1]

The same evening, Susan B. Anthony addressed a congregation that packed the pews in the First Unitarian Church of Rochester. The famed suffragist argued, as she had done for years, not only for equal rights but for the legal and social independence of single women. "Man will not at once be able to surrender his time-honored supremacy over women," Anthony declared. "Not until women shall have demonstrated their ability to equality of work, not until they shall have won equality in every respect, will the superior sex lay aside their assumption. The woman who will not be ruled must live without marriage." Yet Lillie Davy, staring into the evening through the barred windows of the Industrial School, was not part of Anthony's middle- and upper-middle-class audience. Although as an adult she would absorb those very teachings, Lillie's needs upon her release were far more basic and immediate: how to be safe from an abusive father, how to live with a dishonest and unstable husband, how to find a job when she had no skills, and how to get food to eat.[2]

Meanwhile, Anna Davy, with her husband constantly drunk and her three eldest children behind bars, could barely cope with her youngest ones. A week later neighbors heard the cries of children inside the Davy house. Reported a city journalist, "From the history of the family it was generally supposed that the children were being beaten." John Garrett, employed by a child-welfare charity, visited the home and found "that the two younger children had lately recovered from the chicken pox, and that one of them is now suffering from kidney difficulties, which requires the assistance of a physician several times each day. It is the operation upon the child that causes it to cry." The doctor probably had to catheterize the youngest boy, two-year-old Acle. Garrett reported that "Mrs. Davy appears to be an industrious woman, doing all she can for her little ones."[3]

A month later, Albert Davy, in a drunken rage, kicked his wife and children out of the house and ordered them to live on the street. The police soon arrived and took Davy to jail, and a police-court judge sentenced him to fifteen days. Meanwhile, Lillie served her term in the State Industrial School, located in what is now Edgerton Park in Rochester. Previously known as the Western House of Refuge, it had been founded in 1849. According to New York law, its purpose was "to gather into the school, vagrant and destitute children, who from the vice of their parents, are unable to attend the public schools, and who gather a precarious livelihood by begging and pilfering, to give them ideas of moral and religious duty, to instruct them in the elements of learning, and in different branches of industry, and thus enable them to obtain honest and honorable support, and to become useful members of society."[4]

It was then a revolutionary approach to caring for delinquent, disadvantaged, or abused children. Previously, the government had provided no care at all for impoverished and neglected children. In 1876 girls were admitted into the Industrial School for the first time, and a separate building to house them was erected. The emphasis was supposed to be on education and training, including cooking and sewing for the girls and woodworking and other skills for the boys. Although hard work was intended to instill strong character traits, a contract-labor system soon developed, in which the children manufactured furniture, shoes, buggy whips, and other items for outside companies. Those who disobeyed were subject to floggings. An 1884 investigation by the New York State Assembly resulted in major reforms. Contract labor was abolished, corporal punishment was gradually discontinued, and children were segregated according to their age and behavior. Most important was a renewed emphasis on education and job training. And a year before Lillie was admitted, legislators changed the name from the Western House of Refuge to the State Industrial School.

Lillie seems to have absorbed some of the education, because she became adept at reading, writing, and composing poetry. But a childhood of abject poverty and abuse had made its profound effect. When Lillie was released in early September 1887, she returned to her housebreaking husband, Charlie Dean. A few weeks later, on October 7, she and Dean "engaged in a free-handed fight in a house in the Eighth ward" with a man named Wilson. Rochester police officers quickly arrived, placed Lillie and Wilson under arrest, and released Dean. According to a colorful newspaper report the next day, "They were given a ride in the noisy phaeton [paddy wagon], and passed the night on iron cots. They will probably go over the hill in the shoemakers' [prisoners'] wagon this afternoon." In the slang of that era, convicts were called shoemakers because many of them worked in prison shoe shops. The judge heard Lillie's case, then sent her back to the State Industrial School for three months.[5]

John Garrett was one man in town who was a friend to the Davy family. Rochester had an active branch of the New York Society for the Prevention of Cruelty to Children, founded in 1874 to battle child abuse and neglect. Garrett, its local agent and child-welfare officer, was a former Rochester policeman. He carried a revolver, had the power to make arrests, and handled about fifty child-abuse cases a month. As Garrett once explained, "I come in contact with so many cases of destitution, desertion, and devilishness that at times, accustomed to it as I have become, my very heart is sick." He knew the Davy family well.[6]

On October 10, two days after Lillie returned to the Industrial School, Garrett received a pathetic note from Anna Davy. "Please Mr. Garrett, can't you do something for me? My man is all the time threatening to run away and I am not able to work and have nothing for my children, aged 14, 12, 10, 8, 5 and 3 years, to eat." Garrett proceeded promptly to the Davy home where he "found the family in as deplorable condition as the note had suggested." He reported, "The father had already 'run away,' else he would have been arrested for non-support." Garrett also noticed that Anna Davy was again pregnant, and he concluded that "the family would have to be cared for by the poor officials."[7]

But with virtually no social services, there was a limit to what Garrett could do for the Davys. Two weeks later Lillie's ten-year-old brother, Henry, spotted a velocipede—an early, large-wheeled version of a bicycle—in a Rochester store. Bicycling was becoming popular, and with mechanical improvements in the next few years, a craze for biking broke out. During the 1890s, the Golden Age of Bicycles resulted in cultural and transportation changes, especially for women who found an independent way to travel while wearing comfortable—but scandalous—

clothing. Henry, however, was not out to change society when he decided to steal the velocipede and ride off with it. The storekeeper managed to get it back but declined to press charges against the boy. A week later, young Henry stole another velocipede. Two officers found him and took him to police headquarters. He was sentenced to thirty days and joined Lillie in the State Industrial School. Soon after that, police lodged Albert Davy in the Rochester jail, apparently on charges of public drunkenness. The exasperated judge gave him two months behind bars.[8]

In mid-November Henry was released from the Industrial School. Just a week later, on November 23, he and his younger sister, Jennie, age seven, were arrested for disorderly conduct. The pair told police officers that they "want to go where they can get something to eat." They were fed, kept in jail overnight, and then appeared before the police-court judge. He gave them a lecture and set them free. Two nights afterward, Henry led his three younger siblings, Jennie, Mary, and little brother Acle, ages seven to two, outside in a driving rain. They slipped into a nearby church where Henry stole a Bible, an armful of fans, and a hymn book. Police officers quickly arrested him and found three stolen watches in his pockets. They locked Henry in jail and Detective Thomas Lynch took the three younger ones to the Industrial School. Lynch told a reporter, "The case of this family is a sad one, and the little homeless children should be taken care of and not allowed to run about the streets." The police-court judge found Henry guilty of vagrancy and sent him back to the Industrial School.[9]

Soon afterward, the secretary of the State Industrial School issued its annual report, which included a graphic description of the travails of the Davy family. "It was after ten o'clock at night when recently three of the Davy children were brought to this shelter. They had been trailed through mire and slush by their remarkable brother Henry, himself scarcely ten years old, but precocious almost beyond belief in ways that are dark. He has again been sent to the State Industrial School, from which institution he had only recently been liberated. The children thus brought under our care are aged respectively six, four, and two-and-one-half years. They were in a shocking plight as the police officer brought them in. The rags they wore were so drenched from the rain to which they were so long exposed and the soggy leather that did service as shoes had so stained their feet that they might have belonged to Malay children. Their wretched apparel was stripped from them and they were all given a bath, the youngest, the two-and-a-half year old boy [Acle], acted as if terrified at the idea of being put into the water—had never been there before probably—and resisted emphatically with loud screaming, until the matron took him up *nolens volens* [like it or not] and plunged him into the rare element. Once there he was subdued and after thorough ablution was attired in a clean, white night-dress, placed snugly in bed, and as soon as his head touched the pillow was fast asleep. His poor little body, in addition to the filth attached to it, was all scarred and sore, as if he had been burned badly."[10]

Lillie was released from the Industrial School early in 1888. She rejoined her husband, Charlie Dean, but their reunion was short-lived. Sometime after midnight on February 18, Dean, with two eighteen-year-old burglars, George McMullen and George McCauley, broke into a grocery store on Rochester's West Side. They escaped with a measly six dollars. Less than two weeks later, on the night of March 1, the trio entered a grocery store on Spring Street. Unfortunately for the burglars, an alert police officer spotted them forcing their way inside. He immediately summoned help, probably by using the time-honored policeman's telegraph: pinging his nightstick against the cobblestone sidewalk. Three other officers rushed to the scene. Dean and his comrades fled on foot, closely pursued by the four patrolmen. One officer caught McMullen, but Dean and McCauley managed to outrun their pursuers.

The policemen apparently recognized Dean, for he was located and captured the following night. The officers searched him and found that he was carrying a double slungshot—a cord with weights at each end, used as a bludgeon—and a candle for nighttime burglaries. His captors reported, "Dean has a bad reputation, and has been arrested on a similar charge before. He took the matter very coolly, and said he had been married three times, and was now living with his last wife." Early the next morning police arrested George McCauley at his home. Incredibly, he had been married only hours earlier. After a thorough grilling, McCauley admitted participation in both store break-ins. All three pleaded guilty to third-degree burglary and were sentenced to terms of two and a half years each at hard labor in the county penitentiary, known as the Rochester Work House.[11]

Lillie did not long mourn the loss of Charlie Dean. She soon began running with Thomas O'Hara, a young Rochester thief. On the night of April 24, 1888, a policeman stopped O'Hara on Maple Street and found that he was carrying some women's clothing. He locked O'Hara in jail on suspicion of stealing the clothes. O'Hara insisted that he had traded the garments with Lillie Davy for men's wear and that she "was now about the city palming herself off for one of the sterner sex." When it turned out that O'Hara had told the truth, police officers released him from jail. He rejoined Lillie, then the pair beat their way by freight train to Hamilton, Ontario. Their journey to Canada was later described by a Hamilton newspaperman who interviewed Lillie. She claimed that in Rochester "five or six boys got her 'full' [drunk], had her hair cut off, dressed her up in boys' clothes, and suggested that they would all go to Chicago. She consented, and all the boys but Thomas O'Hara backed out, so they had to start alone. The fellow who got her the clothes had lots of money, and she regretted that he did not accompany them on the trip. It was at O'Hara's suggestion that they alighted from a freight train and tarried at Hamilton. She had been here before and did not want to fall into the hands of the police."[12]

Lillie spent the next week, according to another reporter, "masquerading in male clothing and associating with young men of low instincts in the city of Hamilton." Police soon jailed Thomas O'Hara on suspicion of burglarizing a hotel. A few days later, on the night of May 6, Lillie was at the Grand Trunk Railway station where she traded hats and overcoats with a young ruffian, James O'Leary. Detective Sergeant James Castell of the Hamilton police spotted her. As Lillie recalled, "A policeman came up on each side of me, and one said, 'My girl, you had better com wid me.' I says, 'What do you want wid me? I ain't no girl.' Den they arrested me." Castell took Lillie and O'Leary to the police station and booked them for vagrancy. The next morning a reporter interviewed Lillie, writing that "she was seated on a stool at the police station with her feet cocked up on the rungs. She had on a rather good suit of clothes and appeared to be quite at home in them." He added, "She is so well disguised that Sergeant Castell's perceptive faculties must be unusually keen in order to have been able to spot her at night. With rather a plain face and coarse features, she is broad in the shoulders and has the swagger of a young tough."

Hamilton's colorful chief of police, Hugh McKinnon, a famous athlete, had taken over for Chief Stewart. He was a huge man for that era, six foot three, 225 pounds, and a champion of the Scottish Highland games—especially the caber toss—in Canada and the US.

McKinnon had previously served as police chief of Belleville and knew the Davy family well. He provided a detailed account of the Davys to a reporter for the *Hamilton Spectator.* "Had it not been for a drunken father the youngsters might have been better," the journalist told his readers. "The children were all born and brought up in Lindsay. Their father was very dissipated and continually abused his wife. From Lindsay they went to Orillia, and for a time the chief lost sight of them. The next word he received was that Mrs. Davy had succeeded in getting her husband sent to jail for abusing her."

Chief McKinnon described to the journalist the various escapades of Lillie, Katy, and the other Davy children and even gave a brief account of the gang rape of their mother near Campbellford. The chief also remarked that Katy "is the best looking one of the family." When the reporter asked Lillie about Katy, Lillie claimed that her younger sister had recently married. "Her husband has lots of boodle and she is awfully stuck up," she declared. But Katy was only fourteen and there is no evidence that she married that young, for in New York the age of consent was still sixteen years.[13]

Another journalist who saw Lillie in the Hamilton jail observed, "She is an extraordinary young person, and in her masculine dress looks the picture of a young boy of the 'tough' species. She is bright and intelligent looking, but chews tobacco, smokes a clay pipe, and has the general appearance of a young rowdy." Lillie was then brought into court with the two young hardcases, Thomas O'Hara and James O'Leary. O'Hara testified that "he got acquainted with her in Rochester, and they left together, walking twelve miles." O'Hara falsely claimed that he "did not find out that she was a girl until they got to the Canadian side of the Niagara River. They then stole a ride on a freight train to Hamilton, and were there a week last Friday. They slept around the city in barns and sheds." O'Leary then took the witness stand to testify on behalf of Lillie, but he damaged her case by admitting that he knew she was a girl when they exchanged hats and overcoats.

The magistrate promptly found Lillie guilty of vagrancy. Because she had already served several terms in the New York Industrial School, he sentenced her to a whopping twenty-three months in the Mercer Reformatory in Toronto. As Lillie left court, Chief McKinnon told her, "Hold on to O'Leary's good overcoat. He has made such a miserable witness in the case he is not deserving of it."

A reporter who attended the hearing said, "Her appearance in the police court today caused considerable excitement, and a crowd assembled to see her taken away in the patrol wagon. She seemed to enjoy the sensation she was creating, and laughed and waved her hat as the wagon drove off."[14]

AUTHOR'S COLLECTION.

The Mercer Reformatory in Toronto. Canada's first female prison, it was Lillie Davy's home from 1888 to 1890.

Lillie always claimed that when she was sixteen she attended a boarding school in Canada. Her boarding school was in fact the Mercer Reformatory for Women, located in the West End of Toronto. It was a huge, foreboding brick building, four stories high and topped with neo-Gothic spires. Mercer had opened in 1872 as Canada's first women's prison. In many ways, it was similar to the other two institutions that had held Lillie, the Erring

Women's Refuge in Chicago and the State Industrial School in Rochester. Lillie joined about one hundred and forty inmates in Mercer. When she was booked into the prison, the female guards, called matrons, took away her street clothes and issued the standard uniform, a blue denim dress with a long white apron. The inmates were kept busy with work, in the expectation that honest labor would instill good character traits. They made their own uniforms and performed all cleaning, cooking, and maintenance in the prison.[15]

Unlike the State Industrial School, Mercer provided only minimal opportunities for education. The girls were taught reading and writing only in the winter months, and then just for an hour and a half each day. The classes were given in the sewing room and were purely voluntary. Physical punishment was not allowed, and women who violated the rules were placed in a "dark cell" in the dungeon where they were kept in solitary confinement, sleeping on a straw pallet. As the chief matron of Mercer observed in 1888, "The dungeon, with bread and water diet, will generally reduce the most refractory to obedience, but we have rarely to resort to such expedients. Months may go by without one punishment, and this ward is often vacant for a long time." One-third of Lillie's fellow prisoners were under the age of twenty, and fifty were serving time for prostitution. The rest had been found guilty of larceny, vagrancy, and drunkenness. Among such bad company, Lillie Davy settled in for a long stay in the Mercer Reformatory.[16]

Two months after Lillie entered Mercer, her brother Willie, then eighteen, caused more trouble in Rochester. The police began hunting him after getting a report that he and an accomplice were peddling stolen watches. Willie and his comrade managed to elude the officers, then stole a locket from a jewelry store and fled seventy-five miles east to Oswego, on the shore of Lake Ontario. The pair then pulled a burglary in

Oswego and landed in jail. On July 30 the guards put them to work outside in the jailyard, and Willie managed to escape. He returned immediately by train to Rochester, but the next day policemen spotted and arrested him. Willie joined his father—who had once again been convicted of drunk and disorderly conduct—in the city lockup. Willie was then returned to Oswego to serve out his jail term.[17]

It turned out that the Oswego County Jail was especially porous. A few weeks later, on August 22, Willie and six other prisoners dug a hole through the brick wall and escaped. Willie fled to Canada and managed to avoid capture for three months before slipping back into the US. Finally, on January 24, 1889, police detectives captured him in a house in Rochester. He claimed that during the jailbreak, he had been lying in his bunk and had only joined in after the others had escaped. "I did not intend to go until I saw de jailer lookin' 'round for de men and didn't find me," he declared. "When I saw what an old mutton-head he was, I thought I'd give him de go-bye and put 'im in de soup." Once again officers returned him to Oswego.[18]

Willie caused his jailers no end of trouble. "Davy is one of the sharpest little thieves and jail breakers ever confined in the Oswego County jail," a local newspaperman reported. "Several times since Davy's arrest he has been searched and each time there were found concealed upon his person small files and saws, showing conclusively that he was being supplied with tools by sympathizers on the outside." Willie was also extremely crafty. Although he was nineteen, he told fellow prisoners that he was twenty-two. But to the district attorney he claimed that he was only fifteen. He said that he was willing to plead guilty to charges of burglary and larceny provided that he was sentenced to the Industrial School instead of the state penitentiary. Willie knew that inmates sixteen and older could not be admitted to the Industrial School.

The gullible district attorney agreed, the judge accepted Willie's plea deal, and the county sheriff took him to the Industrial School in Rochester. The school's superintendent, however, knew Willie well. He refused to receive him, saying, "Davy is too old and too hardened a criminal to be placed with boys younger than he." The flummoxed district attorney then complained, "The boy swears that on his last birthday he was fifteen years of age, and I think that unless something different is positively known, his statement should be taken. I understand the Rochester superintendent bases his opinion that the boy is sixteen years old on his appearance. In law, however, appearances don't go."

The district attorney was extraordinarily naive, and the dispute turned out to be academic. The sheriff took Willie back to the Oswego jail. On the morning of March 15, 1889, the guards allowed Willie to exercise in the jail's north corridor. Its windows were covered by half-inch-thick iron bars. The chief turnkey kept an eye on Willie, but at one point he had to go to another side of the jail. The jailer was gone for forty-five minutes, and that was all Willie needed. Using a smuggled file, he severed an iron bar at the bottom of a window, then cut partway through the top of the bar. He then bent the bar up until it snapped off. Willie managed to squeeze through the gap. Dropping to the ground, he scaled the seven-foot jail fence and vanished. It would be more than a year before he was recaptured.[19]

Like Willie, Saphronia's husband, Andrew Wahl, was no stranger to the Rochester police. On October 27, 1888, he stole a coat and soon found himself under arrest. A policeman took him to the station house and sat him in a chair in the captain's office. Despite the fact that he was guarded by two officers, Wahl suddenly sprang to his feet and jumped toward an open window. As the patrolmen tried to seize his coattails, he flung himself through the window, landed safely on the ground, and sprinted away. The officers pursued him on foot, but Wahl managed to escape. They eventually caught him, but he apparently was not punished. The following June, police hauled him and Saphronia into police court for fighting with each other. The judge released the couple on their promise of good behavior.[20]

COURTESY OF RENEE GALLAGHER AND HEIDI RICHARDSON.

The earliest existing photo of Lillie Davy, alias Pearl Hart, taken about 1890.

Meanwhile Lillie whiled away the days, weeks, and months in the Mercer Reformatory. Each day she arose at six o'clock, dressed in her denim uniform, and waited for a matron to unlock her cell door. She then proceeded to the huge dining room where she downed a breakfast of porridge, bread, and black tea. From there Lillie went to her daily assigned work: sewing, knitting, laundering, ironing, washing, and cleaning the floors. At seven thirty each evening, she was locked back in her cell. Throughout the day, however, she labored alongside prisoners young and old, innocent and corrupt.

A journalist who visited Mercer the same year Lillie entered the prison complained, "There is absolutely no classification of the inmates. They mingle freely in recreation hours, work together, eat together in one large, gloomy dining room, and sleep in adjoining cells. For vagrancy, larceny, and assault, drunkenness and prostitution of a greater or less degree, these women are sentenced to mingle together for a period of months or years. Many are first offenders, guilty only of minor evil, sentenced mayhaps by some county judge at the request of an anxious father who desires the reformation of his erring child. Many others, alas, are hardened criminals who have lived a life of the vilest sin that womanhood can compass."[21]

Lillie Davy already was much too wild to be tamed by Victorian principles of thrift, labor, and religious duty. Though she became a skilled seamstress in Mercer, she wanted only her freedom.

4

Becoming Pearl Hart

Lillie Davy's transformation into Pearl Hart began in Buffalo, New York. She completed her term in the Mercer Reformatory early in 1890 and immediately set out to find Katy, who had moved from Rochester to Buffalo. There, sixteen-year-old Katy—with little education or job training—had obtained work as a prostitute. Buffalo, with a population of 255,000, was the largest industrial city of the Great Lakes region. Following the completion of the Erie Canal in 1825, Buffalo—at that time a frontier town accessible only by horse and wagon—became the western terminus of the important waterway that connected it to New York City. The canal allowed for cheap, fast transportation and shipping to and from the Midwest. Buffalo exploded as laborers and their families poured in, attracted by a myriad of jobs. Then, beginning in the 1850s, railroad lines joined the city with the Eastern Seaboard, and as a result, manufacturing and shipping boomed. A huge influx of young, single, male workers encouraged the proliferation of saloons and brothels in Buffalo.[1]

There were then very few occupations available to women, other than housecleaning, washing, dressmaking, running boarding houses, and, in industrial communities, working in mills and factories. Educated women had better opportunities, such as schoolteaching and stenography. But women lacking education or employable skills often drifted to brothels, commonly known in that era as houses of ill repute, bagnios, bawdy houses, and sporting houses. Their inmates were called women of ill fame, bawds, sports, courtesans, lewd women, painted ladies, soiled doves, and pretty waiter girls. Because respectable women did not have sexual relations outside of marriage, unmarried men could not have sex unless they visited a bordello. As a result, prostitution flourished. And prostitutes, just like today, lived vulnerable and precarious lives and frequently coped with their physical and emotional pain by abusing alcohol and drugs.

Fanny Fern, one of the preeminent female journalists of the nineteenth century, described how many of New York's working girls drifted into prostitution. "There are no sufficiently decent, cleanly boarding houses within their means, where their self-respect would not inevitably wither and die. As it is, they stroll the streets, and who can blame them? *There* are gay lights, and fine shop windows. It costs nothing to wish they could have all those fine things. They look longingly into the theaters, through whose doors happier girls of their own age pass, radiant and smiling, with their lovers. Glimpses of paradise come through those doors as they gaze. Back comes the old torturing question: Must my young life *always* be toil? *Nothing* but toil? They stroll on. Music and bright lights from the underground 'concert saloons,' where girls like themselves get fine dresses and good wages, and flattering words and smiles beside. Alas! The future is far away; the present is only tangible. Is it a wonder if they never go back to the dark, cheerless tenement house, or to the 'manufactory' which sets their poor, weary bodies aching, til they feel forsaken of God and man?"[2]

An observer of that era explained that Buffalo was "one of the roughest and most dangerous towns in America. It was sown with saloons. Along the waterfront were solid rows of dives of the worst order—barrel houses [cheap saloons], dens selling Monongahela whiskey [Pennsylvania rye] at four cents a glass, brothels, and gambling joints. Cutting affrays were a daily affair. There were streets where the police walked at mid-day and only in pairs, for an officer who came along might shortly be found floating face down in the Canal. The Irish longshoremen loved nothing more than a fight and the prostitutes numbered in the hundreds."[3]

Buffalo's Canal Street district, also known as "the Hooks" after the cargo hooks used by longshoremen, boasted seventy-five brothels and more than a hundred saloons. One of its best-known madams called herself Pearl Hart. She was about twenty-three and ran a sporting house in the Hooks. A Buffalo journalist described her as "a big, fleshy woman" and explained, "Pearl is a heavy drinker. She is a morphine-eater also, according to the police and denizens of the street." She first arrived in Buffalo about 1887, opened her own bordello, and made a lucrative living. Her common-law husband was a saloonkeeper, Joe Hart.

Within a few years, Pearl's earnings in Buffalo allowed her paramour to open a popular saloon and concert hall on Canal Street. She closed her brothel and lived with Joe in rooms above the saloon. But later, in the mid-1890s, Pearl's heavy drinking and morphine use, coupled with Joe's infidelity, led her to make several attempts at suicide, and she finally succeeded in 1900. Her name inspired the aliases of the Davy sisters. Katy, after arriving in Buffalo in 1889, identified herself as Minnie Hart and began working in the brothels. Given that the custom in that era was for a prostitute to use the last name of her madam or her pimp, it seems possible that she worked in Pearl Hart's bagnio. And Lillie Davy would later adopt the name Pearl Hart.[4]

There was a distinct hierarchy in nineteenth-century prostitution. At the top were courtesans, the stylish, beautiful women who serviced wealthy men. Next were parlor girls who worked in so-called female boarding houses, patronized by upper-middle-class men. Below that were cheap brothels, called bawdy houses, and concert saloons staffed by pretty waiter girls who sold drinks and sex. Next were the cribs, lines of wood shacks or low brick buildings, where the soiled doves displayed themselves from the front windows or porches. An occupant of a crib could service as many as thirty men a day. At the bottom of the ladder were streetwalkers, who loitered in doorways and dark alleys.

By the time of Katy's arrival in Buffalo, the city police conducted a revolving-door campaign against prostitution. Although some officers accepted bribes to allow brothels on their beats, honest policemen raided the bordellos and brought the women into court. The prostitutes received cash fines of five to twenty dollars, then simply returned to work. Katy had ambitions greater than being a parlor girl or occupying a crib. As a Buffalo journalist wrote in 1890, "She quickly opened a house of her own under the name of Minnie Hart, and the place became noted as one of the most disreputable dives in the city. The inmates were of the youngest and most depraved and the place was continually under police surveillance. Time and again the raids of the police resulted in the capture of criminals who frequented the place, although it was often necessary to break open the doors to effect the seizure. Minnie, or Kate, was a handsome young woman who, though nineteen, looked scarcely seventeen years old. The housekeeper was a girl not over fifteen and several ineffectual attempts were made to remove her from the place but she hid away from her parents."[5]

Katy, in fact, was then only sixteen. The fact that she ran her own bagnio at that age speaks volumes of her sophistication. At that time the 400 and 500 blocks of Michigan Street (now Michigan Avenue), located east of the Hooks, were lined with saloons and brothels. Katy established her bordello in rooms above a saloon at 492 Michigan Street, located at the present-day corner of Michigan and Arsenal Place. Several girls worked for her. The main door had a peephole so she could observe any visitors before admitting them. Once, when a customer knocked on the door, she peered through the peephole, only to see that the man was trying to look inside through the other end of the aperture. Katy became enraged, as the Buffalo journalist reported: "She seized a carving knife from the table and plunged it through the peep-hole. There was a cry in the darkness and the man hurried downstairs. No complaint was ever entered as the man was probably unwilling to admit having been in such a neighborhood." The writer added that Katy "was once arrested for attempting to 'clean out' a saloon while she was masquerading in male garments."[6]

RENEE GALLAGHER COLLECTION.

Lillie Davy (Pearl Hart) as she looked in the mid-1890s.

Lillie found Katy in Buffalo and worked with her as a prostitute in the Michigan Street bagnio. Soon they were joined by their brother Willie, who was still on the lam following his escape from the Oswego jail. From time to time the trio would leave the city and venture into the surrounding countryside. As a Buffalo reporter explained, "It is said that one of their games was working the country, by selling and stealing cattle. They would steal a cow in a village, take her to the next, and sell her to some honest yokel, and before he had really come to consider himself the owner, the animal would be again stolen by the trio and resold."[7] On one occasion Katy was the victim, rather than the perpetrator, of a crime.

Charles Liebendorfer, whom a Buffalo reporter called "a sleek young man wearing a private detective badge," was actually a swindler who had been loitering about the neighborhood. On March 22, 1890, he knocked on Katy's door at 492 Michigan Street. She, thinking that he was a customer, let him in. But Liebendorfer was there to get money, not to spend it. As it was reported, "His presence became oppressive to the woman but she stood it until a late hour when, to give him the hint that it was time to leave, she drew out her gold watch to see the time. The fly detective asked to see the watch, and taking it, he coolly walked out of the house and disappeared." Katy, using her alias of Minnie Hart, reported the theft to the police, who quickly collared Liebendorfer. The officers went to his boarding house, searched his room, and found Katy's watch under the bed. Liebendorfer appeared in police court a few days later, pleaded guilty to petty theft, and received twenty days in jail.[8]

A month later the three Davys were joined by their fourteen-year-old sister, Amy. A reporter, who interviewed a witness to their reunion, wrote, "The conversation of Amy is a singular mingling of childish prattle and horrible oaths. While she is a mere child who scarcely seems fourteen years old, she is disguised with a yellow wig." The journalist described the Davys' discussion as "a garbled grist of slang and profanity. The boy wanted some money as he said he had given all he had to his father to pass him up the lakes." What Willie meant was that he paid for Albert's fare so he could return to his old home in Canada's Kawartha Lakes. Willie had obtained an old suitcase and told his sisters that he was going to fill it with bricks and pretend that he was an honest traveler. Willie boasted that he would "'work' a boarding house for a week's board" and then skip out without paying.[9]

But Willie could not outsmart the Buffalo police. On May 7, officers received a report of a young man offering to sell silver spoons on the street at cut-rate prices. That night two patrolmen spotted a suspect who matched the description carrying a large bundle. They shadowed the youth for a time, then stopped him on Elm Street, about a block from the Michigan Street bordello occupied by Lillie and Katy. The officers searched him and found two packages of cooking utensils and a supply of silverware. The young man turned out to be Willie Davy. In his pocket was a letter from Katy that read, "Dear Will: Lill and I have got a chance to go to Rochester and we are going right away. I am afraid to let you stay in Buffalo as the detectives here are too sharp. Write to me. Minnie."

Her warning had been too late to help Willie. The officers, after locking him up in the precinct station on a vagrancy charge, discovered that he was an escapee from the Oswego jail. Buffalo journalists heralded the arrest, declaring that Willie Davy "is a noted crook" and that "two of his sisters reside in Michigan Street sporting houses and have bad reputations." One reporter who saw Willie remarked that he was "extraordinarily youthful in appearance and fairly good looking." He was kept behind bars until Oswego authorities could take him back him to jail to serve out his sentence. Lillie, Katy, and Amy had had enough of Buffalo, and they returned by train to Rochester.[10]

By this time Lillie and Katy realized they were too well-known to the police in Rochester and Buffalo. They decided to head to Toledo, Ohio, a bustling city of eighty thousand on the western tip of Lake Erie. The girls were probably drawn to Toledo because some of their mother's large Duval family had settled there. Lillie later said that it was in Toledo that she met Dan Bandman, a tall, slender, German-Jewish piano player. Bandman, the black-sheep son of a prominent family, made a living playing in saloons and gambling halls. He was then performing with a traveling theatrical company that visited Toledo, and Lillie quickly became infatuated with him. In her recollections, she made no mention of the fact that she had been working as a prostitute. Instead, as she would later claim in the Tucson lockup, "I was easily impressed. I knew nothing of life. Marriage was to me but a name. It did not take him long to get my consent to an elopement. We ran away one night and were married."[11]

Her beau was born Daniel E. Bandman, the son of Charles Joseph Bandman, a German-born physician who had anglicized his surname by dropping the last *n*. Dr. Bandman had joined the Comstock Lode silver rush to Nevada with his wife Emma in about 1860. They settled in Virginia City, Nevada, but soon moved across the Sierra Nevada Mountains to Coloma, California. That was where gold had first been discovered, sparking the Gold Rush of 1849. In Coloma the couple greeted their first child, Daniel, on April 12, 1863. Dr. Bandman proved to be more interested in mining, engineering, and inventing than in practicing medicine. The following year the Bandmans returned to the East Coast and made their home in Union, New Jersey. The elder Bandman patented a new type of cement and founded the New York Stone Works, with headquarters in New York City. Later he became a contractor, building railroads in Venezuela and operating mines in Mexico. His younger brother was the hugely popular Shakespearean actor Daniel E. Bandmann, who from the 1860s until his death in 1905 performed extensively on the stage throughout the US and abroad.[12]

Lillie was greatly impressed with Dan Bandman's pedigree, but unfortunately he did not follow in the luminous footsteps of his father and uncle. As a teenager he lived in Venezuela with his father and became fluent in Spanish. When he was seventeen his parents sent him to New York City, where he resided in a boarding house and studied engraving. But young Bandman was highly musical—and a talented piano player—and he had no interest in working as an illustrator for newspapers and magazines. When his parents decided to return to California in 1890, he went with them. They lived together in an opulent, three-story Victorian home on Sutter Street in San Francisco, but Dan forsook a comfortable upper-middle-class life. Instead of performing as a pianist with his thespian uncle, he struck out on his own and headed back east. Dan Bandman became an itinerant musician, tinkling piano keys in saloons, card rooms, and bordellos.[13]

In 1891 Bandman landed in Toledo, Ohio. Lillie first met him when he was performing in a local theater. She had good reason to be impressed. He was well-educated, well-spoken, and well-traveled. As he once said, "I speak, read, and write Spanish, German, and French." Lillie, always a lover of music, was particularly attracted by his skill as a pianist. Unfortunately, that was one of his few positive traits. Bandman was then twenty-eight, erratic, lazy, ill-tempered, and addicted to opium. She had chosen a man who was not much different from her father. Perhaps Lillie, who had been subjected to extreme neglect by and abuse from Albert Davy, sought affection from the same kind of man. In so doing, she became doomed to repeat the same experiences of her childhood. Modern psychologists believe that this is why many troubled young women marry men much like their abusive fathers.[14]

Despite Lillie's claim that she and Bandman married, their union was probably a common-law relationship, without any legal formality. Nonetheless, she went by the name Lillie Bandman. She recalled that they soon went to Chicago. "We lived together for three years, and I was happy and good, for I dearly loved the man whose name I bore," she said. "I was happy for a time, but not for long. My husband began to abuse me, and presently he drove me from him. Then I returned to my mother, in the village of Lindsay, Ontario, where I was born." But at that time Anna Davy lived in Rochester, not Lindsay. Lillie continued, "Before long, my husband sent for me, and I went back to him. I loved him, and he promised to do better. I had not been with him two weeks before he began to abuse me again, and after bearing up under his blows as long as I could I left him again. This was just as the World's Fair closed in Chicago, in the fall of 1893."[15]

It was then that Edward "Doc" Kelley claimed that he met her. Kelley, a handsome, twenty-eight-year-old Canadian, ran a traveling medicine show. He later said that he had first encountered Lillie six years earlier when she came to see his show near Lindsay. Kelley explained that "on amateur night, a fifteen-year-old farm girl came up on stage and won first prize with a dance." He saw her next near Chicago in 1893. Kelley had created a new show that he called "Kelley's Lady Minstrels" which featured a bevy of beautiful female performers. He claimed that the farm girl was then working in a restaurant. "She neglected her job, practically haunting the show grounds, and it was evident that she had set her cap for 'my dear fellow Canadian.'" Kelley recalled that he did not return her affections, and when she wrote to his home in Canada, he did not respond. Though Doc Kelley told many stories that should be taken with a grain of salt, Lillie was certainly in Chicago that year, separated from Dan Bandman. As it later turned out, she indeed liked medicine showmen just like Kelley, and, years later, would marry one.[16]

AUTHOR'S COLLECTION.

An artist's depiction of Lillie Davy, alias Pearl Hart, based on an 1899 photograph.

While Lillie was with Dan Bandman in Chicago, her siblings continued to plague the city of Rochester and its police. In the spring of 1892 officers arrested Jennie Davy, then twelve, and a judge ordered her to serve a term in the State Industrial School in Rochester. Soon afterward, police collared her brother Henry, fifteen, and he joined her in the Industrial School. Neither of them planned on staying there long. On the night of April 19, 1892, Jennie crawled out a dormitory window, climbed down the fire escape, and fled to her mother's house at 158 Pinnacle Avenue. Veteran police detective Thomas Lynch began a search. He was the same officer who had arrested the Davy children before, and he knew the family well. Lynch quickly found Jennie at home and returned her to the Industrial School. Two weeks later, on March 4, the school's staff foolishly allowed Henry to step outside for fresh air. He promptly vanished, but Detective Lynch got on his trail. Lynch knew that Saphronia and her husband, Andrew Wahl, had recently opened a saloon at 187 Front Street in Rochester. They lived in rooms connected to the saloon with Amy Davy, now sixteen. Detective Lynch watched the saloon off and on for two weeks. On Saturday night, March 19, he collared Henry in Saphronia's place and hauled him back to the Industrial School.[17]

By this time Amy was also in trouble. A Rochester police captain explained that "she has been arrested innumerable times." Like the other Davy girls, Amy had probably been sexually abused by their father and had come to view sex as a commodity. On the night of October 24, 1892, less than two weeks after her seventeenth birthday, Amy was working as a prostitute in the Railroad House, a hotel and saloon on Front Street. This was near Saphronia's saloon. A policeman arrested her for stealing seventeen dollars from one of the male customers. She insisted that her name was Amy Duval—she used her mother's maiden name as an alias—and that she "was an adopted sister of Jennie Davy, who was sent to the State Industrial School some time ago." A journalist met Amy at the jail and described her as "a rather pretty girl, about twenty years of age." When a police captain identified Amy as "one of the notorious Davy family," the reporter said that "she denied [it] up and down and crosswise."

The police-court judge found Amy guilty of petty theft and "prostitution and frequenting disorderly houses." He sentenced her to five years in the House of Refuge for Women, located two hundred and fifty miles east, in Hudson, New York. The House of Refuge accepted only young women who had been convicted of petty larceny, prostitution, and habitual drunkenness. They were sent there for indeterminate sentences of up to five years, in order to learn habits of work and honesty. The judge, however, either had a change of heart or he had only sent Amy to the House of Refuge in order to scare her. A week later he ordered her release. The judge's approach succeeded, because after Amy was freed she "sinned no more."[18]

The same could not be said of her brother Henry. In the winter of 1892 he escaped from the Industrial School. Henry was at large for several months while Rochester policemen kept an eye out for him. Finally, on March 6, 1893, an officer captured him in his favorite hideout: Saphronia's saloon. After the policeman returned him to the Industrial School, Henry boasted that he would escape again. He did not have to. Henry was such a troublemaker the school officials voluntarily released him in July. A few weeks later he was arrested for stealing a ride on a freight train. A Rochester reporter attended his court hearing and wrote, "It was intended to send him back to the Industrial School, but as the officials there don't want him longer, and as he claims to be sixteen years of age, he will probably be sent to the penitentiary." Instead Henry served a term in the county jail.[19]

But not all the Davy children were condemned to follow in their father's footsteps. Mary Davy, like her siblings, had been raised in squalor, hunger, and abuse. In 1891, when she was eight, a Rochester police officer found her wandering the streets alone. The police were unable to identify her, and Mary did not enlighten them. No doubt she did not want to return to the family home. The police-court judge sent her to the Industrial School so she could be cared for. A kindly Rochester woman, Mary Apfel, the wife of a railroad man, soon adopted her and took her home to live with her family. As a journalist later commented, "The child was much pleased with her new home. She was sent to school and has led a happy life. She has almost forgotten that her name ever was Davy or that she was not in reality the daughter of Mrs. Apfel."

Anna Davy later claimed that she did not know what had become of her daughter. Then, one day in March 1893, ten-year-old Mary was walking home from school when Andrew Wahl happened by and immediately recognized her. He told Mary that he was her brother-in-law and insisted that she accompany him to his home—which happened to be in the back rooms of the saloon. Mary did not know who he was. Scared out of her wits, she fled to the Apfel home. Wahl then described his encounter to Anna Davy, and she managed to scrape up enough money to hire a lawyer. Her attorney filed a lawsuit in order to void the adoption and return Mary to her mother. Mary Apfel and her husband got their own attorney, and a Rochester judge listened to arguments from both sides. A month after Wahl had accosted Mary, the judge ruled that the adoption was valid and that the Apfels had legal custody of the child. No doubt the judge was also swayed by the Davy family's reputation. As one newspaper reminded its readers, "Mrs. Davy is the mother of the notorious Davy sisters." Thus Mary Davy grew up in a stable household and avoided the trials and traumas of her unlucky siblings.[20]

Meanwhile Katy Davy had settled in Toledo. When Lillie departed with Dan Bandman for Chicago, Katy stayed in Ohio. She soon met Howard W. Allen, a handsome, thirty-year-old actor from Cincinnati. Like Dan Bandman, Allen was long on flash and short on substance. But the Davy girls liked flashy men, and Katy quickly fell in love. She later claimed that they eloped, going sixty miles north to Detroit, where they were married in

January 1893. Katy falsely recalled, "I was very young then and as my parents were well-to-do and my lover was only an actor, I was compelled to run away and wed him. As soon as my folks heard of our wedding they attempted to separate us and have our wedding annulled. They did not succeed, however, at first, but finally they got me and kept me away from him awhile. I then escaped and left home to endeavor to find him and of course was thrown upon my own resources for a living."[21]

But there is no evidence that the couple was wed in Detroit, and Katy's marriage, like that of Lillie, may have been a common-law union. And her parents certainly were not well-to-do, nor could they have tried to separate her from Allen. Albert Davy had left Anna and had returned to his old haunts in the Kawartha Lakes region, where he had little or no contact with his family. The Davys seem to have separated for good by 1893, when Anna listed herself as a widow in the Rochester city directory. In a later interview Katy claimed that she and Howard Allen soon got a divorce. It is far more likely that they simply broke up, and Allen drifted on to pursue his career as an itinerant actor.[22]

By the spring of 1894, twenty-one-year-old Katy had left Toledo and drifted two hundred miles south to Cincinnati, probably in a vain search for her lover in his old hometown. Perennially destitute, Katy resumed her career as a prostitute in the city's tenderloin district, centered around Longworth Street in Cincinnati's West End. According to a journalist of the era, Longworth Street—which no longer exists—had "more houses of prostitution than can be found from end to end of any other one street in the city. Decent people have long since deserted the neighborhood, so that now it is entirely given over to the demimonde, who swarm within the houses on both sides of the street."[23]

On June 20, 1894, the mother of an eighteen-year-old girl, Effie Schuck, complained to the police that Katy Davy and another young prostitute, Maggie Holland, had tried to entice her daughter into a brothel. Officers quickly arrested the three girls and brought them to the police station where Katy gave police her real name. Then a reporter asked her why she was there. Katy motioned toward Effie Schuck, then instantly switched on her street slang.

"I'll tell yer wat's de matter," she declared. "Her mudder is full of tacks."

"Whose mother is full of tacks, Katy?" asked the reporter.

"Not Mag's, but Ef's," snapped Katy, again pointing to Effie Schuck. "Yer see, it wus like dis. I left me home about two months ago and I'm livin' wid me aunt or sister, or whatever yer want to call her, at 1865 Columbia Avenue. Last week I was up at Hamlet [Ohio] visiting a lady frien', and who do you suppose I met? Nobody but Mag Holland. Her right name is Wicks, but she goes by her stepdaddy's name. He's an engineer on de road, but he's a dead tough mug toward dat Mag. Mag wus kickin' about de old man, and as I was comin' to town, I asks her to come along wid me and she did. She put on dat pink dress she's got on and came down. We've been havin' a good time ever since, and last Monday I says to Mag, says I, 'Let's go up and see Ef Schuck, 'cause she's been sick.' You can see she's been sick; look how pale she is. Well, we went up to her house at 211 East Front Street, and we saw Ef. We tuk a walk an' she went home. Den we went up again Chuesday and tuk another walk. Den that mudder of hers begins to chew de rag and says for us to keep away. When we went up yesterday de old woman was kickin'. You see, I tot she was kiddin', but she was on de level, and wut does she do? Nothin', only call in two cops and has us all pinched, and here we are."

"Were you going to take the girl away with you?" asked the journalist.

"Naw! De old woman said we wus going to 'tice er away, but look at her—she's eighteen and I'm only seventeen," Katy lied.

"Guess she can take care of herself. You kin bet she kin. Say, will you do me a favor?"

"What is it?"

"Why, send word down to a elevator man at de Chamber of Commerce and he'll get us out."

"Is that your fellow?"

"Now yer rubber neckin'!" exclaimed Katy. "Naw, he's not me steady."

That ended the interview, and the three girls were locked up on the prostitution-related offense of loitering. Fortunately for Katy and her friends, the police-court judge released them the next day for lack of evidence. Within a few weeks Katy, using her alias of Minnie Hart, was working in the brothel of Betty Houston, a notorious madam, on Longworth Street. On the night of July 24, an officer on patrol heard a woman yelling, "Police!"

He found Katy in a nearby alley, and she claimed that she had been robbed. According to Katy, a man had accosted her, dragged her into the alley, and snatched her purse containing two dollars. The officer took her to the central police station to make a report, but there a sergeant recognized her as a prostitute. He ordered Katy locked up on a charge of loitering, and the next day a judge released her after she paid a fine. [24]

Katy, when not servicing clients in Betty Houston's sporting house, had a tumultuous social life. On the afternoon of July 30, five days after she was released from jail, Katy, with another of Betty Houston's girls who went by the name of Fannie Franks, walked to the Cincinnati steamboat landing on the Ohio River. There they boarded a steamer for the six-mile ride upriver to Coney Island, a popular amusement park named after the resort in New York City. Coney Island featured a giant swing, a Ferris wheel, a "shoot the chutes" water ride, and carnival games. At the large swimming pool, Katy and Fannie encountered two rowdy young men, Ed Critz and George Stitzelberger. As a journalist later reported, "The quartet took in the Island thoroughly, and by ten o'clock all were quite intoxicated. Exhausting the Island, they got a skiff and rowed over to Silver Grove, where they continued their carousal."

Silver Grove was a Kentucky town situated across the Ohio River from Coney Island. There Katy and her friends found that they had missed the last steamboat back to the city. They decided to hike three miles to the suspension bridge that crossed the river to Cincinnati. While Katy walked with Critz, Fannie and Stitzelberger followed behind. Soon Fannie and Stitzelberger got into a drunken argument. Fannie collapsed in the road and refused to go another step. They started quarreling again, and Stitzelberger drew a large knife and he threatened to "cut her heart out." As he stepped toward Fannie, Critz rushed up and convinced Stitzelberger to sheath his knife. The couple continued arguing, so Katy and Critz left them and walked back to Cincinnati, arriving at Betty Houston's bagnio at one in the morning.

By the following night Fannie had not returned. Katy and Betty Houston became alarmed, and they went to police headquarters where they reported that Fannie might have met with foul play. The next day Katy and her madam went to Silver Grove and began searching for Fannie. From witnesses they learned that Stitzelberger had carried the drunken Fannie on his back some distance. He finally dropped her, and she rolled down the riverbank, yelling, "Murder! Police!" Then the two patched up their quarrel, walked to a roadhouse, and had more drinks. Stitzelberger took Fannie back to the skiff, hoping to return home by river. Several men in a fishing camp told Katy that they had seen the pair in the boat about one o'clock. "The woman was crying and nearly naked," they said.

With the help of three fisherman, Katy and Betty searched all the fishing camps near Silver Grove but found no trace of Fannie Franks. Finally the group located George Stitzelberger in a camp on the river and brought him to the police station in

Cincinnati. There he denied harming Fannie Franks, but the officers locked him up as a suspect in her disappearance. The next evening Fannie Franks showed up at Betty Houston's bagnio, unharmed, hungover, and much the worse for wear. The police released a greatly relieved Stitzelberger from jail. For Katy Davy it seems to have been a valuable experience, for she soon abandoned her life as a prostitute. Her sister Lillie, however, was only getting started.[25]

5

Go West, Young Woman, Go West

The West beckoned Lillie Davy. For generations it had offered the American promise of a better life, and now she followed Horace Greeley's time-honored advice. In Chicago during the fall of 1893 she decided to flee, far away from her abusive husband Dan Bandman. "With what money I had saved I bought a ticket to Colorado," Lillie said later. Her decision had been a difficult one: whether to return to her mother or strike out on her own. "Instead of going home to my mother again, as I should have done," she explained, "I took the train for Trinidad, Colorado." The Atchison, Topeka and Santa Fe Railway ran west to Trinidad, in the mountains of southern Colorado. It was a prosperous town of five thousand people and the center of a huge coal-mining region. "There I secured temporary employment as a waitress in one of the large hotels," Lillie recalled.

Yet it is certain that she did not work in a hotel, for she later related, "I was only twenty-two years old. I was good-looking, desperate, discouraged, and ready for anything that might come. I do not care to dwell on this period of my life." In other words, she worked in a Trinidad brothel, not a hotel. Because of the area's large population of unmarried young miners, Trinidad was a hotbed of prostitution. Several hundred soiled doves lived in its bustling red-light district, servicing men from the surrounding towns and mines. The girls were a transient bunch, coming and going on the Santa Fe Railroad, for Trinidad was a popular stop on the journey from Missouri to Southern California. Though Lillie managed to stay out of trouble during her stay in Colorado, she soon chose to move on.[1]

Lillie probably worked for a time in brothels along the railroad line. As she recalled, "It is sufficient to say that I went from one city to another until sometime later I arrived in Phoenix." Although Phoenix today is the fifth-largest city in America, it was then a rough-and-tumble frontier town of about four thousand, situated in the high desert of Arizona Territory. Arizona was then a rugged and sparsely populated frontier. Only two railroads entered the territory, and its far-flung settlements were connected mainly by primitive, poorly maintained wagon roads. To the eastern press, the public, and politicians, Arizona was a remote and dangerous land peopled by wild Indians and desperate outlaws. That portrait proved a major barrier to the territory's quest for statehood, a goal that would not be achieved for many years. And it was not until 1901 that the territorial legislature established the Arizona Rangers, modeled after the Texas Rangers, to assist rural officers in fighting outlawry. The Arizona Rangers suppressed crime—not without controversy—and helped pave the way for statehood in 1912.[2]

Less than a dozen years before Lillie's arrival, the territory had been plagued by a band of outlaws known as the Cowboys. They were the Old West's biggest outlaw gang, boasting about two hundred freebooters, smugglers, and cattle rustlers. Led by such desperadoes as Curly Bill Brocius, John Ringo, and Ike Clanton, the Cowboys raided throughout southern Arizona and northern Mexico. They murdered at least thirty-five men and created a series of international incidents with the Mexican government. Finally they made the fatal decision of tangling with Wyatt Earp, his brothers, and Doc Holliday. The result was the so-called Gunfight at the O.K. Corral, which left three of the Cowboys dead, followed by Wyatt Earp's vendetta ride, in which he shot and killed Curly Bill and two more of the band. The Cowboys then scattered to the four winds.

Arizona Territory had a boom and bust economy. Rich discoveries of silver in places like Tombstone sparked a huge rush in the late 1870s, followed by a sharp decline two decades later as the mines played out. By that time Arizona's wealth in gold, silver, cattle, and grazing land had attracted adventurers, speculators, gamblers, and ruffians of every stripe. All men carried guns—not for show, but for protection from Apaches, outlaws, and drunken ruffians. For in that era, the government provided little in the way of security for its citizens in the West, and the Arizona press routinely lambasted the US Army for its perceived inability to suppress Apache raids. During the 1870s and 1880s, Southern Arizona was one of America's most violent regions. In 1880 Pima County, with Tucson as the county seat, had a homicide rate twenty-eight times higher than the modern national rate. The 1881 homicide rate in Cochise County, which had Tombstone as the county seat, was fifty-five times higher than the nation's current homicide rate. And Gila County, just east of Phoenix, had a murder rate in the 1880s that was more than fifteen times greater than that of today.[3]

Phoenix, though not as wild as Tombstone, was still a tough town. Its first city marshal and most famous lawman, Henry Garfias, rode herd on the ruffians and desperadoes. Garfias was a Californio—a native Californian of Mexican ancestry—and was highly regarded by Anglos and Latinos alike. In 1879 he tracked down and captured the Saber Slasher, a Latino outlaw who ran amok in Phoenix, badly wounding three men with a sword. Three years later a band of cowhands from Tombstone tried to "buffalo" Phoenix, riding through town flourishing their six-shooters and shooting into buildings. Then they made the fatal error of opening fire on Marshal Garfias. He shot back, killing one and wounding another. The police work of Garfias and his fellow lawmen, coupled with a vigilance committee that lynched a number of murderers, eventually tamed Phoenix.[4]

In 1880 Phoenix was a typical Southwestern pueblo with streets lined by low adobes, and almost half of its population was Latino. The railroad arrived in 1887, bringing an influx of Anglos. Many brick-and-wood-frame buildings sprouted up, and the town quickly became both Americanized and designated as the capital of Arizona Territory. The Phoenix that Lillie Davy first saw in late 1893 still had a significant Latino population and was overwhelming male. She found that prostitution was even more common in Phoenix than in Buffalo. In 1890, Arizona's total population was about eighty-eight thousand, only thirty-five percent of it female. This huge gender imbalance left many Arizona males with two choices: to find wives in more populous states and convince them to move to the frontier or to patronize brothels.

Lillie, with no skills or real education, resumed her life as a bawd. To protect her family's name, she used a new alias, Pearl Hart. No one knew her real identity, which she kept a close secret. Phoenix prostitution, like in most frontier communities, was quasilegal, with the women being arrested and fined and then returning to their bagnios. Not long before her arrival, Phoenix police cracked down on the bordellos, and many of their occupants simply moved outside the town's jurisdiction. Reported the *Phoenix Republican* in 1893, "There are now only twelve prostitutes inside the city limits though there are about fifty hanging like a scarlet fringe on the southern border."[5]

In 1894 local officials enacted a law that allowed prostitution only in Block 41, bounded by Jefferson, Madison, Fifth, and Sixth Streets in downtown Phoenix. Many prostitutes moved back into the city limits, and in Block 41 Lillie Davy became well-known as Pearl Hart. She retained her penchant for men's clothing and was often seen in male attire on the streets. A local journalist later wrote, "Pearl Hart is said by those who knew her to have always looked up to the romantic side of life and while a resident of Phoenix was frequently known to have dressed up in men's clothes and paraded in public."[6]

AUTHOR'S COLLECTION.

Pearl Hart as she looked dressed in men's clothes, 1899.

She remained close to her family and kept in touch with them by correspondence. Probably from her sisters, Dan Bandman learned that she was in Phoenix, and early in 1894 he entrained for Arizona in search of her. As she recalled, "I came face to face with my husband on the street one afternoon. I was not then the innocent schoolgirl he had enticed from home, father, mother, family and friends—far from it. I had been inured to the hardships of the world and knew much of its wickedness. Still, the old infatuation came back. I struggled against it. I knew if

I went back to him I should be more unhappy than I was, but I lost the battle. I did go back." Pearl Hart's decision was no different than that made by her own mother.[7]

In Phoenix Pearl became a chain-smoker and got addicted to opium and morphine, a habit she later blamed on Dan Bandman. Explained a Phoenix journalist who later interviewed townsfolk who knew her, "She was formerly of exquisite form and more than usually attractive but was addicted to the use of morphine and cigarettes and these indulgences have taken from her the brightness of her eye and the rotundity of form that formerly marked her bearing."[8]

Then and now, opiate use takes a heavy toll on the human body. Users are frequently disoriented, confused, and have trouble concentrating and maintaining their balance. They easily become drowsy and often nod off in the daytime. They neglect their daily hygiene and frequently suffer severe weight loss and changes to their physical appearance. Opiate users often have dry skin, bloodshot eyes, and bags under the eyes, coupled with a sunken facial appearance. It is no wonder that such changes in Pearl were noted by the newspaper reporters.

A journalist later spoke with people who knew of Pearl's opium use in Phoenix. "She was, and is, an inveterate smoker of cigarettes, in each of which she usually places some of the drug," he wrote, adding, "Though soft voiced and small, her violent temper led her into many scrapes, in all of which she displayed daring a man might envy." Opiate use was then legal in the US and would not be banned by the federal government until 1914. Although morphine was employed as a painkiller during the Civil War, opium smoking did not become widespread until the 1870s. In the West, opium—known as *hop*—was introduced by Chinese immigrants in the 1850s and eventually became popular among criminals, prostitutes, pimps, saloongoers, and gamblers. Pearl Hart's smoking, to say nothing of her use of opiates, was more than scandalous.[9]

In Phoenix, Pearl Hart and Dan Bandman smoked opium daily.

He played piano in saloons and briefly ran a lunch stand in Block 41. Pearl later said that they conceived two children. "During the first year of my married life a boy was born to us, and a girl while we were together at Phoenix." However, as she explained, "He was not content. He began to abuse me as of old." On August 10, 1894, she and Bandman got into a drunken quarrel, and he beat her. By this time Pearl was fed up with his brutality, and she went before a justice of the peace to demand that he be arrested. A local reporter described her as "Pearl Hart who infests Block 41" and remarked, "She was weeping, drunk, and well dressed and had a specification with the sort of relief she wanted." She described the attack to the judge, saying, "I told him that I would have him sent to Yuma one year for every blow he gave me. Now that's all you've got to do. Send for him right away and have him sent down to the pen tonight." But in that era, domestic violence was not taken seriously. A man was considered the king of the household, and an assaultive husband rarely received serious punishment unless he killed his spouse. However, if a man murdered a woman on the frontier, that was beyond the pale, and he faced harsh justice or even a lynch mob. In this case, Pearl was not seriously injured, and Dan Bandman escaped any punishment.[10]

COURTESY HERITAGE AUCTIONS.

Jefferson Street in Phoenix, not far from the notorious Block 41, as Pearl Hart saw it in the mid-1890s.

Ten days later she was arrested, booked under the name Pearl Hart, and brought into police court. A journalist called her "a fille de joie, who erroneously understood that her regular monthly fine as a prostitute covered all her many other shortcomings." She paid ten dollars for disturbing the peace. At the same time a young cowboy, Billy Stiles, was also hauled into the police court and fined two dollars for being "drunk and fighting." Whether the pair had been arrested together or had been in a quarrel is unknown. Billy Stiles would go on to become a noted lawman, and then would switch sides and ride the outlaw trail as one of the Southwest's most notorious train robbers. He and Pearl Hart would cross paths again.[11]

By this time Pearl had decided to separate from Dan Bandman. As she recalled, "I left him for the third time, vowing never to speak to him again. I sent my children home to my dear old mother and went east, where I supported myself by working as a servant. I heard of my husband occasionally. I tried to forget him, but could not. He was the father of my children and I loved him, in spite of all the abuse he had heaped on me." Anna Davy had moved from Rochester to Toledo with her daughters, Amy, nineteen, Jennie, fifteen, and her youngest son, Acle, aged nine. Acle had been in poor health since he was a toddler, when Rochester social workers had found him "scarred and sore" and suffering from kidney disease. Ten-year-old Acle died in Toledo in 1895. In December of that year Amy married a Toledo carpenter named James Taylor. Assuming that Pearl Hart told the truth about joining her mother, it was Toledo where she took her children to live.[12]

Pearl never revealed the names of her two children, and their identities remain unconfirmed to this day. However, a clue to the mystery lies in the family record of her sister Amy. During the late 1890s, Amy had two children living with her and her husband James Taylor in Toledo. The eldest, a son named John, was born on August 13, 1893. His birth took place several years before Amy moved to Toledo and met and married Taylor. Thus it is clear that James Taylor was not the father of John. The second child living with Amy was a girl, Anna Lilly, born on December 15, 1896, one year before she married Taylor. John's birth occurred about a year after Pearl began living with Dan Bandman, thus matching up with her statement, "During the first year of my married life a boy was born to us." And Anna Lilly was conceived in the spring of 1896, a time when Pearl said that they had "a girl while we were together at Phoenix." Many years later, Amy's descendants recalled that Pearl's two children were raised by the Davy family. Although it is possible that they were Amy's natural children, born out of wedlock, it is also possible that John and Anna Lilly were Pearl's son and daughter whom she sent east to be raised by her family.[13]

Meanwhile her sister Katy had also decided to go west for a new start. When Katy told the Cincinnati journalist that she lived with her "aunt or sister, or whatever yer want to call her," she was probably referring to Saphronia, her eldest sister. Saphronia and Andrew had disposed of their saloon in Rochester and moved to Ohio. In 1895, they moved again, this time to Missouri, where she gave birth to a baby son. Meanwhile Katy reconnected with her estranged husband, Howard Allen, and she soon became pregnant. In 1896 she bore a son, Steven, whom she always called Stevie. But Katy and Allen soon separated again. Katy maintained a close relationship with her sisters, and she apparently followed Saphronia from Ohio to Missouri. There Katy met Eugene O. Griffith, a daring thirty-six-year-old acrobat and circus performer from Springfield in southern Missouri. He called himself Professor Griffith and traveled the country performing a stunt in which he dropped from a balloon by parachute. He once wisecracked, "As a balloon ascensionist and a parachute descensionist I covered most of Europe as well as this country, though, luckily enough, not in fragments."[14]

By the 1890s, parachuting from a balloon had become a popular spectator entertainment. Huge crowds gathered at county fairs to see daredevils ascend to great heights, then drop to the ground by parachute. Although some balloons were inflated by hot air, most used gas. Under the bag was a basket, sometimes a trapeze, that held the aeronaut. A silk parachute, fifteen to twenty feet wide, was fastened to the balloon by ropes. When the balloonist reached a height of one thousand feet or more, he would cut the ropes and leap from the balloon. Needless to say, the stunt was extremely dangerous, and many balloonists died when the parachute failed to deploy. During the 1890s, a handful of female parachutists performed the stunt, and at least two lost their lives.

In late 1896 Eugene Griffith was performing in southern Missouri where he was joined by Katy Davy, with her infant baby, Stevie, in tow. Because she began calling herself Mrs. Griffith, she probably had a sexual relationship with the barnstormer. Ever adventurous and still a natural acrobat, Katy decided to try her hand at skydiving. In order to distance herself from her former identity as a prostitute, she adopted the nickname for her middle name of Amelia, and dubbed herself Millie Davy. Though unemployed and impoverished, she was determined to never again work as a bawd. Katy later explained, "Finding nothing to do to make an honest living, I was almost giving up in despair when an opportunity suddenly presented itself. A lady was wanted to make balloon ascensions. The salary was good, but they wanted someone of experience. As I have a steady nerve I believed I could accept the position and I did. I made aerial ascensions that way for several months, using my maiden name, Millie Davy."[15]

She and Griffith entrained for Texas, which he believed was fertile ground for parachute exhibitions. In July 1897 they prepared for a performance in Austin. Long the capital of Texas, Austin had only recently emerged from its years as a rough frontier settlement. In 1880 its citizens had elected the notorious cow-town gambler and gunfighter Ben Thompson as city marshal, or chief of police. He resigned in 1882 after killing a San Antonio enemy, Jack Harris, in one of the most famous of all Texas gunfights. Two years later Thompson and his friend John King Fisher, also a noted Texas gunman, were assassinated in San Antonio by friends of Harris. That same year the townsfolk of Austin were terrorized by the Servant Girl Annihilator, a serial killer who murdered seven women and one man and was never identified. By the time of Katy's arrival, Austin was a booming, modern community of almost twenty thousand, and its days as a mecca for gunfighters and killers was largely over. Four years earlier a huge dam had been completed across the Colorado River, just northwest of town, along with a large public park on the east shore of the reservoir. The dam powered generators that provided lighting and power for electric streetcars and helped usher in the modern era.

On July 22, 1897, in front of a huge crowd in the park next to the dam, Eugene Griffith began the work to inflate his balloon. He used a portable gas machine that mixed water, sulfuric acid, and zinc and iron filings to create hydrogen that was pumped into the billowing bag. With spectators holding the guy ropes, Griffith gave the order to release, and the balloon began to rise. He floated far up into the clouds, then dropped by parachute into the water, much to the spectators' delight. But the real attraction was yet to come. "The professor will make an ascension Sunday afternoon," announced the Austin newspaper. "Miss Millie Davy...will go up one thousand feet more, and then jump from the balloon with her parachute. Both Professor Griffith and Miss Davy are experienced ballooners, and their voyage to the clouds will be worth seeing."[16]

A female aviator was highly unusual, and Griffith ran newspaper advertisements that proclaimed, "Millie Davy will make a balloon ascension and parachute jump. See the little lady go one thousand feet in the air and make a jump for life." On July

25, in front of an even larger crowd, Griffith filled his balloon with hydrogen gas. Volunteers held the balloon with ropes, while Katy perched on a trapeze under the bag. A long tether, attached to a winch, ensured that the balloon could not go adrift. At Griffith's order, the ropes were released and she shot up into the sky. At a height of one thousand feet Katy released the ropes which held her parachute to the balloon. A reporter who watched her wrote, "When she first left the big airship she shot downward with the swiftness of a cannon ball, but before reaching the earth, her parachute, which worked perfectly, checked her flight downward and she landed easily and safely on the mountains west of the lake."[17]

ZOO PARK

At the Dam.

THIS AFTERNOON,

5 O'CLOCK.

MISS MILLIE DAVY

Will Make a

Balloon Ascension and Parachute Jump

ee the Little Lady Go One Thousand Feet in the Air and Make a Jump for Life.

e Management Assures the Patrons That They Will Not Be Disappointed. It is Free.

AUTHOR'S COLLECTION.

An Austin, Texas, newspaper advertisement for Katy Davy's parachute jump in 1897.

The performance was so successful that Griffith bought more ads for another ascension the following week. This time Griffith prepared a small second parachute so Katy could take a pet dog with her. On August 1, streetcars brought more than a thousand spectators out to the park to see the show. As the crowd held its collective breath, the balloon was released from its mooring lines and rose quickly. From her perch under the balloon, Katy held the dog tightly. At a height of two hundred feet, she cut the dog's safety line, and the animal floated gently to the ground. By this time a breeze carried the balloon over the lake, and it quickly began to lose altitude. Katy worked frantically to release her parachute, but the ropes would not work. The balloon dropped to seventy-five feet and drifted over the center of the lake. Katy realized that if it landed in the water, she would be trapped beneath the huge bag and drowned. She quickly drew a knife and cut the ropes that secured her parachute to the balloon. The drop was so short that her parachute did not fully open. She slammed with such force into the water that the impact knocked her unconscious.

Several men in skiffs had sensed the danger and were already rowing to Katy's rescue as quickly as they could pull their oars. They dragged the female skydiver from the water into their boat and soon managed to revive her. Katy would have drowned if not for their quick actions. As a local reporter remarked, "When the crowd saw the aeronaut strike the water the ladies screamed and some of them are said to have fainted, but when Miss Davy regained consciousness and waved her hand from the boat to assure them she was safe, she was given a cheer which almost shook the neighboring hills."[18]

Few women of that era would even consider such a stunt, but Katy Davy—like Pearl Hart—was cut from a different cloth. Now Griffith ran new ads, proclaiming another parachute jump by "Miss Millie Davy, the little woman who came very near drowning last Sunday." On August 8, twelve hundred people flocked to the park to view the spectacle. A reporter wrote that "the crowd was not disappointed, for the little lady went so high that all the people could see was a little bit of a black speck in the air, and when she cut her parachute loose from the balloon she dropped like a shot for a couple of hundred feet, and when the parachute opened the people cheered. It was certainly a pretty sight to see."[19]

Although Griffith made two more parachute jumps in Austin that month, Katy did not participate. While in Austin, she received a letter from her husband Howard Allen, who was then visiting Kansas City. They agreed to meet each other at the halfway point, Oklahoma City. As Katy later explained, "I heard from my husband and went to him and have never since made a balloon ascension." Professor Griffith was unfazed by the loss of his beautiful assistant. He continued to perform but eventually gave up his career as a skydiver and became, alternately, a soldier of fortune in Central America, a ship's captain, and finally, the owner of a motion-picture theater in Tampa, Florida. He then married a woman from Texas, but in 1915 she sued him for divorce. Burdened with debt and facing financial ruin, Eugene Griffith used poison to take his own life in Tampa that year.[20]

In early December 1897 Katy boarded a train at the Austin depot and rode north to meet Howard Allen in Oklahoma City. She apparently left Stevie with friends in Austin. In Oklahoma Katy checked into the Planters Hotel. She told local people, variously, that her name was Mrs. Griffith and Mrs. Davy, and a city journalist described her as "a petite brunette of striking beauty." Soon Allen joined her at the Planters Hotel. Perhaps not surprisingly, he turned out to be more thief than thespian. He told the hotel manager that he was in town to train the cast and chorus of a popular comic opera, "The Hindoo Head Hunters." Allen asked to borrow the manager's gold pocket watch so he could keep time, and the hotelkeeper complied. Allen, still enraptured by Katy's beauty and eager to rekindle their relationship, began showering her with gifts. He presented Katy with a seven-dollar ring, a three-dollar hat, and six dollars in other presents. For an ex-prostitute who had grown up in abject poverty, those gifts must have seemed lavish. The problem was that Allen paid for everything with rubber checks. On the night of December 14 the couple slipped out of the hotel without settling their bill, boarded a train, and fled south to Fort Worth, Texas. The merchants were left in the lurch, and the hotelkeeper never saw his gold watch again.[21]

The Oklahoma City police sent a telegram to officers in Fort Worth, and a few days later they picked up Allen and returned him to Oklahoma City. It turned out that authorities in Stillwater, Oklahoma, wanted him for the then-common crime of check raising. The officials learned that Allen, before meeting Katy at the Planters Hotel, had worked briefly for a farmer near Stillwater. The farmer paid him with a check for $4.35, and Allen "raised" the check value by adding a *5* and making it $54.35. In addition to altering the numeral, he also forged the false dollar amount by adding the word *Fifty* on the check. After cashing the check, he had fled south for his reunion with Katy in the Planters Hotel. Because check forgery was a more serious crime than writing bad checks, law officers returned Allen to Stillwater to face the new charge.

Katy Davy was determined to get her man out of the Stillwater jail. His bond was set at eight hundred dollars, a small fortune, and she did not have that kind of money. Instead, she offered to pay the farmer his fifty dollars back if he would drop the forged-check case. He refused, and by late January 1898 Katy was becoming desperate. She told the jailer that she was Allen's wife, and he foolishly allowed them an unsupervised visit. Katy smuggled in a bottle of acid and several saw blades and managed to slip them to Allen. But a few days later the jailer made a routine search of his cell, found the contraband, and discovered that Allen had been trying to cut through the jail bars. Katy skipped town, and Sheriff O. W. Annis boasted that he would soon capture her. He was wrong.[22]

Katy had some skill as a seamstress, and she stitched together a woman's dress that would fit Allen. She slipped back into Stillwater and secreted the dress and a six-gun outside the county jail. On the morning of March 14, 1898, the guard began his customary cleaning of the jail, which consisted of a row of three large cells. The jailer ordered all the prisoners into one cell, so he could safely clean the other two. Allen hid behind his bunk while the other prisoners all walked into the opposite cell. The jailer locked the prisoners inside without counting them. Then, thinking they were all secure, he stepped outside briefly. Allen pulled off his shoes, crept silently down the jail corridor, slipped out through an unlocked door, and scaled the jail fence. When he could not find Katy's dress and six-shooter, he quickly headed out of town on foot. A huge manhunt swung into action, and searchers soon found the dress and the pistol but no trace of the escapee. Sheriff Annis offered a reward of fifty dollars—about fifteen hundred dollars in modern currency—for Allen's capture.[23]

Two days later Sheriff Annis and a deputy got a tip that Allen had been spotted on foot about twenty miles south of town. When the deputy sheriff drove up on Allen in a buggy, the jailbreaker started to run. The officer threw down on him with a double-barreled shotgun and yelled at Allen to halt. Allen threw up his hands, then asked if the shotgun was loaded with bird shot. The deputy snapped, "You come here or I'll show you!"

Allen complied, saying, "If I thought you had only bird shot in that gun, I would take a chance on it."

Sheriff Annis soon rode up, and the two lawmen returned Allen to the Stillwater jail. It was a crowded and extremely leaky lockup, with thirteen prisoners now occupying the three cells. Five weeks later, on April 24, the jailer allowed the prisoners out of their cells and into the corridor. There, one of the jailbirds pulled out an old fiddle and began sawing away, much to the jailer's delight. While the prisoners stomped and clapped, Allen and a few others did their own sawing. They laboriously cut through an iron bar on their cell window. How they got a smuggled hacksaw is unknown, but Katy Davy is the likely suspect. After an hour of work, they removed the bar, and eight prisoners squeezed through the window. When the jailer finally realized that the birds had flown, he raised the alarm, and a two-hundred-man posse swung into action. They managed to capture three of the escapees, but the rest, including Allen, vanished, some of them riding stolen horses.[24]

Allen, accompanied by Katy, again fled south, this time to Denison, just across the Red River in Texas. Denison, like much of the US, was gripped by patriotic fervor. The Spanish–American War had broken out just three days before Allen escaped jail. Katy's man was now overcome by patriotism or—more likely—he saw a better way to elude capture. Allen enlisted in Troop L of the First Texas Cavalry in Denison. Katy later claimed proudly that Allen was a lieutenant, but in fact he joined up as a private. When Allen left with his troop for Fort Sam Houston in San Antonio, Katy followed. But military life did not agree with him, for within days he deserted and took Katy with him by rail to Laredo on the Rio Grande. They crossed the border but did not stay long in Mexico. The pair returned to Laredo where they legally married on May 19, 1898, in St. Peter's Catholic Church, using their real names, H. W. Allen and C. A. Davy.[25]

Allen was soon arrested as a deserter and returned to San Antonio, where soldiers lodged him in the guardhouse at Fort Sam Houston. There, someone recognized him as a fugitive from Oklahoma. Army officers sent a wire to Stillwater, and Sheriff Annis responded, arriving in San Antonio on July 23, 1898. Katy, learning of the sheriff's arrival, panicked at the thought of her husband going to prison. Once again she became determined to free him. Katy visited the guardhouse and smuggled in a revolver and a fake beard. That night, Allen, who somehow learned that the guards' rifles were—oddly enough—unloaded, made his break. He threatened several sentries with his six-gun, then dashed toward a high fence behind the barracks. He quickly scaled the fence, and, with a defiant yell, dared the guards to follow him. They prudently stayed back, and he disappeared into the darkness.

Allen knew that Katy was staying in a nearby house at 113 Hood Street. Instead of going there, he climbed a tree, donned the false whiskers, and hid high in the branches for hours while the soldiers hunted for him. A San Antonio newspaper report said, "The search was fast and furious during the several hours that it lasted, and gave the people of this city a very picturesque representation of one phase of military life. Squads of men were stationed at the depots watching the outgoing trains and other squads were galloping over the highways and byways of the city and beating the brush in the suburbs."

Major Edward A. Peareson learned that Allen's wife was lodging at the house on Hood Street. He led a patrol to search the place, but Katy told him that Allen was not there. While his men rode off, Peareson slipped unnoticed into the dark backyard and waited quietly. After what seemed like an eternity, he spotted a shadowy figure climbing over the fence. As the man started to crawl on all fours toward the house, Peareson captured him at gunpoint. He pulled off the fake beard and recognized Allen as the wanted man. Major Peareson returned Allen to the guardhouse, and the Army notified Sheriff Annis, who took his prisoner back to Oklahoma in irons. As a San Antonio journalist remarked, "The officers of the army made no objections to giving him up as they explained that they were heartily tired of him."[26]

Katy, beside herself with anxiety, gave a long interview to a reporter for the *San Antonio Daily Light*. She provided a partly fictionalized account of her relationship with Allen, insisted that he was innocent, and mentioned nothing of her efforts to break him out of the Stillwater jail. "The alleged charge of forgery on which my husband is being held is untrue," Katy declared. "The incident occurred in Stillwater, Oklahoma Territory, last winter, where a check which was issued to him for $4.35 was raised to $54.35. The check was drawn by the wife of a man who owed the amount to my husband and was made $54 by her through mistake. Another reason to believe that my husband did not raise the check was the fact that the following morning after it was issued the man drove to the bank early and ordered that the check not be cashed. This looks as if his wife had discovered the raise in the amount. The check was not cashed, but only presented, when my husband was taken into custody."

Katy denied that she had smuggled the six-gun into the guardhouse. "I did not provide my husband with a pistol with which to effect his escape, but knew that he had one. I want you to say that he was not captured in a tree, either, but just as he jumped over the fence into my yard. I stood one man off with a pistol, but let the major [Peareson] take him. He has always been a loving and good husband, true as steel and I'll remain true to him to the last. I am now circulating a petition to have his name kept on his troop rolls until his trial, so that if proven innocent he will get an honorable discharge. We have a little boy, who is now with me."

She also claimed that her problems had all been caused by a mysterious man who had been stalking her. "All our trouble has been brought on us by a man who met me in Chicago while I was forcibly separated from my husband. That man paid his attentions to me persistently upon first meeting me and has since hounded myself and husband all over the country, making his boasts that he would get my husband out of the way and win me yet, but he never will. He followed us to San Antonio and on West Commerce Street told me that he would get that husband of mine in the pen. At the same time he made ungentlemanly proposals to me and threatened my husband more seriously than ever if I did not comply. He is the very man who has worked up all these charges against my husband."[27]

Katy's yarn about the stalker was believed by some of the cavalrymen's wives, who took pity on her and her two-year-old son. They decided to put on a benefit concert for Katy at Muth's Garden, a popular outdoor restaurant, concert ground, and beer garden situated across the road from the officers' quarters at Fort Sam Houston. Katy, ever the entertainer, announced that she had prepared a sketch that she intended to perform with her toddler,

Stevie. She also told a reporter that her husband had arrived safely at the Stillwater jail. The journalist wrote, "She has received two letters from him since he arrived there and he expects to return here in about two weeks, as he thinks he can give bond." The benefit concert, which took place on the night of August 7, was well attended and proved a financial success. A reporter wrote, "The program was varied and was well carried out. The climax of the evening's entertainment was the original sketch written by Mrs. Allen and performed by herself and her little son, Stevie. It was entitled, 'A Message to Dewey'." Katy's performance honored Admiral George Dewey, who had commanded the US naval fleet in its victory over the Spanish Armada in the Battle of Manila Bay. The reporter concluded, "Mrs. Allen also did some fine buck-and-wing [tap] dancing and made a slide with her little son on a wire from the top of the pavilion."[28]

AUTHOR'S COLLECTION.

Katy Davy in a woodcut engraving made from a photograph, late 1890s. She wears her hair down, over her shoulders, because she is posing for a role as a performer.

Meanwhile Howard Allen languished in the Stillwater jail. Because of his prior jailbreaks, he faced a lengthy term in prison. On August 17, ten days after the benefit concert, Allen tried to kill himself by swallowing a dose of arsenic. Doctors managed to revive him, and he was placed on a suicide watch. How he managed to get arsenic inside the jail was a mystery. Despite all of Katy's protestations of his innocence, he pleaded guilty to forgery in exchange for a one-year prison term. In November, Sheriff Annis took Allen to the Kansas state prison in Lansing, which then held convicts from Oklahoma Territory. Katy and Stevie would not see him again for more than a year.[29]

The benefit funds raised for Katy and her son soon ran out. To raise cash, she decided to perform another dangerous stunt: tightrope walking. On September 11 the *Daily Light* announced, "The 'Queen of the air,' Miss Millie Davy, the little lady who had such a narrow escape from drowning one afternoon last summer at the dam in Austin, will give a free exhibition of tightrope walking and also a slide for life at 5:30 p.m. in Riverside Park this afternoon." The slide for life was a popular circus stunt in which the performer slid down a high cable, supported only by a hand or foot loop. A large crowd gathered at the appointed time, but Katy failed to appear. The announcer claimed that she was ill, and the *Daily Light* reported, "She will make it next Sunday, however." Yet Katy either had cold feet or good sense, for she never performed the stunt. Two months later her friends hosted another benefit for her at Muth's Garden, but very few people showed up. With the little money she received, Katy packed her belongings and moved with her son to Kansas City, Missouri.[30]

By this time her sister, as Pearl Hart, had reunited with Dan Bandman, probably in Toledo. They then returned to Arizona. "Two years after I had left him the third time, he found out where I was," she recalled. "He came to me and begged me to go back to the West with him, making me all kinds of smooth promises. I went back. I followed him to Tucson. After the money I had saved had been spent, he began beating me, and I lived in hell for months." Finally, in 1896, Bandman left Pearl and went to the mining town of Jerome, a hundred miles north of Phoenix, where he stayed for a year. Pearl, with no means to support herself, went to work in a brothel in Gay Alley, which was the heart of Tucson's red-light district. Her reputation quickly grew, as a Tucson paper later reported: "Almost every abandoned woman in the territory knows her." A year later, in the fall of 1897, Bandman came to Tucson in search of Pearl, but she rejected him. She decided to return alone to the territorial capital. As Pearl recalled, "I went back to Phoenix and got along as best I could." Simply put, she continued her life of prostitution.[31]

During the 1890s the best-known madam in Phoenix was Minnie Powers. Her true name was Rose Gregory, and she managed a succession of brothels, most notably the Louvre House at 22 East Madison Street. It was supposedly a female boarding house, and her newspaper advertisements offered: "First class furnished rooms by the day, week or month. Well stocked bar of choice wines, liquors and cigars in connection." Minnie Powers was the quintessential prostitute with a heart of gold, and though financially well-off, she gave much of her money to the poor and needy. Pearl Hart went to work for Minnie and became even more notorious as a prostitute. She still liked to dress in men's clothing and used morphine daily to cope with the humiliation and degradation of her chosen profession. As she recalled, "I was tired of life. I wanted to die, and tried to kill myself three or four times. I was restrained each time."[32]

In the spring of 1898 the Phoenix city council passed an ordinance outlawing prostitution in the city limits, thus putting a temporary end to the bordellos in Block 41. In late June law officers began removing the girls. "The women are scattering to all parts of the town," declared the *Phoenix Republican*. Pearl Hart was one of those who left Block 41, but not a life of prostitution. Once again Dan Bandman sought her out, and once again she took him back. They lived together unhappily until the Spanish–American War erupted in 1898. For Pearl, that was a relief. As she later explained, "Finally, he joined McCord's regiment and went to the war." On the Fourth of July, 1898, Bandman enlisted as a musician in the regiment of volunteer infantry raised by Arizona Governor Myron H. McCord.

Two months later, Pearl's madam, Minnie Powers, met a fate so common to many frontier prostitutes. Her lover and bartender was an Englishman, William Belcher, known as the Cockney. In September, due to Belcher's violent and inebriated behavior, Minnie had deputy sheriffs eject him from her brothel. A week later, on the night of September 17, 1898, a drunken Belcher entered Minnie's bedroom while she slept. He drew a .44 six-gun and shot her in the head, killing her. Then he placed the pistol barrel into his mouth and blew out the back of his head. Belcher fell dead on top of his former lover's corpse. Given Pearl's need to survive, Minnie's bloody demise did not dissuade her from life as a bawd.[33]

A month after the murder, Pearl moved two dressers and other bedroom furniture out of Minnie Powers's place. Reported the *Phoenix Republican*, "She said she owned them. A male companion named 'Slim Jim' pretended to be the owner of a horse and cart belonging to the dead woman, and took it. Neither of these parties have ever had enough wealth of any sort to keep them properly supplied with whiskey and morphine. A warrant will likely be issued against them for stealing." But Pearl evidently owned the furniture, for no warrant was issued for her arrest.[34]

She wasted no time in returning to Block 41 where she set up her own illegal establishment, replete with opium-smoking paraphernalia. Her new "lover"—an 1890s euphemism for a pimp—was Frank Miranda, a drug-addicted Mexican-American. On November 23, 1898, a deputy sheriff and a town policeman raided Pearl's bagnio, seized her opium and smoking pipes, and arrested them both. They were tried the next day in police court for "maintaining or frequenting an opium joint." The officers produced the contraband and testified that they "did not see anybody smoking, heard a great scurrying when they broke into the house, found the opium slaves' pallet on the floor, and the bowl of the pipe was still warm." Pearl testified on her own behalf, with a journalist recording that she admitted "that she hit the pipe with pleasure and great regularity for the purpose of working up an appetite. She had understood that it was lawful for any number of persons not exceeding two to meet together to indulge in opium dreams. Three or more persons with this object in view constitute an unlawful assembly."

Pearl was correct about the law. An Arizona statute made it illegal to operate an opium den, but smoking opium was itself legal. The justice of the peace released her but found Miranda guilty of vagrancy and sentenced him to thirty days in jail. Two weeks later, on December 8, Pearl was again caught in the toils of the law. Officers arrested her in her room inside a Block 41 brothel and brought her and another prostitute into police court. Pearl was quickly released, but the crackdown on prostitution in Phoenix made her look for new horizons. Those new ventures would soon make her the most notorious woman in America.[35]

6

Stagecoach Robber

From Phoenix, Pearl Hart boarded a stagecoach for a bone-jarring ride to the isolated mining camp of Mammoth, a hundred and fifty-five miles southeast. The town's six hundred people, most of them hard-rock miners, mill workers, teamsters, and their families, clustered in a sprawling collection of canvas tents, wood shacks, and adobe houses roofed with sheet iron. Mammoth, located on the west bank of the San Pedro River, also boasted six saloons and two general stores. The Mammoth gold mine—the settlement's sole reason for existence—was situated just above the town. Twenty-mule teams hauled the gold ore three miles to a large stamp mill on the river. There the ore was crushed, then smelted into gold.

Pearl recalled that she did legitimate labor in the rough mining town. "I got employment cooking for some miners at Mammoth," she said. "I lived there for a while, living in a tent pitched on the banks of the San Pedro River." But in reality, she was not cooking for miners. Pearl gave another account—and a more honest one—to a reporter in Florence, Arizona, who wrote, "She said she came from Phoenix to Mammoth some time ago in response to a letter from a woman who wanted inmates of a sporting house, but when she found the writer of the letter was a negro woman she refused to have anything to do with her and secured a tent and went into business for herself."[1]

Pearl's refusal to work for an African American madam was not unusual in that era of pervasive racism. But ironically, many residents of Mammoth did not feel the same way. One of the most prominent men in town was William "Curly" Neal, who happened to be African American. Neal—the son of a Black man and a Cherokee woman—was a prosperous Arizona pioneer. A former US Army scout in the Indian Wars and a close friend of Buffalo Bill Cody, Neal owned mines as well as a popular resort hotel in the nearby town of Oracle. He also ran the mule teams and wagons that transported ore from the Mammoth mine to the mill. A frontier journalist called his operation "one of the greatest freighting outfits in the world" and said that each mule team hauled four ore wagons "almost as big as boxcars." Despite the racist attitudes so common in the nineteenth century, Curly Neal was a popular and respected figure among the miners and townsfolk.[2]

AUTHOR'S COLLECTION.

Pearl Hart the stage robber.

In Mammoth, Pearl Hart acquired a six-gun and enjoyed target shooting and hunting. According to a writer who interviewed her later, "All of Pearl's spare time was spent in practicing her favorite pastime. No target was too small or distant to escape the bullet that flew from the nervous pressure of her small, strong hand, and the more dangerous and savage the game she pursued the greater pleasure she found in the chase. Circumstances seemed to have combined to mold the slender young girl into an amazon of undaunted type, fearing neither God nor man." Hyperbole aside, Pearl indeed became adept at the use of firearms in Mammoth.[3]

In January 1899 she met a diminutive, mustachioed miner who called himself Joe Boot—he never revealed his true name. The two quickly became lovers. Joe was twenty-eight, handsome, and stood just five foot four. He hailed from Ohio. Pearl later said that he had been a shoemaker in Chicago. A journalist who met him wrote that Boot "calls himself a gambler, but is nothing more than a poor article of bawdy house lounger, weak-faced and without spirit." He added that "the woman was the leader and the more adventurous of the pair." Joe Boot seems to have worshiped Pearl. And unlike most men in her dysfunctional life, he treated her well.[4]

Eugene Childs, who ran a general store in Mammoth, later recalled her stay there. "I remember Pearl Hart very well. She was around here for a few months and always paid her bills. She had a camp of three or four tents by the San Pedro River and there was a young fellow who did the cooking. She used to hang around the saloons but did not drink to excess; it was said she used dope and smoked cigarettes. The day she left Mammoth she was dressed in boys' clothes (very unusual in those days), her hair put up under a cap. She came into the store, paid me what she owed me and was gone."[5]

Because Mammoth was so small and isolated, Pearl attracted far fewer clients than she had in Phoenix. She managed to save a meager ten dollars, then decided to move sixty miles north to the much larger and more prosperous silver mining town of

Globe. But the road was badly mired by recent rains. As Pearl recalled, "I packed my goods in a wagon and started to go to Globe. I had to return to my old camp because the horses were unable to pull us through. A man named Joe Boot wanted to go to Globe, too, and we made an arrangement with two Mormon boys to freight the whole outfit to Globe for eight dollars."[6]

ERNIE PARKS COLLECTION.

The remote town of Riverside, on the Gila River, as it looked a few years after Pearl Hart was there in 1899.

At that time, travel from Mammoth to Globe was on a rough, steep mountain road. Present-day Highway 77, which serves Globe from the south, did not exist until the 1930s. In 1899 the wagon road to Globe followed the San Pedro River north from Mammoth to its confluence with the Gila River at modern-day Winkelman. From there the road skirted the Gila River west to the stage station of Riverside, now called Kelvin. At Riverside, wagons and stagecoaches forded the Gila, entered the mouth of Kane Spring Canyon, and commenced a long climb through the rugged Dripping Spring Mountains. Another fifteen miles brought travelers to the stagecoach depot in Pioneer Pass, 5,900 feet high in the Pinal Mountains, with a final eleven-mile pull into Globe. The road passed through winding, narrow canyons, surrounded by craggy peaks. The prior year a railroad line from the west had been completed into Globe, and traffic on the road through Kane Spring Canyon dropped drastically. Pearl Hart's journey on the old Globe wagon road would prove an important one in her life.

She later told a journalist that her trip to Globe was a long and slow trudge. The reporter wrote, "In the evening of the last day of the journey the party camped three miles from the latter place [Globe], and while they were there the Globe stage containing several passengers passed the camp. Pearl, whose observant eyes were always wide awake to what was going on around her, had taken a close view of the locality in which they were encamped and noted every rock and declivity with accurate judgment of one who has grown wise in the ways of the wilderness. The girl possessed a wonderfully tenacious memory." Events would soon show that Pearl had indeed closely observed the topography of Kane Spring Canyon.[7]

Pearl and Joe arrived in Globe in mid-April 1899. She recalled, "We camped out three miles from Globe, and next day moved in, and I went to work again in a miners' boarding house." In Arizona, the term *boarding house* was a common euphemism for a brothel, and there Pearl returned to prostitution. Globe, like all mining towns, experienced booms and busts. Pearl explained, "Then one of the big mines shut down and that left me with nothing to do. I had saved a little money. One of my brothers found my address and wrote me for some money to help him out of a scrape. I sent him all I had, and was just about to move on to some other town when my husband appeared again." Dan Bandman's volunteer infantry regiment had remained stateside during the war. He was discharged from the Army in February 1899 and returned to Arizona by rail. Bandman wasted no time in tracking Pearl down and found her in Globe. She later told a reporter that she and Bandman then lived together in Globe for a short time, but he "robbed her of all her savings." How Pearl managed to keep Boot and Bandman apart she did not say. But in another interview, she stated that she quickly got rid of Dan

Bandman. "He had been mustered out of his regiment and had followed me to Globe. He was too lazy to work and wanted me to support him. We had another quarrel and parted. I haven't seen him since and I hope I never shall see him again."[8]

Pearl remained close to her mother and her siblings and kept in touch with them by mail. By this time Anna Davy had moved from Toledo to Kansas City. She now suffered from heart disease. Pearl explained, "On top of all my other troubles, I got a letter just at this time saying my mother was dying and asking me to come home if I wanted to see her alive again. That letter drove me crazy. No matter what I had been, my mother had been my dearest, truest friend, and I longed to see her again before she died. I had no money. I could get no money. From what I know now, I believe I became temporarily insane. Joe Boot, the man who freighted his goods over to Globe with me, told me he had a mining claim and offered to go out with me and try to dig up enough metal to get a passage home to Canada. We went out to the claim and both worked night and day. It was useless. The claim was no good. I handled pick and shovel like a man, and began wearing men's clothes while I was mining there. I have never worked so hard in my life, and I have had some pretty hard experiences, too. When we found there wasn't a sign of color in the claim, I was frantic. I wanted to see my mother. It was the only wish I had."[9]

Pearl later insisted, "I intended to take her back to our old home in Canada and lead a decent life." With a few exceptions, her story was true. Anna Davy may have been ill but certainly was not dying; she would live for many years. And Pearl was not temporarily insane. In order to survive, she had made many reckless choices in her life, and she was about to make another one.[10]

At that time, stage and train robbery remained a significant problem in Arizona. During the 1890s the territory continued to be plagued by bandits, most notably the train-robbing gangs of Thomas "Black Jack" Ketchum, William "Black Jack" Christian, "Bronco Bill" Walters, and Grant Wheeler, as well as by countless stage robbers and highwaymen who infested the back roads leading into Arizona's remote mining camps. The first Far-West stagecoach holdups took place in California during the Gold Rush years of the 1850s. Bandits were attracted by heavy shipments of treasure, generally carried on coaches in the gold-mining regions. Although California experienced scores of stage holdups during the late 1850s and 1860s, the first such robbery did not take place in Arizona until 1875. During the next ten years, gold and silver strikes, especially at Tombstone, brought rapid development to Arizona Territory. The mining riches attracted a disproportionate share of gamblers, saloonkeepers, and hardcases, all looking to make a quick buck. As Arizona's economic development increased rapidly, stagecoaches carrying bullion shipments from the mining camps and cash payrolls for miners became the favorite target of highwaymen.

The road between Riverside and Globe had been the scene of at least seven stage holdups, and Pearl undoubtedly heard some of those stories on her way through Kane Spring Canyon. The first stagecoach robbery in Kane Spring Canyon took place in 1880. A famous frontier lawman, Bob Paul, whom Pearl would come to know well, was then a Wells Fargo detective. He led a determined but fruitless manhunt for the three bandits. The next year the road to Globe was visited by two of the Cowboys, Pony Diehl and Sherman McMaster. They held up a stagecoach near Dripping Springs and galloped off with cash from the Wells Fargo strongbox. Both escaped punishment, but McMaster eventually deserted the gang and became a loyal posseman for Wyatt Earp in his epic battle against the Cowboys. In 1883 Kane Spring Canyon saw one of the Southwest's most notorious stage holdups. The band led by "Red Jack" Almer held up a coach and murdered the Wells Fargo shotgun messenger, an incident that helped inspire the 1967 film *Hombre*, starring Paul Newman, and based on Elmore Leonard's novel of the same name. Once again Bob Paul—by that time sheriff of Pima County in Tucson—took to the saddle. He and his posse tracked down Red Jack and one of his band and killed the pair in a pitched gun battle. Two other members of the Red Jack gang were captured, jailed in Florence, and then lynched by an enraged mob.[11]

In Globe, Pearl began to see stage robbery as the solution to her financial woes. She was distraught by the news of her mother's illness and became determined to raise enough money to visit her. Pearl later said, "One day Joe Boot found me crying and asked what was the matter. I explained that I needed money. He then proposed the stage robbery. I was horrified at first, but the temptation of the riches and the romance got the better part of me and I consented to Joe's plan." In another interview, Pearl gave more details: "Boot sympathized with me, but he had no money and could not get any. He proposed that we rob the Globe stage. I protested. He said it was the only way to get money. Then I weakened so far as the moral part of it was concerned, but said I was afraid to rob a stage. It seemed a desperate undertaking for a woman of my size. Joe finally said it was easy enough and no one would get hurt."

Boot told her, "A bold front is all that is necessary to rob any stage."

To that, Pearl responded, "Joe, if you will promise me that no one will be hurt, I will go with you."[12]

But on other occasions, Pearl admitted that it was she who came up with the plan to hold up a stagecoach. A writer who later interviewed her wrote, "She then thought of the Globe stage and proposed a 'stick up' to her companion. The business was entirely new to him and he strongly objected, but the young woman insisted and he finally gave in. Perhaps he would not have consented had not Pearl overawed him by a timely exhibition in gunnery. She wore in her belt a brace of six-shooters, and drawing them, proceeded to fire at surrounding objects in the most nonchalant way. First naming the target at which she was about to shoot, she would pull the trigger, and in every instance the bullet sped true to its mark. She used her right and left hand alternately, and after she had exhausted the chambers of her two revolvers, proceeded to reload them."

As she did so, Pearl exclaimed, "I guess that will show you I ain't likely to fall down on my part of the game, Joe."

Boot was convinced. "You're the real thing, all right. I'm with you, pal. We'll hit the trail whenever you say so."[13]

Pearl recalled, "We secured Winchester rifles, pistols, plenty of ammunition, and two good ponies. I dressed in a pair of overalls, high heeled boots, buckskin jacket, wore a cowboy hat, and tied a big handkerchief around my neck so my hair did not show from behind, and wore a pair of men's riding gloves. You could not have told I was a woman to save your life. We took with us plenty of provisions, and rode two days and two nights to a place near the canyon where we could watch for the stage. Here we established a camp and waited." Where Pearl and Joe got the money to acquire firearms and horses, she did not say. However, such items cost far more than a thirty-dollar railroad ticket to her mother's home in Kansas City. And it is certain that they did not steal them.[14]

ERNIE PARKS COLLECTION.

Kane Spring Canyon as it looks today, showing the general location of the stage robbery. The remnant of the old stage road is on the right.

Their horseback ride took them south from Globe in late May 1899. They crossed Pioneer Pass, then descended into Kane Spring Canyon. According to a journalist of the day, "The road at that point is one of the worst in the Southwest, following the bed of a creek." The trail was steep and skirted high cliffs. On the side of one cliff someone had used wagon grease to paint an ominous warning sign: *Are you ready to meet your God?* Finally Pearl and Joe rode into Riverside, on the Gila River. It was a small settlement with a stagecoach stop and a population of about fifty. Nearby they made camp and watched the coaches as they came in and out of the station. In that era, Wells Fargo & Co. was the principal express business in Arizona Territory, and it paid stage lines to carry its ubiquitous green strongboxes. If a coach carried a valuable treasure shipment in the express box, it was generally accompanied by a guard, or shotgun messenger, who sat next to the driver. If there was no messenger on board, the strongbox held little of value, and the robbers' main target was the passengers. Wells Fargo shotgun messengers were hired for their sand, or courage, and their gunfighting skill. Only an extremely daring—or desperate—bandit would try to tangle with them. As a result, most stage robbers avoided coaches that had a guard on board.[15]

In Riverside, Pearl and Joe figured out the stage schedule. Coaches left Globe at eight in the morning, three times a week, on Mondays, Wednesdays, and Fridays. The stages arrived at Riverside late in the evening. There the driver and passengers spent the night, then at dawn proceeded to Florence, arriving at eleven in the morning. Pearl and Joe also learned that shotgun messengers did not regularly ride the road from Globe. Several townsfolk spotted the two strangers in Riverside, and one of them insisted that the holdup plan originated with Pearl, not Joe. The witness overheard them discussing a possible robbery, and Boot declared, "I can never do it. Never, never, never!"

"But you must—we must!" she insisted. "And it's easy. All

you'll have to do will be to hold your gun out straight and keep quiet. I'll do the rest."[16]

On May 29, 1899, the pair rode out of their camp near Riverside, splashed their horses across the Gila River, and headed toward Kane Spring Canyon. Pearl later told the story.

"On the afternoon of the robbery we took our horses and rode over the mountains and through the canyons, and at last hit the Globe road. We rode along slowly until we came to a bend in the road, which was a most favorable spot for our undertaking. We halted and listened till we heard the stage. Then we went forward on a slow walk, till we saw the stage coming around the bend. We then pulled to one side of the road. Joe drew a forty-five, and said, 'Throw up your hands!' I drew my little thirty-eight and likewise covered the occupants of the stage. Joe said to me, 'Get off your horse.' I did so, while he kept the people covered. He ordered them out of the stage. They were a badly scared outfit. I learned how easily a job of this kind could be done.

AUTHOR'S COLLECTION.

The stagecoach robbed by Pearl Hart as it appeared in 1899.

"Joe told me to search the passengers for arms. I carefully went through them all. They had no pistols. Joe motioned toward the stage. I advanced and searched it, and found the brave passengers had left two of their guns behind them when ordered out of the stage. Really, I can't see why men carry revolvers, because they almost invariably give them up at the very time they were made to be used. They certainly don't want revolvers for playthings. I gave Joe a forty-four, and kept the forty-five for myself. Joe told me to search the passengers for money. I did so, and found on the fellow who was shaking the worst three hundred and ninety dollars. This fellow was trembling so I could hardly get my hand in his pockets. The other fellow, a sort of a dude, with his hair parted in the middle, tried to tell me how much he needed the money, but he yielded thirty-six dollars, a dime and two nickels. Then I searched the remaining passenger, a Chinaman. He was nearer my size and I just scared him to death. His clothes enabled me to go through him quickly. I only got five dollars, however. The stage driver had a few dollars, but after a council of war we decided not to rob him."[17]

Pearl gave another account in which she provided more details. "When the coach came in sight we rode down into the canyon to meet it. Our masks were lost in going to the camp, but we didn't mind that. So on we rode. As we came upon the coach the driver reined his horses to have a word with us, as travelers out there do, and as the three passengers stuck their heads out to see why the stop was made, we covered them and ordered all four men to line up outside. While Joe kept their hands up at the point of the Winchester, I searched the men. I had to pull off one of my gloves to do this, and in this way the men saw by my hand that I was a woman. I can still see the Chinaman, who was one of the passengers, holding our horses. He was smiling at the thought that he was so kind we would not rob him. You can bet he was smiling on the other side of his face when I was through with him. I left about two dollars for each man, and told them to continue their journey and not to look back under penalty of being shot."[18]

Pearl later claimed that, after returning the driver's money, she told him with a laugh, "You may keep that. I believe you've earned it by driving three such cowards across the hills."

Pearl added that after giving a few dollars back to the passengers, she told them, "Being a good fellow, I kind of hate to see folks dead broke, so I'll stake you all. And now take a run back along the trail for the good of your health."

Then, watching the stagecoach disappear down the canyon, she exclaimed, "Come on, Joe!" The two then walked to the spot where their horses were tied, mounted up, and rode off.[19]

AUTHOR'S COLLECTION.

An artist's conception of the stage holdup.

Pearl's account was reasonably accurate and only differed slightly from the details later provided by the stage driver, his passengers, and lawmen. She and Joe set up their ambush at a spot in Kane Spring Canyon that was four miles from the Gila River. It was a narrow, twisting bend where the driver could not see more than twenty feet ahead of his lead horses. The outlaws waited for three hours for the coach to arrive. A few minutes before the stage pulled into sight, Hank Barton, who ran a saloon in Riverside, rode by. He spotted Pearl and Joe waiting by the road and later said that he "recognized them as hard characters he had seen in Globe." The bandits were not interested in Barton, and they let him pass. It was five in the evening when the stage from Globe came rattling down the rough trail. It was not a large, six-horse Concord coach of the type commonly seen in television and film. Instead the stage was a much lighter conveyance that looked like a carriage, known as a mud wagon. It had three seats, a canvas top, and a four-horse team. At the ribbons, or reins, was stage driver Henry Bacon. He had three passengers: Oscar J. Neil, a traveling salesman; an old man named Harding; and a Chinese passenger whose name was never recorded. Pearl and Joe stepped out from the roadside brush, and Joe called out, "Halt!"

Bacon pulled back on the reins and quickly set his brake.

"Climb out of there!" Joe barked. The driver and passengers meekly complied, even though Bacon and Neil were armed with large revolvers. Pearl and Joe lined the four men up and went through their pockets. From Neil they took three hundred and ninety dollars, his pistol, and a gold pocket watch worth fifty dollars. Henry Bacon coughed up his six-gun and eight dollars, but Pearl handed the money back to him. They relieved the Chinese passenger of thirty dollars. The bandits took forty dollars from the other passenger, Harding. However, before climbing out of the stage, Harding had slipped into his mouth a tobacco pouch holding eighty dollars in gold. A journalist who later interviewed the passengers wrote, "He presented a ludicrous appearance with his cheeks swelled out and the strings of the pouch hanging from his lips. The highwaymen failed to notice it, however."[20]

Joe Boot did most of the talking, probably because Pearl did not want her voice to reveal that she was a woman. The only words she actually spoke were to one of the passengers who was slow in handing over his cash. Pearl barked, "Cough up, partner, or I'll plug you."

After completing the search, Pearl handed back four silver dollars to each of the victims. The passengers later said that they were convinced that "the smaller of the two robbers was a woman. Her figure had only been illy concealed by the crude garb she wore of rough shirt and blue overalls, the latter tucked into coarse boots that were plainly far too large. Under the dirty cowboy hat…there showed a curl or two of dark hair, and the hands that had deftly turned their pockets inside out were small and white."[21]

Joe then ordered the men back into the stage. Henry Bacon whipped up his team, and the coach lurched off toward Riverside. Pearl and Joe then walked a short distance to the spot where they had concealed their horses. Swinging into the saddle, Pearl Hart began a long ride into national notoriety.

7

A Frontier Manhunt

Spurring their horses, Pearl Hart and Joe Boot followed far behind the stage through Kane Spring Canyon. "Joe and I rode slowly up the road for a few miles, planning our future movements," she recalled. "We turned off the well-traveled road to the right. We sought the roughest and most inaccessible region that we could find. We passed at right angles over canyons, and re-passed those same canyons the same day, to cover a trail that we knew would be a hot one before many hours. This undertaking, to throw the officers off the track, was most hazardous, and as I look back upon that wild ride, that effort to escape from the consequences of our bloodless crime, I marvel that we did not lose our lives. As it was, we had many very close escapes. Our horses were likewise in perilous positions several times. It seems to me now that nothing but the excitement of the hour could have carried me through this awful ride, over the perilous trails and the precipitous canyons. Today I cannot tell how we ever got through the ride that day. Many noises in the great mountains and canyons led us to believe that our pursuers were at hand, but these turned out to be the workings of our guilty consciences."[1]

Pearl later explained that they rode into a long box canyon where they heard "an unearthly chorus of hoarse grunts and strident squeals." She reined in her horse and cried, "My God, Joe, ain't that terrible. What can it be? Maybe this place is haunted."

Joe paused for a moment, perplexed. Then a grin of relief came over his face. "It's all right. They're nothing but bullfrogs, gal. Big croaking bullfrogs."[2]

Pearl, much relieved, continued her ride with Joe in the evening dusk. "Just at dark that night we came out on the road near Kane Spring," she later said. "Here Joe left me to take care of the two horses, and went to see if the road ahead was clear. He reported things all right. We then rode toward Riverside, passing that place in the dark about ten o'clock. We continued on for six miles, then crossed the river and camped for the rest of the night and the next day, hobbling our horses as soon as it became dark."[3]

AUTHOR'S COLLECTION.

A newspaper artist's sketch of Joe Boot wearing a cartridge belt and two six-guns.

Meanwhile the stage had arrived in Riverside an hour after the holdup. Oscar Neil left the coach and immediately began his own search for the bandits. In an era when a working man earned one to two dollars a day, his loss of almost four hundred dollars, plus a revolver and a gold watch, was a huge one, and he was determined to help find the robbers. Henry Bacon then boarded his passengers, whipped up his team, and headed up the Kelvin Grade, the beginning of a thirty-five-mile journey west to Florence, the Pinal County seat. When his stage arrived in Florence, Bacon learned that Sheriff William Truman had gone to Phoenix on business. Bacon reported the holdup to the undersheriff, who in turn swore out a criminal complaint before a justice of the peace. By this time Bacon had managed to identify the bandits as "Little Pearl" and "Joe," and the justice issued the complaint against them under those names. The elderly passenger, Harding, took no part in reporting the crime. He also refused to tell people in Florence his name, which was later revealed by the stage-line owner who had sold Harding his ticket. Harding then quietly left town by stagecoach for Prescott. The reason for his reticence seems evident, for he probably recognized Little Pearl from one of the brothels she had worked in. No doubt Harding did not want to have to explain to newspapers how and why he happened to know a notorious prostitute.[4]

Sheriff Truman arrived back in Florence that afternoon, May 30, and promptly rode alone out of town, headed for Riverside to hunt the stage robbers. Truman was a capable lawman. A forty-five-year-old native of New York, he had come to Pinal County in 1879, hoping to make his fortune in the gold and silver mines. Truman worked as a carpenter for the huge Silver King Mine and in 1890 won election as Pinal County sheriff. Contrary to depictions in Western films, there was no such thing as a town sheriff. Towns had a city marshal, and counties had a sheriff. And contrary to popular belief, very few Western sheriffs were gamblers or gunfighters. Most, like Truman, were public-spirited or politically ambitious working men who, due to the rabidly partisan politics and high political turnover of that era, rarely served more than a few terms in office. And this was a time when American policing was still in its infancy. There was no formal training and law officers—Truman included—learned on the job. In 1891 he had been publicly embarrassed when Ham White of Texas, one of the Old West's most prolific stage robbers, escaped his custody. Fortunately for the sheriff, White was quickly recaptured and sent to prison. In 1892 Truman played a prominent role in the hunt for King Ussery, a notorious desperado and stagecoach robber. By 1899 the sheriff had gained substantial experience. He also had a huge advantage over Pearl Hart and Joe Boot: he knew every square mile of Pinal County.[5]

By the time Bill Truman took to the saddle, the fugitives were a full day ahead of him. Undaunted, the sheriff made the long ride to Riverside, arriving in the middle of the night. There he met with Oscar Neil, and at daybreak the two rode four miles up Kane Spring Canyon, where Neil pointed out the site of the holdup. After a brief search, Truman found the tracks of the bandits' horses. From there he and Neil painstakingly followed the trail through rugged terrain and desert canyons as it led back to Riverside. From there they tracked the outlaws south along the Gila River seventeen miles to its confluence with the San Pedro River, then continued farther south along the San Pedro. The latter, more creek than river, flows north from Mexico, winding its way lazily a hundred and forty miles to its confluence with the former. For most of the year it barely has enough water to keep the fish alive, but in the summer monsoon season it can become a raging torrent. From time to time the posse lost the trail, but each time Sheriff Truman rode in a wide circle until he—in manhunter's parlance—cut sign and found the faded hoofprints.[6]

AUTHOR'S COLLECTION.

Pearl Hart with two six-shooters.

Pearl and Joe had left their camp on the Gila River on the night of May 31. Their route south along the San Pedro River would take them through Mammoth and then another seventy miles to Benson, a principal stop on the Southern Pacific Railroad. They planned on boarding a train in Benson and escaping the territory. The pair wisely slept in the daytime and rode at night. As Pearl later explained, "Our horses were much worn, but in the night we came to a big haystack and got a small feed for each of them, then pushed to within six miles of Mammoth. We were well known there and had to be very careful. We first lay down in the bushes, but we heard wagons pass, and, afterward, men on horseback, which made us very uneasy. We kept quiet until the sounds ceased, then crawled and walked up the side of a big sandstone hill where there were many small caves, or holes, of a circular shape, not much larger than a man's body.

"Upon reaching this spot of safety we found it to be the home of wild or musk hogs [javelinas], which abound in this locality. These hogs will fight if they have to. However, our peril was so great that we could not hesitate about other chances, and we selected a hole into which we could crawl. Joe started in and I followed. Of course, we had to look out for rattlesnakes, too, which made our entrance very slow. After we had crawled about twenty feet, Joe stopped, saying he could see two shining eyes ahead and was going to take a shot.

"I confess I felt very creepy, but we were between the devil and the deep sea and I listened to hear Joe, from his point ahead of me, tell of his success. The animal was shot and killed, and proved to be a big musk hog. We soon found the powder-smoke annoying, and as we could not turn around we backed to near the entrance for fresh air. We stayed there all day, and what a long day it was! When it got dark we saddled our horses. Joe stole into Mammoth for food and tobacco, and got back without arousing suspicion."[7]

Pearl later claimed that she mailed some of the stolen cash to her mother. "Joe gave up most of the money to send to my mother. We had a stamped envelope and some paper. I wrapped the paper money in this paper and put it in the envelope. I did not dare to show myself much, so I slipped the envelope addressed to mother at Kansas City in a box at Mammoth, and trusted to luck for it to reach her, which I learned afterward it did." Pearl and Joe made camp north of Mammoth, where they stayed until nightfall.[8]

Meanwhile Truman and Neil rode into Mammoth on June 1. The sheriff made inquiries around the settlement and learned that Joe Boot had been in town earlier that day, buying food and supplies. Truman and Neil—concluding that the outlaws were headed toward the railroad—started out again. Arizona's monsoon season had just begun, and a heavy rain started to fall that night. The sheriff and his posseman sought refuge at a remote ranch house on the San Pedro River, where they spent the night. Truman later said that the rancher assured them "that no one could pass without his dogs giving the alarm." They believed him and slept soundly until daybreak.[9]

At the same time, Pearl recalled that she and Joe broke camp and rode south from Mammoth in the dark. "When we hit the main trail again we put grass and canvas on the horses' hoofs so they would make no sound and leave no marks on the ground by which we could be traced." But that trick did not fool Sheriff Truman. In the morning he inspected the road that passed by the ranch house and was chagrined to find the bandits' tracks plainly visible in the fresh mud. The rancher's dogs had not uttered a sound. Frustrated but unfazed, Truman and Neil started out again, realizing they were not far behind their quarry.[10]

Pearl later explained, "After passing Mammoth, we crossed the river and went as far as the schoolhouse, where we hid ourselves and the horses in the bushes at the farther end of a big field. We secured feed for our animals here, and filled a cotton bag with straw to carry. Tired out, we forgot our troubles and slept soundly. At daylight Joe got some food, and we started on; but after going ten miles our horses showed signs of distress, and I realized how much depended on our animals and would have done anything to secure rest and food for them. I remonstrated with my partner about the condition of things, proposing to put our horses in a field and capture others; also to abandon the horses and walk, or to separate for our own safety. His answer was a peremptory no and we pushed on, passing a Mexican squatter's settlement and coming to a wide ditch. My horse jumped across, but Joe's horse fell in, and for a while I thought they would both be drowned. They finally got out. I sat in my saddle perfectly helpless during the struggle."[11]

AUTHOR'S COLLECTION.

Pearl Hart showing the pistol she used in the stage holdup.

Pearl became exhausted by her flight from the manhunters. "We rode by night and slept during the day while the posse which hit the trail we were following did exactly opposite. As we rested on the sides of the gulches, many times we could see our pursuers as they rode past and below us. It would have been an easy thing to pick the riders off with our Winchesters. We would slip past the posse as they rested and then they would pass us next time. This see-saw game continued five days, when the worry and physical exertion began to tell on me and I became sick." Their horses became so hungry and worn out they had to be walked.[12]

By this time Sheriff Truman had recruited Jose Maria Orosco into his little posse. Orosco owned a large cattle ranch on the San Pedro River. Like Truman, he was an Arizona pioneer. Born in Mexico in 1862, Orosco had come to Arizona with his parents when he was a child. As a young vaquero, he had several close brushes with Apaches. His many years on the Arizona frontier made him an expert tracker, as well as a good man with a gun. In 1891 he had joined a posse in pursuit of the gang of Geronimo Miranda, one of Arizona's deadliest train and stage robbers. In a pitched pistol duel north of Benson, Orosco and the other possemen shot Miranda to death. He was just the kind of man Sheriff Truman needed.[13]

It was now June 2. As Pearl recalled, "This day, which proved to be our last day of freedom, at least for a while, we spent sleeping and cooking. The rain fell in torrents and we were very uncomfortable. At night we again started, and rode until five o'clock in the morning. Just after daylight we came across a mountain lion and gave chase for two miles, but could not get a shot." Truman, Orosco, and Neil tracked the outlaws to a schoolhouse north of Benson. Pearl and Joe had taken refuge inside. Because the schoolhouse could not be approached without his posse being spotted, Truman and his men kept watch from a distance. At daybreak the two fugitives rode away, and the posse followed far behind. Pearl was weak from hunger and exhaustion, after riding a hundred miles through rough country. After proceeding several hundred yards, she and Joe dismounted and made camp in the brush. The pair lay down, side by side under a single saddle blanket, and fell sound asleep.[14]

Pearl recalled, "About three hours after lying down we were awakened by yelling and shooting. We sprang up and grabbed our guns, but found we were looking straight into the mouths of two gaping Winchesters in the hands of the sheriff's posse. Resistance was worse than useless, and we put up hands. At the time of our capture we were within twenty miles of Benson, the railroad station we were making for. Had we reached Benson, I believe we should have escaped." In another account, Pearl said, "I lay down to sleep, and Joe went to sleep on watch. The next morning at daybreak we were startled from our slumbers by a command to throw up our hands. Sheriff Bill Truman of Pinal County and a Mexican stood covering us with Winchesters."[15]

According to Sheriff Truman, the posse did no shooting. Truman had watched and waited for several hours until he was sure the bandits were asleep. While Neil held the horses, Truman and Orosco silently crept forward, clutching their Winchester rifles. A journalist later shared Truman's account thus: "They softly approached until they stood over the sleepers, when they emitted a yell that would have wakened the dead. The woman jumped to her feet and screamed, but the man was slower in responding, and had to be warned a second time before he held up his hands. They were searched and all of the booty, $469, and five six-shooters were secured." Pearl put up a brief struggle and tried to grab her guns, but the burly sheriff quickly overpowered her. If she and Joe had in fact been armed with Winchesters as Pearl had claimed, they had either discarded them or traded them for supplies in Mammoth. The recovered six-guns included Pearl's .45 caliber Colt Army revolver and her .44 caliber Merwin & Hulbert revolver, Joe's pistol, and the six-shooters taken from Bacon and Neil in the stage holdup. Sheriff Truman kept Pearl's Merwin & Hulbert pistol as a memento. And it seems Pearl had not mailed the stolen cash to her mother, for all the loot, including Neil's gold watch, was recovered.[16]

At first Pearl—still dressed like a cowboy—insisted that her name was Dan Goodrich, but she soon admitted she was Pearl Hart. She was furious at their capture and directed her anger at Joe. A journalist wrote that she "reproached him in vile and profane language for his lack of sand and said that if the posse had tried to capture her while she was awake she would have made some holes in it." Pearl recalled, "We were taken as prisoners first to Benson, thence through Tucson to Casa Grande by rail, and then to Florence. We were kindly treated. The worst thing we suffered was from the curious who came to look at and make fun of us. It would have given me pleasure to meet some of these curious fellows as we met the men in the stage, just to see what they were made of."[17]

AUTHOR'S COLLECTION.

Pearl Hart with Sheriff Bill Truman at the door to the Florence jail.

On the train, Pearl admitted to Sheriff Truman that they had robbed the stage. "We were flat broke in Globe and had to get away, and the only way in sight of raising a stake was to hold up the stage," she declared. "We were heading for the railroad to skip the Territory. I was to take about all the money and go to my old home in Canada. I'm tired of this wild rush for fortune in the Southwest." Passengers on the train noticed her and later told a reporter, "The woman was dressed in men's clothes, and seemed not a little pleased at the notoriety she had gained. She laughed and chatted with everyone who came along and freely described the holdup." At the rail stop in Casa Grande the posse and prisoners disembarked and boarded a stage for Florence. News of the arrest had been wired ahead, and a large crowd gathered in Florence to greet the sheriff and the two bandits. Truman lodged the pair in adjacent cells in the Pinal County jail, which was located on the main floor of the courthouse. He also gave Pearl some women's clothing to wear.[18]

The capture of a woman stagecoach robber created a public

sensation. The headline in the *Tucson Star* declared, "We Have a Woman Bandit." The story quickly hit the wires and was published in newspapers nationwide. The *St. Louis Post-Dispatch* trumpeted, "Girl Stage Robber Caught." The Washington, DC, *Evening Times* titled its account "Petite and Pretty but Full of Nerve." In her former New York home, the *Buffalo Evening News* ran a prominent headline: "A Beauty, but a Bandit." And the story was even news in Canada, where the *Ottawa Journal* headlined its report "A Highwaywoman." Yet no one in Canada connected Pearl Hart with its native daughter, Lillie Davy.[19]

Newspaper reporters rushed to the Pinal County jail to see the woman bandit. "The woman is well known in Phoenix, where she was a resident of Block 41," wrote a Florence reporter. "She is a confirmed morphine fiend and requires ten grains a day to keep herself in shape." A Phoenix journalist interviewed Pearl and wrote, "The woman claims to be a native of Canada, twenty-eight years old, though she looks much younger. She makes a striking picture, sitting with a cigarette in her lips, her legs crossed, and telling carelessly the story of her doings. She admits all guilt in the crime, but adds with some disgust that if she were a man held up by a woman she would not say much about it." To another reporter Pearl said, "I got a letter from my mother saying she was sick at Toledo, Ohio, and I was desperate." She added ruefully, "I expect now I am bound for Yuma."[20]

The journalists uniformly noted her physical attractiveness. According to one in Florence, "She is small and slight, weighs about 115 pounds, and is not bad looking." Wrote another from Phoenix, "She is by nature a handsome looking girl, about medium height." A correspondent for the *Los Angeles Times* observed, "The woman is under the average size, and is distinctly dainty and pretty." He called her "a delicate-looking, little, dark haired woman. She has refined features, a mouth of the true rosebud type, a nose slightly and piquantly retrousse, and clear, blue eyes that would be confiding and baby-like were there not a few lines that come through seeing life in its harsher aspects." A San Francisco reporter was somewhat less effusive: "She is about twenty-five years old and still retains a trace of her once remarkable beauty, despite the marks that a reckless life and dissipation have left upon her."[21]

The journalists were not so kind to Joe. As a San Francisco reporter declared, "Boot is a dissolute character who frequented the dives of Phoenix." Wrote the *Los Angeles Times* journalist "Joe Boot is a weak, morphine-depraved specimen of male mortality, without spirit and lacking in intelligence and activity. It is plain that the woman is the leader of the illy-assorted pair. She does not deny that such was the case, and expresses nothing but contempt for her companion." Witnesses who saw Boot being escorted to jail agreed, saying that he was "stoop-shouldered and awkward, with a weak face, quite unlike the ideal stage robber."[22]

The *Los Angeles Times* reporter interviewed Sheriff Truman, who remarked, "One wouldn't think that she is a very tiger cat for nerve and for endurance. She looks feminine enough now, in the women's clothes I got for her, and one can see the touch of a woman's hand in the way she has brightened up her cell. Yet, only a couple of days ago, I had a struggle with her for my life. She would have killed me in my tracks, could she have got to her pistol. Sure, women are curious creatures." In response, Pearl told the journalist, "Truman wonders why I fought him. How can any one wonder I fought who considers that the money I had was to have taken me back to liberty and decency and happiness?" As she explained, "Boot was to have helped me hit a train eastward. In a day more I would have been safe, and in a couple of days more would have been home, my life here left behind forever."[23]

Pearl, puffing furiously on a cigarette, told the *Times* writer, "I shall make no defense. I don't care what the world does with me. I'd do it all over again if I had the chance." Referring to Joe Boot, she declared, "Why, the fellow hadn't an ounce of sand. When I was going through the passengers his hands were shaking like leaves, and he a-holding the guns, too. Why, if I hadn't more nerve than that, I'd jump off the earth." When another journalist told her that she would probably become the only woman convict in Yuma prison, Pearl insisted, "I don't care a rap. If it were all to do over again, I would do just what I did. I don't care what becomes of me and don't propose to make any defense. The man with me hadn't an ounce of sand. Why, when I was going through the pockets of passengers on the stage I had to depend on him to hold both our guns. There he stood on the edge of the road with his hands shaking like aspens."[24]

Yet her anger toward Joe quickly cooled. As one journalist pointed out, "Boot, though apparently weak otherwise, has shown considerable manliness in the way in which he is seeking, in all the interviews held with him, to take to himself the entire blame for the stage robbery of Kane Spring Canyon." Said another reporter, "Pearl Hart was the center of curiosity and many visitors filled the jail every day. A young man from the East even bought her saddle, which he deemed a rare relic of the highways of Arizona. She persistently refused to wear anything except the man's garb she wore when captured, and this caused great consternation among the prison keepers." In interviews with reporters, she admitted that Pearl Hart was an alias and revealed that she had been married to Dan Bandman. But she steadfastly refused to state her real name, probably because of the shame it would bring to her mother. At the same time Pearl basked in the publicity, and when amateur photographers visited the jail, she happily posed for several images, taken on the jail steps at the rear of the courthouse. Those photos are widely published to this day.[25]

The 1890s saw the beginning of amateur photography. Previously, all photos had been taken by professionals who used heavy, unwieldy cameras mounted on tripods, with large glass photographic plates as film. But in 1888 the Eastman Kodak Company introduced a simple, handheld box camera that held a roll of film and was easy to use. It was the precursor to the hugely popular Brownie camera, introduced in 1900. During the 1890s, amateur photography became all the rage, even on the Arizona frontier. Sheriff Truman permitted visitors to bring their box cameras into the jail and allowed Pearl to don her men's clothing and pose with unloaded guns. "The woman is receiving much attention, an afternoon rarely going by without her having a lot of callers and herself photographed," announced a Phoenix reporter. "The camera fiends have taken shots of her with all sorts of firearms on and looking as much the desperado as they can make her. Altogether Miss Hart is good natured and seems to enjoy her situation. She says, however, that if Joe, her partner, were not near she would not be so content. Boot stretches his hands through the bars for the girl to caress and they seem happy. She still wears her overalls, top boots, and the rest of her masculine attire."[26]

AUTHOR'S COLLECTION.

Pearl Hart at the steps to the Florence jail, with male prisoners peering at her through the barred windows.

On June 7, Sheriff Truman and his deputies brought the pair into court for their preliminary hearing. The judge set bail at a thousand dollars each and sent the case to the grand jury to determine if they should be indicted for robbery. Neither Pearl nor Joe could make bail, so they were returned to their cells to languish until the grand jury convened for the November term of court. Then, after Pearl began showing symptoms of opiate withdrawal, Sheriff Truman obtained morphine for her. His jail had no separate cells for female prisoners, so he contacted the sheriff in Phoenix to inquire whether that jail could receive Pearl Hart. When Pearl found out that she might be separated from Joe, she became frantic. She first tried to escape from her cell, but the jailer stopped her. Next, while being watched by a deputy sheriff, she suddenly poured some white powder into her hand. Tossing it into her mouth, she exclaimed, "My troubles will soon be over."

The deputy promptly summoned a doctor, who determined that the powder was not poisonous. The physician concluded that Pearl "was running a prize bluff for sympathy." By this time Sheriff Truman had learned that the Phoenix lockup had no room for Pearl, but the county jail in Tucson did. On June 16 he obtained a court order that she be lodged in the Tucson jail. Two days later he directed her to don feminine clothing, then walked her to the stage depot. The sheriff allowed Pearl to bring her men's clothes along, and the pair proceeded by stagecoach to the train depot in Casa Grande, and from there they traveled south by rail to Tucson. A Florence reporter provided Pearl with a caustic farewell: "For this trip skirts and a hat were provided for Miss Hart and she proved not so good looking a female as she had been as a boy." [27]

"I did hate to leave Joe, who had been so considerate of me during all the ups and downs of the wild chase we had been through," said Pearl later. "His entire trouble was brought on by trying to get money for me to reach mother. We took an oath at parting never to serve out a term in the penitentiary, but rather to find that rest a tired soul seeks. It is, of course, public that I tried to kill myself the day they separated me from Joe at Florence and today I am sorry I didn't succeed."[28]

But Pearl Hart would not give up so easily.

8

Jailbreak

On the morning of June 20, 1899, Pearl Hart stepped into the Pima County jail in Tucson. There, Sheriff Truman turned her over to Undersheriff Robert H. Paul, who ran the jail. Though Bob Paul was one of the most experienced lawmen on the American frontier, in five decades as a pioneer peace officer he had never encountered an outlaw like Pearl Hart. A tall and powerful frontiersman, Paul was then sixty-nine and nearing the end of his adventurous career. Three years earlier, Wyatt Earp had called him "as fearless a man and as fast a friend as I ever knew." Paul had led an exciting life. Born in Massachusetts, as a teenage sailor he made three whaling voyages around Cape Horn to the Pacific Ocean. On his final voyage in 1848, the crew landed in Hawaii only to hear that gold had been discovered in California. Paul and many of the crewmen left their whale ship and boarded a vessel bound for the Pacific Coast. There he became an enthusiastic but unsuccessful gold miner. In 1854 he won election as a constable in the Sierra Nevada foothills of Calaveras County and soon after was appointed a deputy sheriff. Bob Paul proved to be much more successful as a manhunter than as a gold hunter.

In 1855 he took part in two bloody shoot-outs with a band of Mexican robbers, wounding one and killing another. The following year he played a leading role in breaking up the notorious Tom Bell gang, one of the worst outlaw bands of the Old West. Posing as a desperado, Bob Paul infiltrated the gang and learned many of the outlaws' secrets. Based on his detective work, several of the band were sent to San Quentin prison. Tom Bell was not so lucky: he was captured and lynched by a posse. In 1859 a grateful electorate picked Bob Paul as sheriff of Calaveras County, a post he held from 1860 to 1864. During the 1870s he worked as a shotgun messenger and detective for Wells Fargo & Company in California, Nevada, and Utah. Bob Paul was so aggressive in hunting bandits that in 1877 an attempt was made by highway robbers to assassinate him. They ambushed a stagecoach in the California desert and shot and killed a man who was riding next to the driver. The outlaws thought that they had killed Bob Paul. By a stroke of luck, Paul, who had been scheduled to guard that coach, had been instructed to wait for the second stage, and his life was spared.

The next year Wells Fargo officials in California sent him to Arizona Territory to deal with an explosion of stage robberies. The instant he crossed the Colorado River, Bob Paul became the most experienced lawman in Arizona. He wasted no time in tracking down some of the worst stage robbers in the territory, one of whom was hanged in Phoenix for murdering a passenger in a holdup. Paul liked Arizona and brought his wife and children to Tucson, where he lived out his days. One night in March 1881, Paul was riding shotgun on a stagecoach from Tombstone to the rail depot in Benson. His Wells Fargo strongbox held a fortune in gold. Suddenly a band of fearsome Cowboys appeared from the roadside blackness and shouted, "Hold!"

AUTHOR'S COLLECTION.

The famed lawman Bob Paul in 1899 when he was undersheriff of Pima County.

"I don't hold for anybody!" Bob Paul thundered.

Simultaneously, two Cowboys on each side of the stagecoach opened fire with Winchesters. Paul threw his sawed-off shotgun to his shoulder and emptied both barrels. One of the Cowboys staggered with a belly wound. The bandits poured a volley of fire into the stagecoach, narrowly missing Paul but killing the driver and a passenger. The terrified stage team raced off, and the Cowboys rode away empty-handed. The attempted stage robbery proved to be one of the most momentous of the American frontier. Wyatt Earp's efforts to capture the killers led directly to the shoot-out near the O.K. Corral in Tombstone.

By that time Bob Paul had been elected sheriff of Pima County. He fought highwaymen, murderers, and lynch mobs and helped establish law enforcement in the Southwest. In 1888 he led a posse into Mexico after a gang of train robbers. In a pitched gun battle, Paul and his possemen killed all three of the outlaws. His exploits made him one of the West's most noted peace officers. President Benjamin Harrison appointed Paul US Marshal of Arizona Territory in 1890, a post he held for three years. In 1899 Pima County Sheriff Lyman Wakefield made him his undersheriff. In that capacity, Paul ran the county jail in Tucson. Pearl Hart, as the sole woman prisoner, became his responsibility.[1]

Instead of putting Pearl in a jail cell, Paul lodged her in a locked room on the second floor of the courthouse that was used for female inmates. It was well outfitted with a bed, sofa, and other furniture. A Tucson newspaperman soon arrived to see her. "Miss Hart was not in a talkative mood," he reported, "having just run out of morphine, to which drug she is a slave, and seems to writhe in pain when not under its influence. When tossing and rolling upon her couch, she called for Sheriff Truman, being too modest, no doubt, to make her wishes known to Undersheriff Paul." The journalist concluded, "She is of fair form and has a face bearing traces of refinement beneath wrinkles of dissipation, has a rather musical voice, a luxuriant growth of hair, and would be a handsome woman were she not broken down by a life of shame and a profligate use of opiates."[2]

Bob Paul, despite all the violence he had seen on the frontier, was a kind and gentle family man. His three daughters were close in age to Pearl, and he looked upon his new prisoner with fatherly compassion. Paul had a Tucson doctor examine her. The physician recommended that she be given a dose of morphine twice a day, once early in the morning and once in the evening. Paul saw to it that she received the drug daily, as well as hot meals from a nearby restaurant. The next morning Pearl doffed her women's clothing and put her masculine attire back on. She explained that she found men's clothing more comfortable. The Tucson newspaperman visited her again and reported, "Since regular rations of morphine are issued to her she has become more docile and appears to be content with her lot. However, the sheriff's office keeps close watch over her lest she might 'hold out' on the dope and repeat her attempt at self-destruction." Another journalist who saw her in the courthouse added, "She alternates between blissful slumber in the morphine period and wild ravings when the drug is not to be had." But Pearl told the Tucson reporter that she was well cared for. "She says she is receiving better treatment than she ever imagined could be extended to prisoners. Her food is of the best, her room is comfortable, and between reading and singing she manages to while away the time."[3]

ARIZONA HISTORICAL SOCIETY.

The Pima County courthouse, where Pearl Hart was held as a prisoner. The county jail is the two-story wing partially visible and attached to the left, or rear, of the courthouse.

Pearl continued to be an object of great curiosity, and Bob Paul allowed her frequent visitors. Some visited her in her locked room, while others saw her in the jail where she was often kept during the daytime. One of them brought Pearl a bobcat cub, and Paul let her keep it as a pet. Bobcats—commonly known as wildcats—were fairly common in Arizona and grew to about twice the size of a domestic cat.

Despite Pearl's penchant for male attire, the undersheriff got her a new and stylish outfit: a willowy white dress and belt, with a checkered blouse and a white straw hat topped with flowers. Soon two of Paul's friends asked to conduct a long interview and to have her pose for photographs. They were Royal A. Johnson, a prominent businessman, politician, and former surveyor general of Arizona, and twenty-three-year-old Francis Reno, who later became a deputy US marshal and private detective. The pair had been engaged to write a feature story about the woman stage robber for *Cosmopolitan*. The popular magazine, then just thirteen years old, was well on its way to becoming an important journal for women.

Bob Paul permitted the interview, and the two took thorough notes as Pearl told her story in detail. Paul allowed her to don men's clothes so she could be photographed and even supplied Pearl with a pistol belt, two six-guns, and a Winchester rifle—all unloaded. Then, as Reno snapped away with his Kodak box camera, she posed for six images in her cell and the jailyard. In two photos she held her pet wildcat; in others she carried firearms; and in one she posed in a fashionable women's outfit, looking prim, pretty, and proper. These photographs would soon be published not only in *Cosmopolitan* but in newspapers throughout the country. The public was simultaneously fascinated and shocked at the sight of a woman dressed like a cowboy and armed to the teeth.[4]

Francis Reno was not the only person taking photos of the bandit. Reported the *Tucson Star*, "The county jail is besieged by Kodak fiends, seeking pictures of Pearl Hart." She probably recalled her experience twelve years before, when Sheriff Barlow in Minnesota had sold photos of her and Katy. "He was a fool to sell them for a quarter," she had declared. "He might as well have had half a dollar." Now she obtained copies of the photographs and peddled scores of them to jail visitors for fifty cents each. Several people in Tucson befriended Pearl and gave her a little money, which she used to buy cigarettes and other small luxuries.[5]

Pearl's most prominent visitor was Louis C. Hughes, former governor of Arizona Territory and owner of the *Tucson Star.* Hughes was a controversial pioneer and journalist who had founded the *Star* in 1877. His well-educated, well-bred wife, Josephine Brawley Hughes, an early feminist, became popularly known as the Mother of Arizona. She impressed upon her husband views that were especially unpopular on the Arizona frontier: opposition to drinking and gambling, and support of a woman's right to vote. Over the years, Louis Hughes had played a leading role in countless political disputes, sometimes taking positions beyond reason. Probably the most incredible was his bitter opposition to Wyatt Earp and his brothers in Tombstone and his editorial support for the murderous Cowboys. His reason: the Earps were Republicans, and most of the Cowboys, like him, were Democrats. Hughes's political career reached its nadir in 1896 when he supported a bill that was opposed by his own patron, President Grover Cleveland. The president, who had appointed Hughes as Arizona's territorial governor three years earlier, forced him to resign.

Although Hughes was a fierce political enemy of Bob Paul, the old lawman allowed the *Star* editor to visit Pearl. Apparently, she used her charms on Hughes, for afterward, rumors circulated about his behavior in the jail. Hughes denied any inappropriate conduct, as the *Phoenix Gazette* reported: "Editor Hughes, whom it is thought flirted with Pearl Hart, says he would not fool with a girl who had a pistol pocket in her clothes." In response, a Tombstone newspaper insisted, "There is no sort of truth in the report. The governor is a law-abiding citizen and no nymph in calico could prevail on him to shatter the commandments." That was hardly true, for Hughes was a notorious womanizer. Over the years he had been repeatedly accused of consorting with prostitutes, "squandering his money on variety women," and "lallygagging with bewitching actresses." Pearl Hart, as we will see, made a profound impression on Louis C. Hughes.[6]

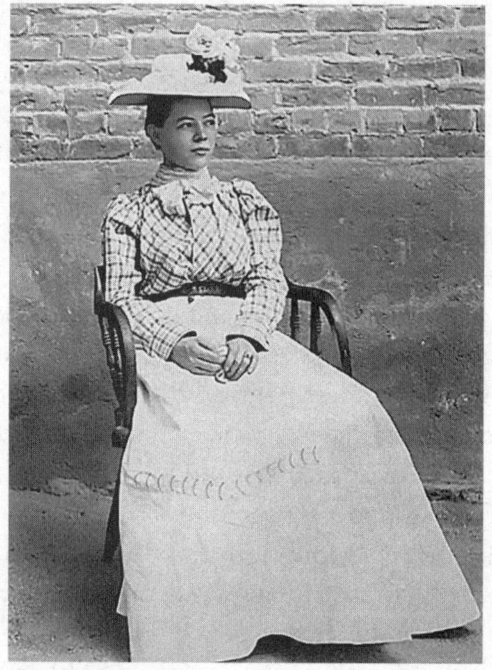

AUTHOR'S COLLECTION.

Pearl Hart looking prim, pretty, and proper. This photo was taken in the Tucson jail by Francis Reno.

Francis Reno visited Pearl a number of times. He explained that on one occasion, Pearl's pet animal was far from gentle. "The wildcat was lying on the cot in the cell at the time. Once the cat got in the woman's way and she lifted it up to drop it on the floor. As soon as she took hold of the animal it sank its teeth through her thumb. With a string of oaths that would shame the worst badman that ever traveled the sands of Arizona, she grabbed the cat by the neck and halfway beat it to death." But Pearl could not have hurt the animal too badly. On August 4 a lawyer visited Pearl in jail and apparently brought his dog with him. As a Tucson newspaper reported, it was a volatile mix. "A pet mountain lion, an innocent canine, an attorney, and Pearl Hart got mixed up on the second floor, rear of the courthouse yesterday. The attorney and the female bandit do not speak now, and the dog has no further use for inside the jail. The story is too long for repetition."[7]

In late September Pearl received even more publicity when copies of *Cosmopolitan* magazine, containing the well-illustrated story about her, arrived in Tucson. Possibly influenced by former governor Hughes, she began expressing feminist views to visitors, declaring, "I shall never submit to be tried under the law that neither I nor my sex had a voice in making." Pearl wasn't fooling, for she soon began planning an escape. She later said, "A prisoner, whose time would be out in about ten days, fell in love with me. He was a trusty and he got it into his head that they were going to take me away from the jail the next day. So he escaped and came back in the night for me. He dug a hole in the wall from the outside of the jail large enough to take me out of. Then he begged me to flee with him until I consented and we ran away together."[8]

But as with so many of Pearl's stories, this one was neither wholly accurate nor complete. The prisoner who fell in love with her went by the name of Ed Hogan, alias Ed Sherwood. He was a morphine addict whom a Tucson journalist called "nothing but a saloon lounger and bum." The previous January, Hogan had gone on a spree of bicycle theft in Phoenix. Among the half dozen "wheels" he stole and sold was one that belonged to the Phoenix city marshal. Officers arrested Hogan, and a judge sentenced him to a hundred and fifty days in jail. In June, less than a week after he was released from jail, Hogan embarked on a second spree of bike-stealing. Two policemen captured him after a foot pursuit in which they fired a warning shot over his head. Hogan pleaded guilty to stealing five bicycles, and the judge handed him a ten-month jail term. Deputy sheriffs then put him to work on the county chain gang. But Hogan was a slippery character. Even though one of his feet was secured by a ball and chain, he managed to get loose and escape from his guards. He was quickly recaptured in Phoenix, returned to the chain gang, and escaped again. Hogan jumped a train for Tucson, where officers arrested him for grand larceny in August. But the sheriff in Phoenix did not want to incur the expense of having the petty thief sent back. Finally, a Tucson judge convicted Hogan of drunk and disorderly conduct and sentenced him to sixty days in the county jail.[9]

AUTHOR'S COLLECTION.

Pearl with her pet wildcat in the Tucson jailyard.

Francis Reno later described how Pearl Hart met Ed Hogan. "While in the jail the young woman bandit made a pet of a young wildcat. She kept the animal in her cell most of the time, but occasionally it roamed out into the corridor and visited the cells of the other prisoners. One day it entered the cell of the short term prisoner [Hogan]. He picked up the cat and held it above his head, and the animal bit the prisoner's hand, badly lacerating it. With a howl of rage and pain, he threw the cat to the steel floor of the cell and killed it. For hours Pearl sat in her cell and cursed the man who had killed her pet, but later, when he had a chance to speak to the young woman, he told her he would get her out." Hogan proved true to his word.[10]

Due to Ed Hogan's good behavior, Bob Paul had made him what was referred to as a trusty, a trustworthy prisoner who was allowed out of his cell to clean and do odd jobs. Hogan worked around the jail and courthouse in the day and was locked in his cell after dark. He had only ten days of his sentence left to serve. But when jailers locked up the cells on the night of October 11, 1899, they found that Hogan was missing. He hid out nearby and after midnight crept back to the courthouse and slipped inside through an unlocked door. Although there was a guard on duty in the jail, the adjacent courthouse had no night watchman. Next to Pearl's locked room was an alcove that led to a stairway to the courthouse tower. Hogan climbed a few steps up the stairway, then used a jackknife to cut a fifteen-inch-square hole through the plaster-and-wood wall. The hole was about ten feet up the wall in Pearl's room, so she held up her bedsheet to catch the falling plaster and prevent the noise from waking anyone. After donning her men's attire, she placed a chair on top of a table, climbed up and, with Hogan's help, squeezed through the small hole. They walked ten minutes to the railroad yards near the train depot. There they found an eastbound freight train ready to pull out. In the dark the pair slipped aboard, hid between two boxcars, and headed for New Mexico.[11]

A jailer entered Pearl's room at five thirty in the morning to bring her the usual dose of morphine. He was shocked to find the chair on top of the table, the hole high up in the wall, and Pearl Hart gone. The jailer immediately summoned Bob Paul, who searched the room and found a rambling, bombastic farewell letter. It was alternately sympathetic to and critical of Pearl's erstwhile holdup partner. "I forced Joe Boot at the point of my gun to help me hold up the stage," her note read. "It is my fault, not his. He loved me and did as I said. If he had not, I sure would have killed him and he knew it too. When I want anything and want it bad I would do anything to get it. I want to see my mother and I will, if it costs me my life, and I shall not be caught asleep again. For I have no bullhead to deal with. I think my head is all right when I am alone and the man don't live that could be my partner again, only when I can use them to my own advantage. I hate both sexes [except] only in my own family. I will be ever on the lookout and will have no mercy on those who come between me and my darling old gray haired mother. I will not ask what is wanted, but kill on sight. In two months if you want me bad, you can go to Toledo, Ohio, and get me. Then I will have seen my mother and then I care not what anyone does to me. If she is alive, well and good. If she has died since my arrest, God pity those who kept me from her. I shall have no pity and shall devote my entire life to killing all who detained me. It was the hope of getting out that has kept me up. I am, yours respectfully, Pearl Hart."[12]

AUTHOR'S COLLECTION.

Pearl with her wildcat in the jailyard. This is another of the six photos taken by Francis Reno.

Respectful or not, neither Bob Paul nor his boss, Sheriff Wakefield, were amused. Wakefield interviewed railroad officials, who insisted that the fugitives could not have boarded a train in Tucson. Wakefield, convinced that the two were headed for Mexico on horseback, went by railroad to the border town of Nogales where he hoped to cut off their flight south. At the same time his deputies found the tracks of horses heading east. Wakefield soon joined them, and they followed the false trail to Bowie, a hundred miles east of Tucson. From there they tracked the horses north toward Globe but soon lost the scent. After almost a week of searching, Wakefield and his deputies returned to Tucson empty-handed. Meanwhile Pearl's notoriety grew exponentially. The jailbreak brought her even more national newspaper attention, and some began seeing the woman outlaw as a folk hero. "The escape caused a sensation," declared the *San Francisco Examiner*, "although the prevailing sentiment appears to applaud the courage of the little bandit." The *New York Sun* added, "Public sentiment appears to be in her favor, and it is said that no very determined effort will be made to recapture her."[13]

Former governor Louis Hughes had been thoroughly hornswoggled by Pearl. Now he threw his support to her in the pages of the *Tucson Star*. "The ease with which she secured her freedom appears as novel as it was surprising. The intelligence of the escape appeared to create a sentiment rather favorable to the prisoner. This comes no doubt from a feeling of chivalry which so largely prevails on the frontier. There is no place where woman is held in such esteem and her protection is so certain as in this region of the United States. Every true frontiersman hallows the thought that his mother was a woman, and he owes respect and protection to her sex, no matter where she may be, nor what her misfortunes may have been.

"Pearl Hart declared in her cell that she would never consent to be tried under a law she or her sex had no voice in making, or to which woman had no power under the law to give her consent. Now there is much in this declaration. Why should a woman be indicted, put on trial, convicted and sentenced for an offense under a law that she nor her sex had no voice in making? That laws should be enacted by the consent of the governed is a fundamental principle of our government. The penalty of a given law is supposed to be consented to by those who are made liable to the penalty. Woman is not given the right to consent to the enactment of the laws which provide these penalties. Then why should she be made to suffer the penalty of acts which by law is declared to be a crime? Pearl Hart in her declaration raised a most important question, which shows the injustice which is visited upon her sex, in requiring her to suffer the penalty of the violation of laws enacted without her consent. To carry out what she deemed her rights under the principles of our government, she struck out for liberty and at this writing she seems to be as free as the birds of the air."[14]

Hughes's portrayal of Pearl Hart as a pioneer feminist did not meet with universal approval. The following day the *Phoenix Republican* offered the opposite point of view in an editorial entitled "Criminal Sentimentalism." Its editor wrote, "The *Tucson Star* in commenting on the escape from jail of Pearl Hart, the female stage robber, prints a sentimental and foolish editorial in her defense. It seems that Pearl, who is a soiled one to say the least, is a woman suffragist and had objected to being tried for stage robbery because women had no part in making laws which would send them to jail. This is natural, in view of the fact that she stood a splendid show of going 'over the road' for a considerable period. The *Star*, however, sees in Pearl's reasoning an argument in favor of woman's suffrage and urges that female offenders be exempted from consequences of crimes because they cannot vote. There would be as much sense in arguing that a Chinese highbinder [gangster] should escape the law, for the same reason. [The Chinese Exclusion Act of 1882 prevented Chinese from entering the US, becoming citizens, and voting.]

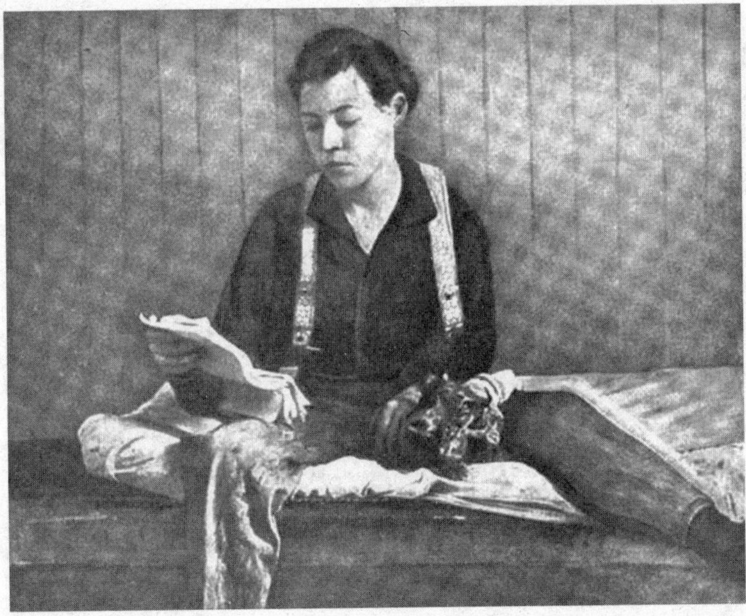

AUTHOR'S COLLECTION.

Pearl on her cot in the Tucson courthouse. Her pet wildcat sits on her lap.

"The cause of woman's suffrage, no matter how meritorious, can gain nothing from such sentimental theorists as the *Star*'s editorial writer. Arizona has already gained too much unenviable notoriety from the escapade of this female degenerate. First, the yellow journals made much of her, printing her picture in outlandish costumes, the photographs for which were obtained by the consent of silly county officials who permitted their prisoner to pose ad libitum. Next, the *Cosmopolitan*, a magazine of otherwise decent tendencies, undertakes to make a heroine of her. After all this silly sentimentalism over a character who during her residence in Phoenix was known to the authorities as a woman of the lowest type, no one should be surprised at her escape from custody. It will be time enough to be surprised when she is caught."[15]

At that time, American feminism was in its infancy. Susan B. Anthony's demands in Rochester for "equality in every respect" were considered radical in an era when women were universally deemed to be naturally subservient to men. But winning the right to vote became an essential goal, embraced by women of all social classes. During the 1890s, women reformers made huge strides in the fight to obtain the vote, primarily in the West. There, women were greatly in the minority, and male civic leaders saw a way to attract female settlers to the frontier. Additionally, the simple fact that a woman lived on the frontier meant that she was independent, tough, and self-reliant. Before the advent of the railroads, the only way to get to frontier regions was a long trip on dangerous trails by covered wagon or stagecoach. And Western women had to have grit just to survive. They used that energy and determination—as well as the respect they earned from men—to get the vote. As a result, women activists first won suffrage in Wyoming in 1869, followed by Utah in 1870, Washington in 1883, Montana in 1887, Colorado in 1893, and Idaho in 1896. By 1914, women could cast a vote in most Western states, but not in a single state east of the Mississippi River. Winning suffrage was an important start and opened the way for a century-long struggle for women's equal rights.

While newspaper editors debated Pearl Hart's significance as an icon, she and Ed Hogan proceeded by freight train to Bowie, Arizona, a hundred miles east of Tucson. There the railroad crew spotted the pair and ejected them from the train. Then, alternately walking and stealing rides on freight trains, the two continued east another fifty miles to Lordsburg, New Mexico. After spending two days in Lordsburg, they managed to slip aboard another train, which took them sixty miles farther east to Deming. Pearl and Hogan arrived in the rough railroad town of thirteen hundred people on October 18, a week after fleeing Tucson. They had no money, so she went to work in a brothel. Their decision to stop in Deming was a poor one, for it was the home of George Scarborough, one of the Old West's most celebrated lawmen. Scarborough was ever on the alert. He—like almost everyone else in the Southwest—knew the pair had escaped from Tucson, and he had seen the photos of Pearl in *Cosmopolitan*. When Scarborough spotted the two strangers come into town—one looking like a slender youth—he immediately recognized Pearl Hart from the magazine illustrations.[16]

The forty-year-old Scarborough was no man to fool with. He had grown up as a cowboy in Texas and in 1884 won election as sheriff of Jones County, just north of Abilene. Scarborough quickly established himself as a crack detective and relentless manhunter. He was also a dangerous gunman. In 1887 he and his younger brother stepped inside the Road to Ruin Saloon in Haskell, Texas, where he sat down at a desk and began writing a letter. Suddenly his deadly enemy, a cattle thief named A. J. Williams, burst in, wielding a double-barrel shotgun and yelling that he was going to kill the sheriff. The Scarborough boys jerked their six-shooters and riddled him with lead. Williams dropped to the saloon floor, blood gushing from five bullet wounds, and died two hours later. The brothers were charged with murder and a jury acquitted them in five minutes.[17]

The next year Scarborough lost the sheriff's election. He then worked as a livestock detective until 1893 when he obtained appointment as a deputy US marshal in El Paso. The border town, popularly called Hell Paso, was widely known for its array of infamous gunfighters. There Scarborough worked closely with his best friend, Jeff Milton, El Paso's chief of police and one of the Southwest's most noted peace officers. In 1895 Scarborough and Milton shot and killed a notorious fugitive, Martin Mrose, while attempting to arrest him on the Rio Grande. Mrose's attorney was John Wesley Hardin, the king of the gunfighters. Wes Hardin had studied law while serving a term for murder in the Texas state prison. Upon his release he became a lawyer but spent most of his time gambling in El Paso. As a result of the Mrose killing, there was bad blood between Hardin and Scarborough, but no bloodshed. It was left to John Selman, a notorious killer and quasireformed outlaw, to deal with Hardin.

While Wes Hardin was playing dice in the Acme Saloon, Selman walked in and shot the celebrated gunfighter in the head, killing him instantly. Eight months later, in April 1896, Selman made the fatal mistake of quarreling with George Scarborough in El Paso's Wigwam Saloon. Scarborough shot him dead and instantly became famous as the man who killed the man who killed John Wesley Hardin.[18]

Despite Scarborough's reputation as a mankiller, he made the vast majority of his arrests without any shooting. On one occasion in 1896 he attempted to collar a pair of Mexican revolutionaries charged with violating the US neutrality laws. One of the Mexicans shot him in the jaw. Although bleeding heavily, Scarborough grappled with his assailant and held him until other officers arrived. Due to the controversy over his killings of Mrose and Selman, Scarborough resigned his commission as deputy US marshal. The next year he moved with his wife and children to Deming, New Mexico Territory, where he served as a deputy sheriff and cattle detective. He and his pal Jeff Milton then played a prominent role in the manhunt for the train-robbing gang of Black Jack Ketchum. In July 1898 the pair teamed up again to hunt down Bronco Bill Walters and his band of train robbers. In a pitched gun battle in Arizona's White Mountains, they shot and captured Bronco Bill and killed one of his gang.[19]

Though George Scarborough had no fear of any man—or woman—he moved cautiously after spotting Pearl Hart in Deming. He first sent a wire to the sheriff's office in Tucson, asking for confirmation that the two jailbreakers were wanted. Bob Paul replied the next day, instructing him "to arrest them at once" and advising that a fifty dollar reward had been offered for their capture. Scarborough then kept a close watch on Pearl's brothel and found that Ed Hogan was staying in her room. At eight o'clock the next morning, October 20, Scarborough and a friend, Archie Rollins, the town barber, quietly entered the bordello. Scarborough unceremoniously shoved open the bedroom door. Pearl and Hogan were in bed together and wisely offered no resistance. Scarborough quickly searched the room and found no weapons. Pearl unleashed a torrent of oaths at the officer but quickly calmed down and said, "Well, I guess the game is all up with me, but if I had a gun I would send one officer to repentance."[20]

AUTHOR'S COLLECTION.

George Scarborough, the noted Western lawman who captured Pearl Hart and Ed Hogan in Deming, New Mexico.

Scarborough ordered the pair to dress, but Pearl had sent her men's clothing to a Chinese laundry. The officer had her don some of Hogan's clothes, then he and Rollins escorted them to jail to await the evening train to Tucson. The arrest created an uproar in Deming. A reporter interviewed their captor and wrote, "Mr. Scarborough says that while he had her locked in the town calaboose he was approached by a couple of nice appearing ladies, who had with them a little girl, who wanted to see the famous bandit. He told them he would take them down and show her to them it they wanted to go, but warned them that she was one of the most foul mouthed persons he had ever seen, and that he could not guarantee but that she would use language to them that no woman ought to hear. They said that made no difference, that they would stand anything to get a sight of her and have her write her name on a card. Mr. Scarborough took the party, who were travelers from the east, en route to California, down to the calaboose, and the woman got the desired autograph. Luckily for the little girl, it made no difference as regards the woman, Pearl behaved quite decently, and made no bad breaks."[21]

In the evening, when the westbound train arrived, a huge, excited crowd gathered at the depot to catch a glimpse of the notorious woman outlaw. Scarborough bundled the manacled pair onto a passenger car, and the train pulled out for Tucson. Later Pearl Hart ruefully described her brief stay with Ed Hogan in the Deming lockup: "The officers put us in one of those little wooden jails that an ordinary wind could blow away. Then they chained our feet together and fastened them to the floor. Outside of the jail and all around the building they stationed fifty rough looking men, each with two revolvers in his hip pocket. Being chained together in that way was worse than being married."[22]

9

The Arizona Female Bandit

Pearl Hart was more than unhappy when George Scarborough took her off the train at the Tucson depot and turned her over to Sheriff Wakefield. "She swears she will never go to the penitentiary, that she will kill herself first," a journalist reported. The sheriff and Bob Paul were taking no more chances with her. Instead of returning Pearl to her former quarters in the courthouse, they locked her in an iron-barred cell in the county jail. And a Tucson newspaperman denied her account of how she was kept secure in the Deming lockup. "There were no fifty rough men outside, each carrying two revolvers, guarding the jail," he wrote. "This was one of Pearl Hart's pipe dreams which looks well in yellow journals."[1]

Sheriff Wakefield was embarrassed—politically and personally—by her escape. Even though Bob Paul was in charge of the jail, Wakefield, as the elected sheriff, bore the brunt of the criticism. In an effort to save face, Wakefield gave an interview to the *Tucson Citizen*, claiming responsibility for recapturing the two fugitives. The *Citizen* asserted, "Pearl Hart and Edward Hogan are now confined in the county jail, thanks to the clever detective work of Sheriff Wakefield." Its story continued, "Sheriff Wakefield started on the trail of the refugees the day following their escape. He had no difficulty in tracking Pearl Hart, but lost Hogan's trail completely. Since the second day after Pearl Hart escaped there has not been an hour that Sheriff Wakefield did not know exactly where she was, for all the time either he has been watching her or else he has had another officer doing it. The reason that the sheriff did not arrest her was that he wished to use her as a decoy. He had no knowledge of the whereabouts of Hogan, but he believed Pearl Hart and Hogan had agreed upon a rendezvous and sooner or later Hogan would join her. Three days ago the sheriff was near Pearl, although she never dreamed that he was around her. Pearl started for Deming. Mr. Wakefield learned where she was going, he telegraphed Deputy Sheriff George A. Scarborough, who lives at Deming, that Pearl Hart was going there and for him to keep her shadowed and not to arrest her unless Hogan appeared, in which case he was to arrest both."[2]

Sheriff Wakefield's account was fiction. He had no idea where Pearl and Hogan had gone, as evidenced by his wild-goose chase to the Mexican border in search of them. Before Scarborough caught Pearl, Wakefield claimed that she had joined a band of outlaws on the Black River in Eastern Arizona. A Deming newspaper promptly debunked the sheriff's yarn. "Pearl Hart and Ed Hogan were in Deming for two days and nights and only one man in this town was aware of their presence, and George Scarborough never received a telegram from anyone regarding them, until he wired to Tucson to know if they were wanted." The Deming journalist explained, "It is customary, throughout this western country, for officers to try to claim all the credit that there is attached to the arresting of bad men or women, in order to hold all the rewards, if there are any to be paid, but in this particular instance it would seem that Sheriff Wakefield has gone a little too fast, and as is usual with such a gait, has overreached himself."[3]

AUTHOR'S COLLECTION.

Pearl Hart in the Tucson jail, 1899.

Bob Paul kept a wary eye on Pearl. As one reporter observed, "Her daily supply of morphine has been closely watched, for fear she would save up enough for a fatal dose." The November term of court in Florence was fast approaching, and Sheriff Wakefield looked forward to getting rid of his troublesome woman prisoner. On November 7, 1899, the Pinal County grand jury in Florence heard the testimony of Henry Bacon and Oscar Neil. The grand jurors issued an indictment against Pearl and Joe for robbery in the classic but cumbersome legal language of that era, charging that the pair "being each armed with a deadly weapon, to wit, a pistol, loaded with gun powder and leaden bullets…then and there feloniously and by means of force and fear did steal, take, and carry away" the victims' property. The same day Pearl pulled on her favorite overalls, bid farewell to Bob Paul, and accompanied Wakefield to the Tucson railroad depot. They boarded a northbound train for Casa Grande, the closest stop to Florence.[4]

The train's passengers included a group of women from Tennessee, on their way to San Francisco to welcome back the state's volunteer troops returning from the Philippine–American War. One of the women, in a letter home, wrote about spotting Pearl Hart on the train between Tucson and Casa Grande. "Some of our party saw her and all wanted to see her but when her presence became known to all she was in such an advanced stage of inebriety that she was unpresentable. Before she had been so liberally supplied with liquor, some of our ladies saw her. She is a petite figure, rather pretty features, and at first showed nothing coarse or revolting. She was dressed in male attire, with short hair and a round skull cap. She sat on the seat beside the sheriff and although she was vigorously puffing a cigarette, was real ladylike in her replies to questions. Her hands and feet were small and effeminate. She was in a car surrounded by twenty-five or thirty men, who soon began to supply her with whisky and tobacco. It was not long before they had their effect and the demoralized nature began to show itself, and we were told that whisky, tobacco, and profanity strived for the mastery. Her life history is what might be expected from the condition she is now in. She has been married, deceived, and has drifted away from all respectability, beyond the reach even of womanly sympathy which would freely have been given her."[5]

That Pearl was a celebrity—and men wanted to treat her to drinks—was no surprise. But it goes without saying that Sheriff Wakefield's permitting her to get drunk on the train was wholly unprofessional, even in that freewheeling era of pioneer policing. At Casa Grande, Wakefield turned Pearl over to a Pinal County deputy sheriff who brought her by stage to the jail in Florence. She rejoined Joe Boot behind bars, and two days later they were brought into court and arraigned on two felony counts. One charge was for robbing Oscar Neil of three hundred and ninety dollars and the other was for stealing Henry

Bacon's six-shooter. Despite Pearl's farewell letter in which she took all the blame for the holdup, she now pleaded not guilty. Pearl and Joe had worked up a clever plan.

Their trial for robbing Oscar Neil began on November 13 before Judge Fletcher Doan in a crowded Florence courtroom. Doan had appointed two local attorneys to represent the defendants. Pearl's lawyer was James Morrison, who also happened to be a physician. First Joe Boot, much to the surprise of everyone present, stood up and entered a guilty plea to robbery. Then Pearl's trial began. It took much of the day to select the all-male jury. Although women in Arizona would achieve the right to vote in 1912, they were not allowed to serve on juries until 1945. Stage driver Henry Bacon first took the stand, followed by his passenger, Oscar Neil. After they told the story of the holdup, Joe Boot stepped forward to testify. He assumed all responsibility for the robbery, even declaring that he had forced Pearl to take part.

AUTHOR'S COLLECTION.

Joe Boot as he looked when he was booked into Yuma prison.

The jurors looked on with skepticism. Then the other bandit, dressed in her best women's clothing, walked demurely to the witness stand. "She played on the feelings of the jurors," one journalist recorded. "Her plea, earnest from the first, became passionate as she told of her longing to return to her home and her mother." A second reporter observed, "She addressed the jury in a passionate and eloquent manner, pleading her desire to return to Toledo, Ohio, and get one last look at her mother, who was not expected to live long, and whom she has not seen in years." According to yet another account, "Pearl flipped her dark eyelashes at the jurymen, rustled her skirts at the bailiff [and] smiled sweetly at the district attorney."[6]

The jurors were simultaneously seduced and overcome with empathy. Pearl's lawyer made a passionate closing argument. As a Florence journalist observed, "Morrison's appeal to the jury was especially touching and affected the jurors as well as those in the courtroom." It was well after dark when they finally retired to the jury room to deliberate. There wasn't much to discuss. In just three minutes they held their first ballot: eleven for acquittal, one to convict. After more deliberations, the lone holdout juror gave in, and the jury filed back into the courtroom. When they delivered their verdict of not guilty, Judge Doan became—according to a reporter—"highly indignant." He ordered Pearl Hart held on the second charge of robbing Henry Bacon. Then Doan dismissed the jurors, first giving them "a tongue lashing almost unequaled in court annals."[7]

Pearl's trial for robbing the stage driver of his six-gun began two days later before a new jury. Her lawyers argued that because she had already been tried and acquitted, a retrial was barred by the legal defense of double jeopardy. Judge Doan rejected that argument on the grounds that the robbery of Bacon was a separate offense. The trial took less than a day, and although the testimony was identical, the outcome was not. The jurors deliberated only thirty minutes before finding Pearl Hart guilty. Two days later, on November 17, Pearl and Joe were brought before Judge Doan for sentencing. Doan handed Joe Boot an extraordinarily stiff punishment: thirty years in prison. Compared to that, the sentence he gave to Pearl was relatively light: five years in Yuma.[8]

The next morning Sheriff Truman brought Pearl and Joe by rail to Yuma prison, situated on the Colorado River in the extreme southwest corner of Arizona. Passengers on the train reported that she had "a big cigar in her mouth, rivaling the efforts of the locomotive to charge the atmosphere with smoke." At Yuma, the prison officers recorded her as "Pearl Hart, alias Mrs. Joe Boot, twenty-eight years old, five feet three inches tall, one hundred pounds in weight, foot size two-and-a-half, black hair, gray eyes, medium dark complexion, bad teeth, used tobacco, alcohol and morphine, no legitimate occupation, married, husband living, two children, parents living, nearest relation Mrs. James Taylor Jr., of Toledo, Ohio." They searched her and found seven dollars in her pockets. The prison photographer took two mug shots of Pearl, front and side. She looked glum and fearful, neatly dressed in a pinstripe blouse, white canvas belt, and matching skirt, with her hair cut short in the front, and her long locks behind held up in a bun. Then the guards took her to her cell. Though Yuma had held a number of women prisoners before, Pearl was then its only woman convict.[9]

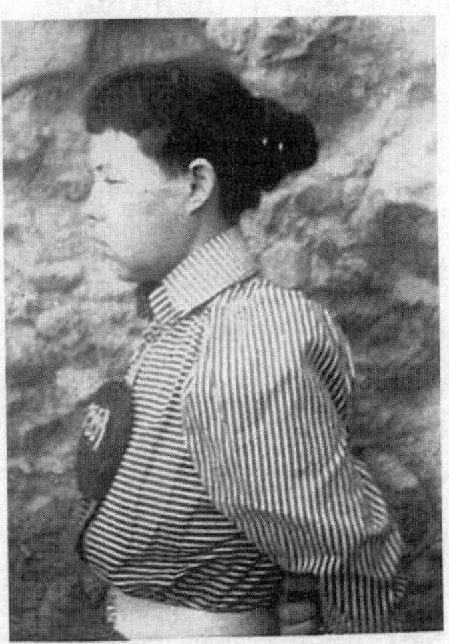

AUTHOR'S COLLECTION.

Pearl Hart looks none too happy in her mug shots taken the day she entered Yuma prison.

While Pearl settled in for a long term in the West's most notorious prison, her sister Katy was having wild misdaventures of her own. A year earlier she had left San Antonio and taken her little boy, Stevie, to Kansas City, Missouri. There she awaited the release of her husband, Howard Allen, from the Kansas state prison. As she told a journalist before he entered the penitentiary, "Our life has been clouded ever since we became lovers, but we were lovers true and nothing that ever came up has affected either of us in the least."

A reporter who met Katy around this time observed, "Mrs. Allen is twenty-eight years of age and a remarkably pretty woman, having large, expressive brown eyes and dark wavy hair." Her glamorous good looks attracted numerous suitors, and Katy preferred actors and showmen. Despite the fact that she was married, Katy soon became involved with Earl Meyers, twenty-four, who went by the stage names of Earl Lighthawk and, occasionally, Jack Earle. He worked as an itinerant actor and acrobat and claimed to have performed with Buffalo Bill's Wild West show. Sometimes he posed as an American Indian and traveled with a medicine show, selling snake-oil remedies. For a few months, Katy lived with him in St. Joseph, Missouri, and professed to be his wife.[10]

But early in 1899 Earl Lighthawk left Katy. She always needed money, so in April, a month before her sister's fateful stage holdup, Katy returned to Texas to resume her career as a pioneer parachutist. Before a fascinated crowd in Houston, she made a single ascent by balloon, then skydived into a large lake below. This was Katy's final aeronautic stunt, and she returned to Kansas City to again wait for Howard Allen's discharge from the penitentiary. But when her husband was released from prison, he did not go back to her and instead began performing with a traveling opera company in small towns in Kansas. In September 1899 she sued Allen for divorce on grounds of desertion. When a reporter asked her about the divorce, Katy said nothing about Allen being an ex-convict and insisted that he was just an actor.[11]

By this time Katy had learned that her sister was in jail in Arizona. Pearl had kept up a correspondence with her siblings, telling them of her troubles, and they read more details of her criminal career in the newspapers. But Anna Davy had no idea that her daughter had become a stage robber. Because Anna was illiterate, she could not read the newspapers, and her children did not enlighten her. As a Phoenix reporter noted, "Pearl has kept the story of her life from her mother, and since her brothers and sisters have learned it through the Arizona papers, they too are holding the secret lest the breaking of the news kill their mother." To spare Anna's feelings, none of the Davy siblings publicly admitted that they were related to Pearl Hart. And given the Davy family's perennial lack of money, there was little they could do to help her.[12]

In the meantime Katy foolishly reconciled with Howard Allen. Then, using the name Millie Allen, she began writing plays and performing on the stage. A Midwestern journalist remarked, "She has been a member of various third-rate dramatic companies and has given considerable of her time to dramatic composition, an art in which she displayed great perseverance and some skill." Theater was hugely popular in that era, for it had almost no competition. There were very few professional sports, no motion pictures or television, and little in the way of entertainment. Every community had its playhouses, which often featured acting troupes and vaudevillians who traveled the theater circuit and performed for enthusiastic crowds. Playwriting and performing were big business, and Katy was determined to achieve success.

With her earnings she managed to purchase a cottage she called Queen's Rest in Mount Washington, a neighborhood in Independence, about seven miles east of Kansas City, Missouri. Katy later explained that her friends and family had taken to calling her Queenie, which inspired the name for Queen's Rest. Situated on a large lot, the house had four rooms and a well that supplied water. Katy was proud of her house and even prouder that she could provide a secure home for her mother. In 1898 Anna had finally divorced her abusive husband on grounds of desertion. Soon afterward she married an honest laborer named Daniel Perry, whom she had probably met in Toledo. Anna and her new spouse moved into the Queen's Rest cottage where they lived with Katy, Howard Allen, and little Stevie.[13]

But Allen soon returned to his larcenous ways. He was frequently absent from home, and Kansas City police suspected that he had joined an organized gang of horse thieves. On the evening of August 10, 1900, Allen drove a stolen team and buggy into California, Missouri, midway between Kansas City and St. Louis. He sold them to a townsman for sixty dollars, but when the buyer became suspicious, Allen suddenly departed without collecting the money. A sheriff captured Katy's husband the next day and took him to jail in Kansas City. Allen, despondent, pleaded with deputies to send word to Katy and their son. The officers did so and told Katy that Allen wanted to see them. Katy, upset by his arrest, finally decided that she would not have a husband who was a criminal. Nonetheless, a few days later she and four-year-old Stevie arrived at the county jail. Allen peered out of his cell and spotted his wife and child walking toward him in the jail corridor. His dejected manner instantly changed to one of joy. He thrust his arms through the bars and leaned forward to try to kiss her. Katy hesitated for a moment, then drew back in visible disgust.

"You won't kiss me?" Allen exclaimed.

"No," she replied firmly.

"You'll let me kiss the child?" he pleaded.

"Yes, you may do that."

She held up little Stevie and he reached through the bars and kissed the boy repeatedly. At that, one of the jailers turned to Katy and said, "This man is your husband. He's in serious trouble. It's your duty to comfort him as much as you can."

"I don't care," she snapped. "He ought never to have been where he is."

Then she scooped up her child and stormed out of the jail. For seven years she had stood by Allen through numerous breakups. She had broken him out of jail twice, once in Oklahoma and once in Texas. Now he was facing another long prison term, and she had had enough. Although Katy still liked flashy men, she thought that she had learned her lesson about consorting with criminals. But her vow to avoid bad company would not last.[14]

Howard Allen, just as he had done in the Oklahoma jail, now contemplated suicide. He occupied a cell with several other prisoners and began weaving a rope from bits of twine and ribbon. Three days after Katy's visit, one of Allen's cellmates awoke to find him hanging by the neck from his bunk, his feet just touching the lower cot. The prisoners broke the rope and released him. The guards immediately summoned a doctor, who managed to revive the despondent prisoner. Then a reporter came to the jail to interview Allen, who declared, "I tried to do it because there was nothing left in life for me. She came here and turned away in disgust. Why should I care to live longer?"[15]

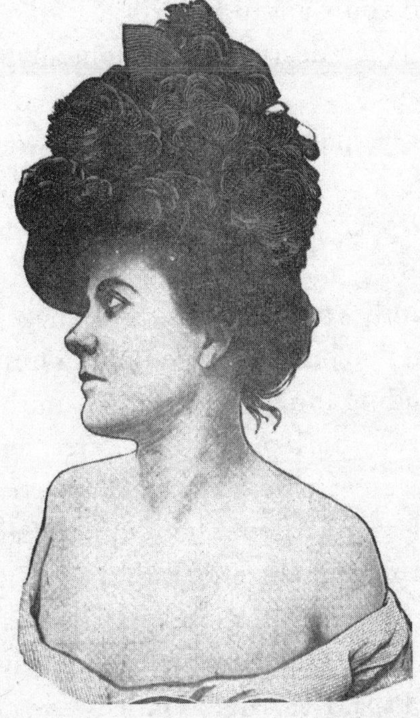

AUTHOR'S COLLECTION.

Katy Davy dressed in the height of fashion, 1901.

But Katy eventually changed her mind about her larcenous husband. Three months later, when Allen's trial began on November 13, 1900, she sat next to him in the Kansas City courtroom. A journalist observed, "Evidently he and his wife had effected a reconciliation, or his lawyers had planned some theatrical effects, for the young couple sat all during the trial with their hands clasped, as if their very existence depended upon the jury not separating them." Given that Katy was an actress, it may have indeed been for show. Either way, her reputation as a wild woman was no secret to the Kansas City authorities. The newspaper reported that during the examination of one witness, the prosecutor "asked a question which touched upon the morality of the prisoner's wife."

Allen immediately leaped from his chair and roared, "What's that? How dare you!"

The judge, in a decided lack of decorum, barked, "Hold on, young man. Do you want to fight?"

"Yes, I do!" Allen declared. "I'll fight anybody who makes such insinuation."

"Is there anyone in particular whom you would care to tackle first?" asked the judge, in a decidedly nonjudicial manner. "If there is, we will take you into the waiting room and try to accommodate you."

Allen reluctantly sat down, but the damage had been done. The jury deliberated briefly before finding him guilty of grand larceny and handing him a two-year jolt in the Missouri state prison. But Katy—just like Pearl—was resilient. She returned to her budding career as an actress and playwright and quickly forgot about Howard Allen. She rejoined Earl Lighthawk in St. Joe and told acquaintances that they were married and that Stevie was their son. Stevie, whose real father had been in prison for much of his young life, thought that Lighthawk was his father and called him Papa. Katy and Lighthawk, with Stevie in tow, took to the road and performed in a number of small theaters in rural Iowa and Nebraska. But Earl Lighthawk was of a roving disposition, and in the spring of 1901 he left Katy to embark on a theatrical tour. In early June Katy and Stevie moved into the Thurston Hotel at Fifteenth and Jackson Streets in Omaha.[16]

There Katy was joined by a thirty-one-year-old housepainter, Thad Brookings, whom she had met in Kansas City a year earlier. Brookings was suave, handsome, immaculately dressed, and wildly in love with her. He also happened to be married. Brookings had visited Katy and her mother at the Queen's Rest cottage in 1900, at the same time Katy's husband Howard Allen was away from home—either acting in theaters or stealing horses. Katy seems to have enjoyed the attentions of Brookings. She let him paint her house and build a fence around the lot. Although Katy later insisted that they did not have a romantic relationship, she promised Brookings that when she took one of her plays on the road, he could be part of the cast. She may not have known that he had an extensive criminal record.[17]

In 1891 Thad Brookings had pulled several house burglaries in Des Moines, for which he received a two-year sentence in the Iowa state penitentiary. Upon his release he embarked on a second spree of burglary in Des Moines. This time he got a twelve-year term, but the governor commuted his sentence and ordered his release in 1896. Brookings got a job in a hotel, but a few months later he stole forty dollars from the cash drawer and fled. When the police caught him, they found forty-two house keys in his pockets, the principal tools of a professional burglar. The governor revoked his commutation, and Brookings found himself back in the Iowa state prison. He was released in 1900, left his wife in Des Moines, and got work painting houses in Omaha. Soon after his release, he met Katy while on a visit to Kansas City.[18]

Katy was fascinated by her sister's misadventures on the Arizona frontier. She wrote a play inspired by those exploits, with a few of her own misdeeds thrown in for good measure. Katy titled it "The Arizona Female Bandit," and she planned to play the lead role at a small theater in Omaha. To protect the Davy family from further embarrassment, Katy used fictional names in the narrative and said nothing about Pearl Hart being the basis for the story. And she kept her promise to Thad Brookings by inviting him to meet her and Stevie at the Thurston Hotel in Omaha. There, Katy's stunning good looks quickly caught the attention of Burt Adams, a lodger at the hotel. He was a twenty-two-year-old teamster with a police record in Omaha for petty theft, burglary, and robbery. Katy probably did not know about his record, either, for she recruited the lovestruck Adams as part of her cast.[19]

Despite Katy's insistence that she did not have a sexual relationship with Brookings, that may not have been true. She and Brookings, with five-year-old Stevie, took a train to St. Joseph, Missouri, where they stayed at a hotel on the Fourth of July, 1901. A witness who saw them in St. Joe later said that Brookings "seemed to be desperately in love with her." A few days later, Katy, with Stevie and Brookings, returned to Omaha so she could rehearse and perform the play. Burt Adams was waiting for her, and he offered to pay for a room for Katy and her son. Given her ever-precarious financial straits, Katy jumped at the offer, and the three checked into Anna Lowe's lodging house on Capitol Avenue in downtown Omaha. This was a respectable place, and Adams told Mrs. Lowe that Katy was his wife.[20]

Thad Brookings was apparently unaware that Burt Adams also had designs on Katy, and she kept her relationship with Adams a secret from him. She wanted to ensure that nothing would interfere with the success of her play. Katy also kept secret the fact that Pearl Hart was her sister and instead named her stage-robbing heroine Noma Schultz. That was a tribute to her sister, for Noma was the nickname for Lillie's middle name of Naomi. In Katy's play, Burt Adams played Bill Desmond, an undercover detective who, although hunting the lady bandit, is in love with her. Thad Brookings had the role of Sam Queakler, a St. Louis millionaire who had been jilted by Noma, and little Stevie performed the part of a young girl. The melodramatic story line featured Noma as a twelve-year-old girl with a physical disability who nonetheless "can ride bucking broncos, engage in hand-to-hand fights with the villain, and finally scale a prison wall to rescue her friends." In the final scene, Noma believes that Bill Desmond has been slain while pulling a bank robbery, but it turns out that he is not dead and that she has been faking her disability all along. Noma rushes into his arms, exclaiming, "Oh, Bill, Bill! This is the happiest moment of my life!" Then the two embrace and the curtain falls. It was the kind of overheated melodrama that Americans of that era loved.[21]

By this time Earl Lighthawk had learned that Katy was in Omaha, and he followed her there from St. Joe. As unfettered by sexual mores as Katy was, being pursued by three men at the same time was probably too much, even for her. The Omaha police spotted Lighthawk and arrested him as a vagrant, but Katy went to the chief and begged for his release. She insisted that she was his wife and that Stevie was his son whom she had adopted. As a local newspaperman reported, Lighthawk "succeeded in convincing the police that this was not the case, but she still alluded to him as her legal husband." The chief ordered Lighthawk released, and he returned to St. Joe, leaving Katy and her two other suitors behind. Not long after, on July 22, the Omaha police picked up Thad Brookings as a "suspicious character" and took him to the station house to be photographed. He admitted being an ex-convict. "I have quit the business now, though," he told the desk sergeant. "There's nothing in it, and I'm straight from now on. A burglar takes big chances in his stealing, and then when he gets the stuff, he can't get anything for it. People he sells it to suspect it is stolen and won't give a decent price. An honest life is easier than that of a burglar, and hereafter I'm honest."[22]

The police sergeant released him. About four days after Katy moved into Mrs. Lowe's lodging house, Brookings showed up and began working his handsome charms on her. Katy quickly succumbed. Burt Adams became furious when he learned of Brookings's attentions to her. He promptly informed Mrs. Lowe that he would no longer pay Katy's room rent. When Adams announced to Katy that he "was going to quit," her pocketbook took sudden control of her heart. According to an Omaha journalist, "She began to make desperate efforts to get rid of Brookings." On August 3, Katy and Brookings had a loud quarrel in her room, and he seized her by the neck, choked her, and threw her to the floor. Then he stormed out, and Katy fled to a nearby hotel where she telephoned Adams to come and stay with her.

RENEE GALLAGHER COLLECTION.

Katy Davy in her role as the Arizona Female Bandit.

That night Brookings returned to Mrs. Lowe's rooming house on Capitol Avenue where he found Stevie alone. He decided to take him across the Missouri River bridge to neighboring Council Bluffs, Iowa. In Katy's room Brookings left behind an angry letter. "My Darling Queen: I have kidnaped the boy, Stevie, and have him with me at the hotel in Council Bluffs, and if you ever expect to see him again you'd better come over, and don't bring that fellow, 'Mr. A' [Adams] with you or there will be trouble. I've got a gun and know how to use it. I know I'm a thief and a low, degraded whelp, but for all that I love you better than my soul. I love you better than God. Now, you better come, for I can tell you I'm a desperate man."[23]

The next morning, Katy and Adams returned to her room at Mrs. Lowe's, only to find Stevie gone and Brookings's letter in his place. Katy did not think Brookings would hurt Stevie, as an Omaha journalist remarked: "The threat failed to bring any great worry to the mother's heart." Soon afterward, Brookings arrived at Katy's door with Stevie in tow. In an apparent effort to defuse the tension and placate the two rivals, Katy began an impromptu rehearsal of the final act of "The Arizona Female Bandit."

With Adams, Brookings, and Stevie looking on, she clutched the script in one hand and began reading lines from the climactic scene in which Noma believes that Bill Desmond has been killed while robbing a bank. Assuming the heroine's character, she cried, "I thought I heard a shot!"

Following the script, she looked around and spotted Desmond's body outside the bank. "Why! What's this? Bill Desmond? What can it mean? Here by the bank with this mask, wig, and revolver?"

Then, peering into an imaginary bank window, Katy exclaimed, "Oh! I see it all now. 'twas he—and yet I am blamed! Bill Desmond a thief? No, no—it cannot be! He was the embodiment of honor! And yet, it must be!"

She raised her hand toward heaven and declared, "But I swear I shall never bear witness against him. Because I love him!"

Katy knelt beside Desmond's body and moaned, "Dead! Dead! Good God! Too impossible! Oh, Bill! Speak to me! Say you are not going to die! I cannot bear it! Bill! Bill!"

But Desmond, of course, was not dead. Burt Adams, playing the part of Desmond, embraced Katy, and the two exchanged a passionate kiss. At that, Brookings angrily interjected, "Oh, cut that out. That don't go in rehearsal!"

Katy's clumsy effort to placate the pair had the opposite effect. An enraged argument erupted between Adams and Brookings. Adams rushed from the room and sought out Mrs. Lowe's burly husband. The two seized Brookings and forced him downstairs to the entrance hallway. Brookings suddenly yanked out a .38 revolver and barked at Adams, "You come out, and I'll settle with you right now!"

But Adams was unarmed, and he discreetly retreated back upstairs to Katy's room. Brookings stormed out the front door and walked one block east on Capitol Avenue. Then he whirled around and rushed back to the lodging house. Knocking on the door, he asked Mrs. Lowe in a polite tone if he could go back to the room and retrieve some clothes that he had left inside. She consented, and Brookings climbed the staircase and reentered Katy's room. He found her sitting on the bed, and next to her stood Adams and Stevie.

"I have come for my clothes," Brookings announced dejectedly. Then he stepped to the front of the bed and reached down for a pile of soiled linen. Katy told him, "If you don't go away and stay away, I'll call the police. I don't want to see any more of you!"

Brookings jerked upright, his face beet red with fury. He threw the bundle of clothes onto the bed and shouted, "Well, you'll see this much more of me!"

He reached for his hip pocket and whipped out the pistol.

Katy shrieked in terror and raced for the door. At a distance of six feet Brookings fired once, and the .38 caliber slug tore into her back, just below the right shoulder blade, and lodged in the muscles near her lung. She dropped like a stone, bleeding heavily, and tumbled a few steps down the stairs. Then, without another word, Brookings pressed the muzzle of the revolver against his breast and fired again. The bullet slammed into his heart, passed through his body, and ripped out his back. Brookings collapsed to the floor, instantly killed.[24]

Katy lay in a pool of blood, still clutching the script in one fist, as police officers raced to the rooming house. They rushed her to a hospital, where doctors reported that she could not live more than a few hours. Newspaper reporters descended on Anna Lowe's boarding house. They found little Stevie, who innocently told one journalist, "My mama worked for a detective agency and had to work late nights. I was so mad at the man who shot her that I wanted to shoot him myself. I'm glad he's dead."

Mrs. Lowe complained that although all of her rooms had been rented, right after the shooting her boarders all moved out. Reporters rummaged through Katy's trunks and found one of them filled with her writings and scripts, plus letters which showed that her maiden name was Davy. Despite their snooping, none of the journalists connected her with the real Arizona female bandit, Pearl Hart. The next day reports of the tragedy appeared not only on the front page of Omaha's dailies but in journals throughout the country. The *New York Times* headlined its story "Double Tragedy on Stage." The bloody climax to a deadly love triangle fascinated readers, and exaggerated and semifictional accounts quickly appeared in the so-called yellow journals.[25]

In the hospital, Katy struggled for life. Doctors probed for the bullet, but could not find it. They thought that it had lodged in her back muscles. A telegram was sent to her mother, and Anna rushed by train to Omaha. For several days Katy hovered between life and death. But she was both lucky and tough, and doctors soon announced that her wound was not fatal. The coroner took Thad Brookings's body to the morgue and sent a wire to his wife in Des Moines, asking her to claim the corpse. When she responded that she did not want the body, a lady friend of Brookings paid for his burial. Earl Lighthawk received news of the shooting and entrained for Omaha to see Katy, bringing with him another woman who turned out to be his real wife. He went alone to her hospital room and said nothing to Katy about the other woman. As Lighthawk sat at her bedside, Katy managed to gasp, "I will not die. But if I should pass away, I want you to take little Stevie and take good care of him. I also want you to have all my possessions."

Lighthawk stepped outside Katy's room. In response to a question from a reporter, he declared, "The papers have been mistaken in referring to Millie Davy as my wife. I was never married to her and never really lived with her. My wife is now with me, and was formerly Miss Edith Marston of St. Louis. We were married some two years ago. She came with me to Omaha when the news came that Millie was shot. When it was believed that Millie was dying, my wife was willing to keep silent, but now that she is recovering justice should be done to my wife."[26]

Then Lighthawk left the hospital and went to Mrs. Lowe's rooming house, where he found Stevie asleep in Katy's room. He woke the boy, who jumped into Lighthawk's arms, crying, "Papa! Papa!" When Lighthawk asked him how the shooting happened, Stevie held out his right hand, pointing the index finger and pulling an imaginary trigger. "He shot Mama that way," Stevie said. Then, pushing his index finger into his chest, he exclaimed, "And then he shot hisself this way." After caressing Stevie, Lighthawk put the boy back to bed.[27]

Within a few days Katy began a rapid recovery, and in late August her doctors decided that she could be sent home from the hospital. Several days before her release, a reporter interviewed her in her hospital room. She declared that her husband was "Lieutenant Allen of the Sixteenth Texas Cavalry" and truthfully admitted that he was serving a term in the Missouri state prison. "My name is not Lighthawk, as the newspapers have been calling me," she said. When asked if she had been married to Earl Lighthawk of St. Joseph, Katy answered coyly, "Well, I believe there was a little escapade away back there, but I'd rather you wouldn't say anything about it. Lieutenant Allen is my husband and we are on good terms. He writes to me twice a week."

AUTHOR'S COLLECTION.

Thad Brookings, who shot and almost killed Katy Davy in Omaha.

When the journalist asked about Thad Brookings, she gave a partly fictional account: "He was helping me get my new play, 'The Arizona Female Bandit,' on the road. We had been having some trouble because he wanted to play a leading part in it and I wanted him to take the part of a Chinaman, to which he objected. I don't pretend, of course, that he shot me on account of this, but I'm sure that if he was infatuated with me, as he certainly was, I never gave him any encouragement. The same is true of the man Burt Adams. I had a deal pending with Adams whereby he was to take the company on the road as manager. Just as soon as I can reorganize my company I'm going to launch 'The Arizona Female Bandit,' making our initial performance probably in Denver. Then I'm going to put on another piece, 'The Little Turncoat.' I wrote both of these plays and feel encouraged that they will make a hit."[28]

Doctors released Katy after four weeks in the hospital, and she returned to her room at Mrs. Lowe's boarding house. There an Omaha reporter met with her and remarked, "Mrs. Allen has the figure and appearance of a child. She is not more than five feet in height and looks not to exceed eighteen years old. Her desperate struggle for life in the hospital has reduced her to an appearance of extreme fragility." Katy told the journalist that she still carried the bullet. "The doctors wanted to cut it out but I wouldn't let them. I didn't want to be operated on."

Katy was eager to portray herself as a woman of good repute, and she expressed no ill will toward Thad Brookings. "It is not true that Mr. Brookings had been a convict in Iowa, or that he had a home and family in Des Moines," she insisted. "Neither is it true that his relations with me were ever improper. He did want me to get a divorce and marry him, but while he was my good friend, I did not love him. Last year he visited me at my mother's home in Missouri, and he has always treated me with consideration and respect. Thad was a good, kind-hearted boy, and when he fired those shots that Sunday morning he didn't know what he was doing. I am very sorry for him and am so sorry he killed himself. I am all alone in Omaha, and have no friends here, but I wish you would believe me when I say that neither with Mr. Brookings nor with Mr. Adams did I ever do anything that was wrong."[29]

Katy soon left Omaha and returned to the Queen's Rest cottage where her mother could care for her and Stevie. As she gradually regained her strength, her thoughts turned to her closest friend. Katy was determined to do something to help her sister who languished in Yuma prison under the name Pearl Hart.

10

The Yuma Hellhole

Pearl Hart found the territorial prison at Yuma bleak and foreboding. As a visitor of the time explained, "Of all the prisons in the United States, the Yuma penitentiary is probably the most repulsive hellhole. It is little more than a hideous adobe bull-pen in which are corralled together two hundred and sixty criminals, many of them among the most hardened and desperate known to crime. So far as the men are concerned, they are perforce herded together indiscriminately, and if there be women convicts, it is next to impossible to keep them separate at all times from the men."[1]

Yuma prison was perched on a rocky bluff overlooking the swirling waters of the Colorado River. It stood adjacent to the village of Yuma, then home to only fifteen hundred people. The prison was extremely isolated, surrounded by hundreds of miles of arid desert and situated just ten miles from the Mexico border. It was opened in 1876 and held felons convicted by courts throughout Arizona Territory. At various times Yuma held some of the most notorious desperadoes of the Southwest, including "Buckskin Frank" Leslie, who once rode with the

Earp brothers; train robber and former lawman Billy Stiles; and Jerry Barton, a deadly member of the Cowboys.

Over the years Yuma prison gradually expanded. By the time of Pearl's arrival, its main cellblock was enclosed by a thick stone-and-adobe wall, three hundred feet square and sixteen feet high. Rifle-toting guards patrolled the walls, and two towers were each mounted with a Gatling gun. This fearsome weapon—precursor of the machine gun—featured multiple rotating barrels turned by a hand crank, capable of firing two hundred rounds a minute.

The main cellblock held thirty-four small cells, with six convicts crammed into each, sleeping on iron bunks stacked three high. Other cells had been excavated from the rocky bluff above the river. Next to the cellblock was a large dining room, kitchen, and laundry. Just outside the main gate, between the cellblock and the river, stood the guards' quarters and the warden's house. The grounds were lit at night by half a dozen electric floodlights, mounted on a pair of towers, forty-five feet above the prison yard. A steam pump delivered water from the river. Convicts performed most of the work inside the prison, including making their own shoes, striped uniforms, and civilian suits for inmates about to be discharged.

AUTHOR'S COLLECTION.

Yuma prison, on the Colorado River. The superintendent's house is at right, and the guards' quarters at left. The cellblocks are barely visible behind.

Escape was more than difficult. As a journalist who toured the prison in 1896 wrote, "The great gates of the prison walls stood wide open, and there were a dozen or so stupid convicts moving here and there about the prison, apparently as free as employees in any factory enclosure. But the Gatling guns, glistening in the sunshine, the guards walking slowly up and down the top of the stone walls, and the awful desert, stretching way to the horizon, tell the most careless observer how practically impossible escape from the penitentiary would be."[2]

Among the two hundred and sixty prisoners then in Yuma, Pearl Hart was the only woman. During its thirty-three-year history from 1876 to 1909, the prison received just over three thousand male convicts, but only twenty-nine women. During all those years, Pearl Hart was by far its most notorious convict of either sex. The men wore stripes, but the women were allowed to don blouses and skirts. Pearl was forced to abandon her men's clothing. The guards tried to keep the convicts away from her. Yuma's women's quarters were set apart from the main cellblock. In 1891 three women's cells had been carved into the rock embankment on the southwest corner of the grounds, separated from the cellblock by a high fence. If male prisoners tried to enter the women's section, they faced solitary confinement in the dark cell, known ominously as the Snake Den.

Outside the women's cells was a private yard, thirty feet square, where Pearl could get exercise and fresh air. She stayed alone in the women's quarters where at first she struggled with her addiction to morphine. The prison superintendent, Herbert Brown, unlike Bob Paul and Sheriff Truman, had no supply of the drug, so Pearl smoked cigarettes incessantly in her effort to ward off the withdrawal symptoms. Initially she was, according to her guards, "rather hard to get along with." But her condition gradually improved. "Pearl is a very docile prisoner at Yuma," reported one newspaperman, who told his readers that she "does not wear stripes." Another journalist noted, "She seems fairly content with her lot, and has not attempted suicide, as she said she assuredly would were she sent to Yuma."[3]

Two months after Pearl entered the prison a Phoenix reporter was allowed inside to interview her. He observed, "Pearl occupies a cell as large as an ordinary bedroom, which is excavated in the hill side. And she has a 'house yard' in which to take her constitutional, whenever she is so minded. She is evidently living on the fat of the land, as there was a pound roll of butter on the table in her cell the morning I called on her. Several weeks of prison life have relieved her physical system of its load of opium, for Pearl was a 'hop fiend' of insatiable appetite, but her wicked face is sallow, for she has not been deprived of her cigarettes, which she consumes in wholesale quantities." Pearl was determined to improve her life, and within a few months she had entirely kicked the morphine habit.[4]

The Phoenix journalist also saw that Pearl lacked companionship. The assistant superintendent, Ira Smith, had a fox terrier named Judy, and he allowed his dog and her puppies to roam the main yard and play with the convicts. "Pearl is lonesome," the newspaperman remarked, "and she wants Ira Smith to let her have Judy's pups in her prison yard. Mr. Smith declined. He says Judy is a lady and her pups are well bred, and he doesn't propose to have their morals contaminated by association with Pearl. Any horse thief or Mexican murderer can fondle the pups, but Ira draws the line at Pearl." Needless to say, the reporter's attempt at humor came across as cruel instead of comical.[5]

Soon after entering Yuma, Pearl learned the fate of her final Arizona lover, Ed Hogan. Undersheriff Bob Paul had revoked Hogan's status as a trusty in the Tucson jail and lodged him in a four-man cell that included Luis Chavez, the most dangerous prisoner in the lockup. Chavez, a miner from Sonora, Mexico, had fled to Arizona after murdering his wife and beating a man to death with a shovel. In 1897 he killed a Chinese brickmaker and escaped, then found work as a railroad section hand. A year later Chavez quarreled with his foreman and killed him with a knife. Having slain four people, he was finally captured and lodged in the Tucson jail to await trial.

AUTHOR'S COLLECTION.

The Yuma prison yard as it looked in Pearl Hart's day.

On the morning of November 27, 1899, just ten days after Pearl stepped inside Yuma prison, Ed Hogan and Luis Chavez made a daring break. They shared their cell with two Mexican smugglers. As Bob Paul and his jailer opened their cell door to allow a trusty to enter and empty the night buckets, Chavez attacked Paul. The old lawman, still possessed of great strength despite his sixty-nine years, threw Chavez to the floor and held him down. At the same time, one prisoner knocked the jailer unconscious with a chunk of firewood. Hogan and the two smugglers dragged him into the cell and locked the door. Then they overpowered Paul, beating him with the firewood club and locking him inside another cell. The escapees ran into the jail office where Hogan stole a pistol and Bob Paul's hat, then all four fled Tucson on foot. Five days later Sheriff Wakefield tracked down Luis Chavez on horseback. When the murderer pulled a six-shooter, Wakefield killed him with a single blast from his shotgun. Ed Hogan was captured the following year, and a Tucson grand jury indicted him for aiding in the jailbreak. But Hogan was lucky. He only received additional time in the county jail and avoided joining Pearl Hart in Yuma.[6]

Meanwhile the Davy siblings grew increasingly anxious about Pearl's fate. Unaware that she had entered Yuma prison, they thought she was in the Phoenix jail. Her sister Amy's husband, James Taylor, wrote a pleading letter to the sheriff in Phoenix. Because the illiterate Anna Davy still did not know the news, Taylor was careful to refer to Lillie as Pearl Hart, rather than by her true name. "I see by the papers that you have Miss Pearl Hart in custody in Arizona for some misdemeanor," he wrote. "Now as I am her brother-in-law I am interested in her welfare. It has been a long time since we heard from her and we did not know what had become of her. The paper stated that she wanted to go to her mother. I assure you that her mother would be glad to have her at home, for I have seen her sit and cry when we were talking about Pearl and wondering what had become of her. Since she has unfortunately become an opium fiend we all have more sympathy for her. She is the only one in the family that has ever become addicted to such habits. Now, I would beg of you to be as easy with her as you can, for we have not dared to let her mother know that we have heard anything of her, and much less that she is a prisoner, as she is troubled with heart disease and the news might affect her seriously. I enclose an envelope with my address for return. You will do me a kindness to answer and tell me all the particulars about her case."[7]

But there was little that the Davy family could do, and Pearl made the best of her stay in the Old West's most infamous prison. For Pearl and her fellow prisoners, the worst thing about Yuma was the heat. A visitor once declared, "This is the hottest place in the world; so hot in the summer time that the wings melt off the mosquitoes, and the flies die from the excessive heat of the scorching sun. The Indians cover themselves with mud, the Mexicans crawl into their little huts, while the Americans stand in the Colorado River half the day and keep drunk the rest of the time to avoid death from melting." He added that it was "so dry that you are compelled to use short sentences in speaking, and those most frequently used are, 'Yes, I'll take a drink.'" A common story claimed that a soldier stationed at Fort Yuma died and went to hell, but immediately returned to Yuma to get his blankets.[8]

Although attempted breakouts were frequent, successful escapes from Yuma prison proved rare, averaging only one a year. The bloodiest break took place in 1887, when seven Latino convicts seized the superintendent, Thomas Gates, and held a knife to his throat. Using him as a shield, they forced their way out the main gate. As they marched Gates to the superintendent's office, a guard opened fire and wounded one of the prisoners. Two of the escapees burst into the office, seized a six-gun and ammunition, and rushed back to their comrades, who were struggling with Gates. Unfortunately for the convicts, a noted lawman, Frank Hartlee, was one of the guards on duty in the nearest gun tower. Hartlee was a dead shot. As chief of police of Los Angeles in 1874, he had shot and captured the infamous bandit chieftain Tiburcio Vasquez. Now Hartlee opened up a deadly fire with his Winchester rifle, killing two of the convicts. As another prisoner began to stab Gates in the neck, a notorious desperado, Barney Riggs, who was serving a life term for murder, raced to Gates's help. He seized the six-gun from one escapee and shot the knife-wielding convict. As the prisoner staggered, Hartlee shot him in the back, killing him. When the smoke cleared, one convict lay wounded, and four were dead. Arizona's governor pardoned Riggs for his courageous act.[9]

The futility of trying to escape from Yuma soon became clear to Pearl Hart. She had been in the prison only four months when a group of cons made a desperate break for liberty. On the evening of March 14, 1900, Pearl and the other prisoners heard the dull thud of gunfire outside the stone walls. Three guards were marching a work detail of twenty-one convicts from the town of Yuma back to the penitentiary. As they approached the west side of the prison, five prisoners suddenly made a break and rushed toward the Colorado River. A guard opened fire, but his shots missed, and the cons kept running. The guards pursued, and one called several times for the escapees to halt. Finally he shouldered his rifle and sent a bullet into the back of a fleeing prisoner. The convict dropped like a stone, and the rest immediately surrendered. The guards brought the wounded man to the prison hospital where he died the next day. The other four escapees were sent back to the work detail, each wearing a ball and chain.[10]

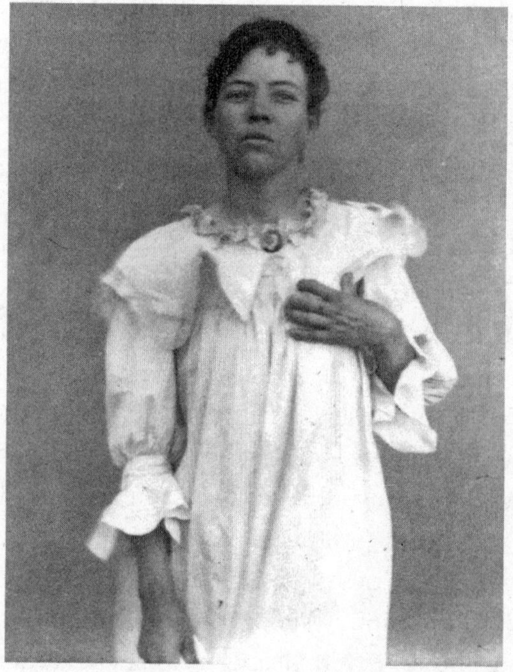

ARIZONA HISTORICAL SOCIETY, TUCSON.

Pearl looks alluring in this snapshot taken in Yuma prison.

Pearl realized that Yuma was not a leaky jail like the lockups in Tucson and Deming. Although her rock-walled cell was little better than a cave, she soon found that the prison was not entirely primitive. It had a library stocked with more than three thousand books and magazines. Pearl whiled away the lonesome hours reading material from the library, and she sewed fancy lace items that she sold to prison visitors. She also wrote poetry about her adventures. Pearl penned a poem she called "The Girl Bandit" and another titled "When She Was Young and Knew No Sin, before the Tempter Entered In." Only one of her lyrical compositions has survived, a ballad sung to the tune of "The Fatal Wedding," a popular song of the 1890s:

The sun was shining brightly on a pleasant afternoon.
My partner speaking lightly, said, "The stage will be here soon."
We saw it coming round the bend and called to them to halt.
Then to their pockets we did attend, if they got hurt, 'twas their own fault.

While the birds were sweetly singing, while the men stood up in line,
And the silver softly ringing as it touched this palm of mine.
There we took away their money, but left them enough to eat.
And the men they looked so funny as they vaulted in their seat.

Then up the road we galloped quickly, then through the canyon we did pass.
Over the mountains we went swiftly, trying to find our horses grass.
Past the station we boldly went, then along the river side.
And our horses now being spent, of course we had to hide.

Now for five long nights we travel, in the day time we would rest.

Now we would throw ourselves on the gravel, and to sleep we try our best.
Around us now our horses stamping, looking for some hay or grain.
On the road the posse tramping, looking for us all in vain.

One more day they would not get us, but my horse got sour and thin.
And my partner was a mean cuss, so Bill Truman roped us in.
Thirty years my partner got, and I was given five.
He seems contented with his lot, and I am still alive.[11]

The prison library also stocked the latest newspapers, and in April 1900 Pearl read about the fate of her captor, George Scarborough. Early that month Walt Birchfield, a rancher and deputy sheriff, sent a wire to Deming asking Scarborough to help him track down some cattle thieves. Birchfield had found a stolen and slaughtered cow in the San Simon Valley in southeastern Arizona, and Scarborough promptly took a train from Deming to Arizona. The two lawmen mounted up and tracked the culprits south to the Chiricahua Mountains. They assumed that the thieves were Mexican smugglers, but that would prove a fatal mistake. In fact the men they were tracking were members of Butch Cassidy's Wild Bunch, some of the most dangerous outlaws of the Old West. The gang of five included the notorious bandits Will Carver, Ben Kilpatrick, known as the Tall Texan, and his younger brother, George Kilpatrick. A week earlier the outlaws had ambushed and killed two young possemen who had been on their trail. Scarborough and Birchfield followed their tracks along the east side of the Chiricahuas and then up Triangle Canyon to a spot now known as Outlaw Spring. That was the dead end of the canyon, and the Wild Bunch was determined not to be taken alive. In a long-range gun battle with high-powered Winchester rifles, they shot George Scarborough in the leg, badly wounding him. The desperadoes escaped, and

Birchfield brought the veteran lawman back to Deming. He died there two days later, leaving behind a wife and seven children. Scarborough's death created headlines, and newspapers reminded their readers that Pearl Hart was the last noted outlaw he had captured.[12]

AUTHOR'S COLLECTION.

The notorious Billy Stiles, right, pretends to hold up newspaperman George Smalley. Smalley claimed that Stiles got Pearl Hart pregnant in Yuma.

In Yuma, reading, composing, and sewing were not Pearl's only pastimes. As the sole woman among the sex-starved convicts, she became a supreme object of desire. It was impossible for the guards to keep her entirely separated from men, for prison trusties had the run of the grounds to perform their chores. In July 1900 Billy Stiles, one of the most notorious characters in the territory, was booked into Yuma. Pearl had known him in Phoenix six years earlier when she and Stiles were hauled into court and fined for disturbing the peace. Stiles—handsome and dashing, with an outrageous sense of humor—was five months younger than Pearl. He had spent his early years working as an Arizona cowboy and had become an expert hunter and tracker. That led several lawmen to employ him as a posse rider and manhunter. In 1899 Billy's friend Burt Alvord, constable of Willcox, Arizona, appointed him a deputy. The pair were law officers in name only. They organized a gang of bandits who robbed two trains, but the band was captured in the spring of 1900. Stiles agreed to testify against his cohorts, but instead he broke Burt Alvord and one of the gang out of the Tombstone jail, shooting a guard in the process. In July, tired of being on the run, Stiles surrendered and again agreed to be a witness against the other bandits.

Billy was a slippery customer, and the law officers did not trust him. They wanted Stiles jailed separately from the rest of the band, so they lodged him in Yuma where he could be kept safely until the trial began in October. Because Billy was a witness and not a convict, the Yuma guards gave him numerous liberties. According to Tucson journalist George Smalley, who knew Stiles and once posed for a photograph with him, "He had the run of the yard and had visited Pearl." Smalley said that Pearl and Billy had sexual relations, and she became pregnant with his child. However, neither the prison records nor contemporary newspapers made any mention of that. And her celebrity was so great that if she was visibly pregnant and gave birth to a child or lost a baby in childbirth, that fact could hardly have been kept a secret from the convicts and guards.[13]

Nonetheless, Pearl could not have been happy when Billy Stiles left the prison in October 1900. Two weeks later she had new company in the form of Elena Estrada, the second female prisoner to enter Yuma at that time. Pearl's new cellmate would become a notable figure in the folklore of the Southwest. According to an account published thirty years later in the *Los*

Angeles Times, "The luscious Elena was the only daughter of a famous Mexican general of the days of Porfirio Diaz. Her romantic disposition ran away with her judgment. Without benefit of clergy she ran away with a dashing lover to Tucson. One night, during a family discussion, he drew a Bowie knife and threatened to cut her heart out. He didn't know Elena's valiant soul. From the mysteries of her silk stocking Elena drew a knife and they fought a long and terrible duel—parry, thrust, retreat. As quick as a cat, Elena drew her lithe, slender young body back from a deadly thrust, and before the cavalier could recover, she had slashed his body open from starboard to port. As he fell weltering in his gore, the vivacious Elena thrust one tiny, delicate hand into the open wound, tore out his living heart, and slapped it in his face."[14]

The story of Elena Estrada the Heartbreaker would be repeated for years in books and magazines. But perhaps not surprisingly, the yarn contained not a word of truth. In fact, Elena Estrada was a twenty-five-year-old prostitute from Hermosillo in northern Mexico. On the Fourth of July 1900 she got roaring drunk in Gay Alley in Tucson's red-light district, where Pearl had worked five years earlier. As Elena walked down the alley toward her crib, she saw Refugio Bindiola, also drunk, blocking the doorway. Although married with children, Bindiola was a ruffian with an arrest record for knifing a man in Phoenix. A quarrel broke out, which ended when Elena whipped out a knife and stabbed the unarmed Bindiola in the stomach. He died the next day, so it is self-evident that his heart could not have been ripped out. Elena was quickly arrested and charged with murder, but she pleaded guilty to manslaughter in exchange for a seven-year term in Yuma.[15]

Pearl seems to have been happy to have some female companionship behind bars. A month after Elena Estrada joined her, the two enjoyed a sumptuous Thanksgiving dinner provided by the guards. The male prisoners were served large portions of fresh pork, with sauerkraut, sweet potatoes, and relishes. But Pearl and Elena fared even better, dining on roast turkey with cranberry sauce. They may have thought—however briefly—that perhaps Yuma was not such a hellhole after all.[16]

AUTHOR'S COLLECTION.

Elena Estrada, notorious as the Heartbreaker, who served time with Pearl in Yuma.

Pearl apparently had little if any contact with Joe Boot. He proved an exemplary prisoner, always obedient and never giving the guards any trouble. Within a year the prison superintendent, Herbert Brown, made Boot a trusty. That was foolish, given the fact that Boot had something to hide, for he refused to reveal his true name to the prison officers. Brown assigned him to work as a cook in the superintendent's house, located just outside the prison gate and overlooking the Colorado River. It was a large adobe structure, with multiple bedrooms, a meeting hall, kitchen, and something that was a luxury for frontier

Arizona: a bathroom with running water. Each day Boot would exit the main gate, walk to the superintendent's home, and dutifully perform all the cooking and cleaning. At night he would return through the gate, and the guards would lock him in his cell. On the evening of February 6, 1901, Boot served dinner for Brown, his wife, and children, then industriously cleaned up the dining room and kitchen and headed back to the prison. Superintendent Brown never saw him again.

The guards did not notice that Joe was missing until the following day. They started a manhunt and soon found his tracks along the Colorado River. His escape received widespread newspaper attention. Wire-service reports declared, "It is believed that the stage robber is attempting to make across the desert to Los Angeles, and stations where he would be likely to stop for water have been notified that he is at large." The Yuma County sheriff telegraphed to Phoenix for good trackers and bloodhounds, but no trace of Boot could be found. Reporters interviewed Pearl in prison, and she told them that she "is anxious for Boot's escape, because he was not responsible for the stage robbery near Florence." Pearl added that she "proposes to compose a poem extolling the virtues of Boot and his gallant escape." Joe Boot was never recaptured, and his fate—as well as his real name—remain a mystery.[17]

Neither prison records nor Arizona newspapers made any mention of Pearl ever attempting to escape. However, decades later, two different ex-convicts told a similar story about her. One of them went by the name of Adam Monroe, though he said he served time in Yuma under another name. According to the cons' story, Pearl was assigned to help the baker in the prison kitchen, where Monroe was a cook's helper. The two quickly began a passionate affair but were unable to have sex until Pearl bribed a guard named Nochols to let Monroe into her cell. Pearl had flirted with Nochols but kept him at arm's length, and at first the guard jealously refused to admit Monroe to the women's quarters. But Pearl managed to convince Nochols that she only wanted to talk to Monroe about the possibility of living in Mexico when her term expired. Nochols finally agreed and allowed Monroe into her cell. When they were alone, Pearl asked Monroe to help her escape from Yuma. She pointed out that the wagon that brought beef to the prison arrived every Saturday morning and left around noon, with the empty bed covered with sheets of canvas. Pearl told Monroe that it would be a simple matter for them to slip out of the kitchen, hide under the tarps, and exit the front gate undetected. At first Monroe was skeptical and asked, "What about the guards?"

Pearl responded that Nochols was in love with her. She said that she would promise to marry him in Mexico if he made sure that no one searched the wagon before it left the prison. On the fateful day, Pearl and Monroe finished their kitchen duties, then sneaked into the back of the wagon and hid under the tarps. Suddenly Pearl whispered that she had prepared some food for their journey and had left it behind in the kitchen. As she jumped out of the wagon bed, Monroe mumbled, "For God's sake, hurry!"

In moments Monroe heard someone close the tailgate, then the wagon began rolling toward the main gate. Just as the huge gate closed with a loud clang, he heard Nochols's distinctive voice.

"Hold it up, driver. There's a prisoner hiding under your tarps in the wagon bed."

The tailgate swung open, and Monroe saw the guard standing before him, sporting a broad grin. "All right, Monroe, jump down," ordered Nochols. "For a man supposed to be a smart con, you're just one big sucker."

The guard took Monroe to the Snake Den, where he was kept on bread and water for two weeks. Monroe soon learned that Pearl had double-crossed him in hopes of getting a pardon or a reduced sentence. But Pearl, because she had helped engineer the escape attempt, was rewarded with neither. Although stories told by convicted felons should be taken with a generous grain of salt, this one was recalled by two former prisoners with substantially similar details. Despite the fact that solid proof is lacking, it sounds just like something Pearl Hart would have tried. And this would not be the last story about Pearl employing her sexual wiles to get out of Yuma.[18]

In November 1901, Pearl Hart and Elena Estrada were joined by two new female convicts. Rosa Duran was a sixteen-year-old Latina prostitute from Prescott who had robbed one of her johns. A judge gave her three years in Yuma. Alfreda Mercer had a much more complicated history. She was thirty-seven, with a loyal, hardworking husband and two children in Phoenix. In 1900 she began a sexual affair with a teenage boy named Fred Crosley. His exact age is unclear, for records show that he was either thirteen or eighteen. Their relationship, according to a Phoenix newspaper, "became notorious all over town." Finally the boy's mother sought the help of the police, who arrested both Alfreda Mercer and young Crosley. Both were charged with violating the Edmunds Act, a federal law that banned polygamy, bigamy, and even adultery. Because Alfreda had young children, the charges against her were dropped. Fred Crosley, however, was convicted and sentenced to six months in Yuma. As the Phoenix newspaper reported, the prosecuting attorney hoped that Fred "would be cured of the infatuation for the woman on his release from the penitentiary."[19]

That is not what happened. When Fred was freed in June 1901 and came back to Phoenix, Alfreda began pursuing him again. She was promptly rearrested and charged with adultery. At trial her husband took the stand and testified in her defense, but on cross-examination he sunk her case. He admitted that during their sixteen-year marriage, Alfreda had engaged in numerous extramarital affairs, and they had separated several times. A Phoenix reporter gave blunt details: "She got to frequenting the lowest saloons and roadhouses and for weeks at a time lived at the latter resorts." The jury found Alfreda guilty, and the judge gave her six months in Yuma. The seriousness of the situation now became clear to Alfreda Mercer. "She was overcome with grief as she was taken downstairs and she passed the greater part of the day in weeping," observed a reporter. "Her husband was with her nearly all day. He called late in the afternoon again, accompanied by one of their children, a little boy, and remained with her until the officer came to take her to the penitentiary."[20]

Until Alfreda Mercer completed her term six months later, Pearl Hart had three companions in the women's quarters. On one occasion, Pearl, with Rosa Duran and Elena Estrada, posed for a photo just outside their cells, with Rosa clutching a guitar. But their relationship was not always cordial. One squabble took place in 1902. Rosa Duran and Elena Estrada got into a violent altercation which landed them both in the Snake Den. Rosa got three days on bread and water, and Elena five. Whether Pearl caused the trouble between them is unknown. A Yuma journalist later observed, "Pearl was not a very desirable prisoner. She took particular delight in making petty trouble for the other female convicts."[21]

AUTHOR'S COLLECTION.

Pearl Hart, standing right, in Yuma's female quarters. Elena Estrada is at left and Rosa Duran is seated with a guitar.

In May 1902 she was overjoyed when her sister Katy arrived for a visit. Katy had fully recovered from her gunshot wound nine months earlier. Somewhere she had picked up yet another lover, Claude P. Frizzell, a former soldier and railroad man from New Mexico. They came by train to Tucson, where they checked into a hotel as Mr. and Mrs. C. P. Frizzell. Then they continued on to Yuma prison, where the sisters had a happy reunion. They had not seen each other in more than five years. Katy told prison officials and a Yuma reporter that she was Pearl's sister and that Frizzell was her husband. As was their custom, neither sister revealed their true family name. Katy explained that she was both an actress and playwright and said that she had written a play, "The Arizona Female Bandit." She announced that her sister would star as herself in the production when she was released from prison. Katy then returned to her home in Kansas City, and left Frizzell, like so many of her lovers, in her wake. An account of her visit to Yuma was published in numerous newspapers in Arizona and New Mexico. And despite the fact that she had been shot while rehearsing the same play in Omaha—an event that had been featured in dailies around the country—not a single journalist connected Mrs. Frizzell with the performer known as Millie Allen and Millie Davy.[22]

Five months later, in October, Pearl was joined by another female prisoner. Elizabeth Trimble was one of the most despicable convicts in Yuma. She had helped her husband, Walter Trimble, rape her own daughter, and both had been sentenced to life imprisonment. The victim was Elizabeth's eleven-year-old child from a prior marriage. She had forcibly held the girl down while her husband committed the rape. Later, Judge Fletcher Doan—the same judge who had presided over Pearl's trial—conducted a bungled investigation and convinced himself and Arizona's governor that the child had lied and that the Trimbles were innocent. Elizabeth and Walter Trimble were both eventually freed from Yuma. But that was a gross miscarriage of justice, for it turned out that Judge Doan had relied on perjured witness statements and the girl had told the truth.[23]

Two weeks after Elizabeth Trimble was booked into Yuma, a fifth woman convict joined Pearl. She was nineteen-year-old Jesus Chacon, who had been convicted of arson and sentenced to a one-year term. She had been infected with smallpox while in the Graham County jail but showed no symptoms. However, right after she entered Yuma she became violently ill, causing a smallpox panic in the prison. Arizona's territorial governor, Alexander O. Brodie, noted in his official annual report, "In November last smallpox was introduced in the prison by Jesus Chacon, a female prisoner, sentenced from Graham County. The disease broke out on the patient three days after her arrival. Although confined in the female ward or yard with four other prisoners of the same sex, the disease was almost miraculously confined to the one case. Heroic and prompt measures were taken to prevent an epidemic, resulting in complete success. When the case had fully recovered the quarters were thoroughly disinfected, and such articles as garments and bedding destroyed by burning." Pearl Hart must have been hugely relieved by her close call with smallpox, for in that era it was often fatal.[24]

In later years a widely published story held that Pearl had used sex to get out of prison. Its source was George Smalley, the Tucson reporter who knew Billy Stiles. When Alexander Brodie was appointed governor of Arizona Territory in 1902, he hired Smalley as his private secretary. Fifty years later Smalley claimed that he had inside information about Pearl Hart. He said that because Billy Stiles got Pearl pregnant, Governor Brodie was desperate to avoid a scandal. Brodie issued Pearl a pardon and ordered her release from Yuma. "As secretary to Governor Brodie, I wrote the pardon," declared Smalley. "But he asked me not to tell the newsmen about it." However, Smalley's account was fiction, for Stiles had left the prison two years earlier and never returned. He could not have impregnated Pearl Hart in 1902.[25]

Nonetheless, common rumor among the convicts insisted that Pearl had become pregnant. According to a journalist who interviewed a former Yuma prisoner years later, "She'd been assaulted by force by one of the guards and was sure she was pregnant. She refused to reveal the name of the guard, or give further details. 'You take this up with the governor,' she added significantly, 'and tell him if he don't do something about it, the *New York Journal* will print the whole story. And you'd better keep this to yourself, don't tell the warden.' When the official returned to Phoenix and told the governor, a hurried call went out to the top officials, and a speedy and stampeded conference was held. Pearl Hart was granted a quick parole, provided she leave the territory and withhold publication of her story to the press. Pearl, of course, agreed." As the former prisoner recalled, "All of us older cons knew it. In the pen there are no secrets. You know everything that goes on. And I'll say this: The warden and prison officials were mighty happy to be shed of Pearl Hart."[26]

The fact is that by late 1902 Pearl Hart was not visibly pregnant. Although it is certainly possible that she could have tried to fake a pregnancy, the prison doctor would likely have seen right through such a charade. The official—and most reliable—account of Pearl's freedom is that due to the smallpox scare, coupled with the fact that the women's quarters were considered to be crowded, the prison superintendent recommended that Pearl Hart and Rosa Duran be released on parole. As Governor Brodie explained in his annual report on Yuma prison, "At the beginning of the year there were three females in confinement in the institution. During the second quarter two additional ones were received, one under sentence for life and the other under sentence for one year. These acquisitions, with the three already in confinement, caused a rather cramped condition in the female ward, and with the presence of the smallpox infection…made the situation more difficult still. In this connection it must be borne in mind that the prison has no matron to personally look after the needs of the female prisoners. Because their conduct while in prison was such as to merit executive clemency, and to relieve the congested condition in that ward, I recommended the parole of Pearl Hart, No. 1559, and Rosa Duran, No. 1818, which was granted, and they were released from confinement on December 15, to the material betterment of the condition of those remaining."[27]

Pearl received news of the parole two days before it took effect. "The sudden release came as a surprise to everyone familiar with the case," noted a Tucson reporter. "In fact, it must have been an agreeable surprise to the prisoner, because she confidently expected to have to serve her full sentence." A Phoenix journalist added, "She learned the art of making laces and many other fancy goods which she has sold, visitors to the prison have been kind to her and have donated a dollar now and then, so she will not leave the institution penniless." Pearl happily packed her clothes and prepared to depart Yuma. She planned to go to Kansas City to live with Katy and their mother. Reported the *Yuma Sun*, "Pearl requested from the prison authorities the addition of only a pair of kid gloves to her wardrobe to fit her for traveling in style, while Rosa demanded a new and complete outfit of paraphernalia."[28]

After three long years, Yuma was about to lose its most infamous prisoner.

11

A New Stage

Pearl Hart stepped into the bright light of freedom on the afternoon of December 15, 1902. The terms of her parole required that she leave Arizona Territory, something she was more than willing to do. Prison officers escorted Pearl to the Yuma train station, where they bought her an eastbound ticket. "She left on Monday night's train for Kansas City," reported the *Yuma Sentinel.* "Quite a large number of people were at the depot to get a glimpse of Arizona's famous female ex-bandit and they were not disappointed, for she was there, and if there is one thing more than another that Pearl is not 'shy on,' it is a fondness for notoriety. Her ticket was bought straight through for Kansas City, where her mother and sister live, and the latter has written a drama in which Pearl will assume the leading role, arrangements having been made to play the Orpheum circuit, the initial performance to be given in Kansas City." The newspaper concluded, "She will try to elevate the stage instead of robbing it."[1]

Pearl's train stopped briefly in Tucson so the passengers could alight and eat, but she attracted little attention at the depot. The train crossed Arizona and New Mexico and arrived in El Paso the following night. A journalist met Pearl at the station and shook hands with her. "Her hand was hard and calloused," the reporter noted. "Its grip was like that of a bronco buster." Pearl told him that several reporters had hounded her at rail stops on the journey to El Paso. "I have met a bunch of them at every town I've come to," she exclaimed. "Tell them to stand off. I ain't armed now, but I might hurt some of 'em!"

Then Pearl stepped into a hotel to eat supper, and while sitting at her table she allowed a newspaper artist to sketch her portrait. The journalist observed, "She is not much of a woman to look at. Her old hat and clothes were faded from long usage and the cloak she wore was of the fashion of several seasons ago. She is not old, but the lines about her mouth are hard and her jaws give to her face a determined expression. She is small and comparatively slender in build. Her eyes have a steely glitter and their stare is bold, rather than frank. When walking about on the depot platform her stride was like that of a cowpuncher wearing top boots." Another El Paso reporter interviewed Pearl and wrote, "Miss Hart is quite an agreeable person to talk to," adding, "She says she is now on her way to the east to go on the stage." While waiting for her Chicago, Rock Island and Pacific Railroad train, Pearl stepped into a saloon with a "gentleman friend" to take a drink and celebrate her release from prison.[2]

Years later a waiter in the saloon recalled that Pearl's friend was "an enterprising man about town" named Jim. The waiter explained, "Jim flagged her with all the food and drink in the house. She ate like a starved wildcat, showing, I guess, that they didn't feed 'em any too fancy over at Yuma. But all the likker she'd take was a coupla' little glasses of sour wine. And every once in a while Jim'd try to get real affectionate. An' then I'd hear her say, low and hissing-like but mighty fierce: 'Now you get over there on your own side of this here table an' stay there. I thought you was a gentleman.' An' Jim would git. Once I came in with some little order while this was goin' on and then I understood how Jim, who wasn't usually that way, was getting buffaloed. God, the look she gave him! It was hard as a killer's and mean as a plungin' bronc's."[3]

AUTHOR'S COLLECTION.

Pearl Hart as sketched by a newspaper artist at the railroad depot in El Paso.

Pearl then left her amorous companion and boarded her train. It proceeded north through New Mexico, stopping in Albuquerque. A newspaperman found her at the depot, and they discussed how she felt about leaving Arizona Territory. "Pearl is getting as far away from it as she can with all possible speed and says that she has no desire to return," he reported. "She has aspirations to go on the stage, the stage of foot lights and grease paint." He also noted that prison had changed her appearance. "Pearl Hart is not a prepossessing looking woman. Her face, while still young, is hard and carries deep lines that are not attractive. Her eyes are a light blue and not overly clear and she walks with the stride of a man."[4]

Pearl then continued with her journey, ending in a tearful reunion with her mother, Anna, and sisters Katy and Amy in Kansas City. Amy had left her husband, James Taylor, in Toledo, and had joined the Davy family. She brought along her two children John and Anna Lilly—the ones who may actually have been Pearl's son and daughter. If they really were Pearl's, the family kept it a closely guarded secret. Pearl now met Anna's new husband, Daniel Perry, for the first time. They invited her to live with them and Katy in the Queen's Rest cottage. What became of Katy's son Stevie is unknown. After 1901 there is no record of him living with Katy, her siblings, or her mother, and he vanished from history. Given the high child-mortality rate of that era, the likely guess is that Stevie died.

Kansas City, located at the confluence of the Missouri River and the Kansas River, had long been the jumping-off place for people emigrating to the West. During the 1840s and '50s, wagon trains poured out of town to the Oregon and Santa Fe Trails. The railroad first arrived in 1865, setting off a huge boom. From 1870 to 1895 its principal lawman was chief of police Tom Speers, one of the great peace officers of the Old West. Among his many exploits, Speers arrested Wild Bill Hickok for vagrancy, befriended Wyatt Earp, and hunted the Jesse James gang. By the time of Pearl's arrival, Kansas City's Wild West days had ended, and it was a prosperous transportation center of about two hundred thousand. Numerous cross-country railroads served the city, with twenty thousand travelers coming and going every day by train. It was the perfect place for Pearl Hart to enter a new stage in her life.

Pearl later said that upon rejoining her family in Kansas City, she got a job working in a store. In the fall of 1903 she moved across the Kansas River to neighboring Kansas City, Kansas. Pearl opened a cigar shop in a small, one-story wood-frame building at 519 Central Avenue in the southern part of town. At about the same time, Katy also moved across the river, leaving her mother in the Queen's Rest house. If Stevie had died in that home, it may have been too painful for her to continue living there. Katy ran a small grocery store at the corner of Quindaro Boulevard and Thirteenth Street in the Rattlebone Hollow neighborhood in the northern part of Kansas City. She lived in rooms connected to the store.

In November a local reporter heard rumors that the lady tobacconist was Pearl Hart, the paroled stage robber. He visited her shop and found Pearl remarkably friendly and talkative. "She has her parole and discharge papers, which she says she will have framed," he told his readers. "The little ex-bandit says that Pearl Hart is an alias, but she refuses to tell her real name. She says her mother and two sisters live in this city." Pearl gave the journalist a detailed account of her stage-robbing adventures in Arizona. She also explained that Katy, whom she called "Mrs. Millie Lighthawk, an actress whose stage name is Millie D. Allen," had indeed written a play about her, "which she intends putting on the road next season." Pearl also briefly abandoned the Davy family's penchant for secrecy and admitted that Katy was the same Millie Allen who had been shot in Omaha. The reporter concluded, "Mrs. Allen still carries the bullet, but thinks she will be able to go on the stage again."[5]

RENEE GALLAGHER COLLECTION.

Katy Davy, dressed in buckskins and perched on a buffalo robe, was the very picture of a glamorous actress.

It did not take Pearl long to attract a new—and much younger—man in Kansas City: Elihu P. Keele, a twenty-three-year-old mason. He was a flashy dresser, and a journalist who met him a few months later wrote, "Keele claims to be a stonemason, but his hands and general appearance indicate that he has not worked for some time at his trade. The police are of the opinion that Keele is a professional confidence man." Though Pearl was now thirty-two, she lopped nine years off her age and told Keele that she was also twenty-three. On November 28, 1903, just a few days after the interview with the reporter in her cigar shop, she and Keele took out a marriage license. Pearl entered her real name on the certificate: Lillie N. Davy. The two got married the same day in a small ceremony in Katy's home on Quindaro Boulevard. Then Pearl closed her tobacco shop, and she and her new husband moved into Katy's place.[6]

By this time the two sisters had received news about the most evil man in their lives. Albert Davy had stayed in the Kawartha Lakes region in Ontario and had had no contact with any of his family for at least six years. He lived in an isolated cabin about fourteen miles north of Lindsay. It was situated on an island at the mouth of Emily Creek, where that stream enters Sturgeon Lake. There Davy became well-known as the Hermit of Emily Creek. He eked out a living paddling his canoe around the lakes, hunting and fishing. Advancing age had done little to change his behavior. In 1899 police in Lindsay arrested him for drunk and disorderly conduct; he served ten days in jail. He remained physically robust, and two years later won a local canoe race. On October 2, 1903, the sixty-two-year-old Davy paddled to the village of Fenelon Falls, at the upper reaches of Sturgeon Lake, where he got roaring drunk. That night he clambered back into his canoe and started for his cabin on the opposite shore of the lake. Men at a fishing camp heard him singing loudly as he paddled down the lake. He rounded Sturgeon Point, then headed north toward Emily Creek. Davy never got there. Two days later his canoe was found amid some tree stumps on the shore, about two miles across Sturgeon Lake from his cabin. A week after that, a search party found his body floating in the water nearby. Davy was apparently so drunk that he missed his home in the dark, then fell out of his canoe and drowned. Pearl Hart surely did not mourn his passing.[7]

Albert Davy's death seemed to underscore the fact that his daughters could not resist the compulsion to associate with disreputable men. A few weeks later, at five in the morning on New Year's Day, 1904, the sisters were awakened by a knock at the front door of Katy's store. Katy was not dressed, so she asked Pearl to answer the door. Pearl did so and greeted two young brothers, Walter and Roy Shaw, who said they wanted to sell Katy some heavy bags of sugar. Previously the youths had sold Pearl cans of salmon and packets of tobacco. Katy now bought the sugar, which was not a good decision, for she must have known it was stolen. It turned out that the Shaw boys had burglarized a railroad freight car and made off with twenty-eight sacks of sugar, weighing a hundred pounds each, which they peddled in both Kansas Citys. The bags were worth about six dollars apiece. Police detectives began investigating the theft and picked up the Shaws. The brothers made a full confession and admitted that they had sold the purloined sugar to Katy and to a saloonkeeper in Kansas City, Missouri. A week after the sale, police searched Katy's store and found several of the stolen sacks of sugar. They arrested her and lodged her in jail with the Shaw boys. Katy spent several days behind bars before she managed to post five hundred dollars bail and returned to her home to await trial.[8]

Meanwhile the Davy family had been joined by their youngest brother, Henry, then twenty-seven. Henry was a self-proclaimed hobo who drifted about the Midwest stealing rides on freight trains. He had inherited his father's temper and propensity for violence. On the evening of March 17 the Davys were eating dinner when Henry spilled gravy on the table. When Pearl upbraided him, he struck her a heavy blow. Pearl, no shrinking violet, immediately slapped him in the face. Elihu Keele jumped to his wife's defense, and a no-holds-barred donnybrook broke out. Henry bit Keele on one hand, then seized Keele's stone-mason hammer and brandished it at the couple. Other family members sent for the police, and two officers quickly arrived. They found the fight over and Henry hiding behind a curtain in one room. The policemen arrested Henry and Keele and lodged them in jail until their tempers cooled.[9]

Three weeks later, on April 6, Katy had a very unwelcome visitor at her Quindaro Boulevard home. Her ex-husband, Howard Allen, had served out his term in the Missouri state prison. He was an inveterate thief and in 1903 had been again convicted of horse stealing and sentenced to a year in jail in Independence, Missouri. After serving four months, he managed to break out, and three days later he knocked on Katy's door begging for help. Someone in the household—most likely Elihu Keele—notified the police. They rapidly responded, clapped the jailbreaker in irons, and returned him to the Independence jail. Keele started having second thoughts about the family he had married into.[10]

Now Francis Reno, who had interviewed Pearl for *Cosmopolitan* magazine, gave an even more detailed account of her life to a Chicago newspaper. His story was based on the notes he took while talking with her in the Tucson lockup. Reno did not know Pearl's true name, but he explained how she, at thirteen, had run away from home with her younger sister and the pair had gone to Buffalo, disguised as boys. Then he provided a long account of the second time they had run away, wearing men's clothing, and ended up in Chicago. Reno even described their escape by rope from the upper floor of the women's reformatory. His story quickly hit the wires and was published extensively throughout the nation. However, no one—not the townsfolk in Windom, not the Chicago police, not the staff of the Erring Women's Refuge—connected Pearl Hart with the teenaged Lillie Davy who had made newspaper headlines seventeen years before.[11]

Soon afterward, Pearl and Keele moved to rented rooms above a saloon on Minnesota Avenue, where they could live alone. The Kansas City police and railroad detectives continued to investigate the boxcar-burglary case, and five weeks later, on May 13, 1904, they arrested Pearl and her husband in their rooms. The couple was taken into police court and charged with vagrancy, which was simply the time-honored tool that police used to hold someone while they investigated a crime. A reporter visited the jail to interview Pearl, who insisted that her name was Mrs. E. P. Keele. The newspaperman told his readers, "Mrs. Keele denied that she is the Pearl Hart of stagecoach robbery fame, but the detectives say they have the original bandit in their custody. The detectives found in her possession Pearl Hart's parole and discharge papers from the Arizona territorial prison at Yuma."

When the journalist pressed her, she slowly smiled. Crossing her legs, she rolled a cigarette and finally replied, "No. I am not Pearl Hart. Do I look like a bandit?"

"Is it not true that you have Pearl Hart's parole papers in your possession?" he asked.

"Yes, but I gave them to my sister, Mrs. Millie Allen, who lives at 1290 Quindaro Boulevard, to keep for me and I was keeping them for my sister."

"Then, you knew Pearl Hart?"

"Yes, I have known her all my life," she answered, with a significant grin.[12]

The next morning Kansas City's police chief interrogated her, but Pearl continued to insist—truthfully—that she was Lillie Keele. Finally, when the chief told her that he would have her photograph taken and sent to Arizona for identification, she admitted that she was Pearl Hart. However, she firmly maintained that she was innocent of receiving stolen property. By the time another reporter came by, Pearl had loosened up, and she regaled him with stories of her stage-robbing and jailbreaking exploits. She even put a new spin on her motive for the holdup. "I have never told this before, but my real object in robbing the stagecoach was to escape the morphine habit," she declared. "I had heard of so many people coming out of these places and going crazy or dying. The habit was wrecking me. I decided that the best place for me would be the penitentiary, where I could not get hold of morphine. I started in by taking the drug to kill pain. Since I have been out of the penitentiary I have never gone back to that awful habit."[13]

Meanwhile, her brother Henry seethed with anger over his arrest, which he blamed on Pearl. When he learned that Pearl and Keele had been jailed, he saw his chance for revenge. He went to the saloon on Minnesota Avenue, showed the proprietor a fake police badge, and demanded to search their rooms. Henry said nothing about being Pearl's brother and insisted that he was an officer. It turned out that he wanted to steal her parole papers, which she kept locked in a trunk. The proprietor got suspicious and called the police, who arrested Henry for impersonating an officer. The charge, however, did not stick, probably because Pearl was not willing to testify against him. Henry was soon released from jail. Pearl and her husband were also freed after spending several days behind bars. Apparently there was insufficient evidence to prove that they had purchased any of the stolen sacks of sugar.[14]

A month later Katy appeared in the Kansas City courthouse for her trial. She was represented by a young lawyer and Spanish–American War veteran, Augustus C. Durham. He knew the Davy family and had also represented Katy's former husband, Howard Allen, in his horse-stealing case a year earlier. Durham later said that Katy and her ex-husband were two of his first clients. He knew Katy as Millie Allen, the name she was charged under, and later told a reporter, "Mrs. Allen was unusually pretty and less forward in manner than Pearl Hart." He also claimed that in Kansas City, Katy led "a dissolute life, though less depraved than Pearl Hart." Yet there is no other evidence that either of the sisters had returned to prostitution. In court, the district attorney dismissed the case against Katy, but before she could leave the courtroom, officers arrested her on two new charges connected to the stolen sacks of sugar. Her trial was continued to the next term of court, and she was released on bail. A journalist spoke with her and reported, "Millie Allen denied last night that she was a sister of Pearl Hart." Katy obviously felt that her family's reputation would work against her in court.[15]

About this time Katy's former lover, Earl Lighthawk, returned to Kansas City. He soon reconnected with Katy, and through her he met Pearl. Lighthawk later said that he had medical problems, and Pearl nursed him back to health. Since the two sisters had always shared everything, perhaps it was no surprise that Pearl became attracted to Lighthawk. When he returned her affections, that was too much for Elihu Keele. His marriage to Pearl had twice landed him in jail, and now he was a cuckold. Whether he divorced Pearl or simply left her is not clear, but in October Keele departed for Topeka, Kansas, where he enlisted for a three-year stint with the US Army.[16]

Lighthawk, unlike in his relationship with Katy, decided to make an honest woman out of Pearl. Three weeks later, on October 27, 1904, they married in Kansas City, Missouri. Instead of providing their real names—Lillie Davy and Earl Meyers—they used their pseudonyms of Pearl Hart and Earl Lighthawk. They did this, no doubt, because each of them was still legally married. Lighthawk lied about his age, stating on the marriage license that he was twenty-eight rather than thirty. The thirty-three-year-old Pearl did even better, chopping ten years off her age and making herself twenty-three once again.[17]

The next year saw good and bad news for Pearl and Katy. In January 1905 Katy completed and copyrighted the script for her play "The Little Turncoat," which she described as "a military drama in four acts and five scenes." Two months later she finally stood trial for receiving stolen property. The jurors concluded that Katy did not know that the sacks of sugar she had bought had been stolen, and they found her not guilty. After Katy's acquittal, their brother Willie showed up in Kansas City. Then Pearl, with Lighthawk, Katy, and Willie, decided to produce Katy's play "The Arizona Female Bandit" and take it on the road.

RENEE GALLAGHER COLLECTION.

Katy Davy performs in her stage drama, "The Little Turncoat."

Katy and Lighthawk had previously performed in small playhouses in Kansas and Iowa and had developed many connections in the business. Early in May 1905 they booked a theater in Paola, forty miles south of Kansas City. Based on Pearl's input, Katy had rewritten the melodrama and made it more true to life. Katy accurately placed the holdup in Kane Spring Canyon, and she assumed the starring role as Pearl Hart, with her sister and the rest as the supporting cast. A local reporter summarized the semifictionalized plot: "The wife of a banker who is forced into the terrible opium habit by her husband, who then deserts her, she works as an office boy in her husband's bank, is falsely accused of robbery, and arrested. She escapes and flees to Arizona. She hears of her mother's destitution and resolves to hold up a coach for the money, as she has no other way of obtaining it. The lone holdup, the chase, battle at her cabin, capture, trial, sentence and her escape are correctly depicted in the play."[18]

But "The Arizona Female Bandit" was not a hit and had a very short run in Paola. As a result, the little company went north to Keokuk, Iowa. They took rooms in the Grand Hotel and began working on a local production of the play. Then, on the night of May 29, Pearl and Lighthawk got into a bitter quarrel in their hotel room. He accused her of infidelity and hinted that he might return to a former mistress. Pearl insisted that she loved him, and that seemed to placate Lighthawk. Desperate for sympathy, he told Pearl that he had not seen his parents in fifteen years. That was false, for he had been living with them five years earlier in New York City. Lighthawk sat down at a desk and began writing a letter to his father and mother in Manhattan. "I am writing this letter with the lightest heart held for many days. I have been an invalid for many a day but thanks to my own dear little wife I am able to get around again. My wife and I are coming to New York in as quick jumps as possible and my own dear little one says we will get there if she has to put on men's clothes and freight there."[19]

Lighthawk wrote a few more rambling lines, then suddenly sprang to his feet and rushed to a dresser. Pulling open a drawer, he snatched up a .38 caliber revolver, pressed the barrel against his head, and fired. The bullet slammed into his head near his right ear and lodged in the skull. The gunshot, followed immediately by Pearl's screams, aroused all the lodgers on the third floor. One of the hotelkeepers ran to the room and found Lighthawk sprawled on the floor, with his head near the doorway and blood flowing from the wound. Two doctors quickly arrived, administered aid, and took him to a hospital.

Then a reporter tracked down Pearl and Willie, who identified himself as Harry Golf. The pair gave a quasitruthful account of the incident, as the journalist reported: "The wife said her name was Lillie Davy and that she was reared in Kansas City, where her parents now reside. The man who gives the name of Harry Golf claims that Mrs. Lighthawk is his sister, but when questioned as to the difference in names he claimed that 'Golf' was his stage name. The woman said that she was married to Lighthawk some fifteen years ago in Arizona, and that they had led a happy domestic life." Pearl also told the reporter that she, Lighthawk, and her brother "are known as the Earle family and have traveled with Ringling's circus" and that she "could not account for the attempt at suicide unless it resulted from jealousy or remorse."

The whole affair had been eerily reminiscent of Thad Brookings's suicide in Omaha. On the way to the hospital, a semiconscious Lighthawk managed to tell the doctors that the trouble arose over a "love matter." His prognosis was not good. A journalist noted, "Late reports from the hospital last night were to the effect that Lighthawk would probably die." But Earl Lighthawk was lucky, and he began a rapid recovery, with Pearl staying at his side. But unlike Katy's choice of men, Earl Lighthawk was not an ex-convict. Earl and Pearl reconciled, and less than three months later she became pregnant with his child. When Lighthawk was well enough to travel, he began another entertainment tour, and Pearl went with him. The couple was in Milwaukee on May 15, 1906, when Pearl gave birth to a daughter. They named the baby Saphronia Millie Lighthawk, after Pearl's sisters, and called her Millie.[20]

By this time Katy had met a small-time vaudeville producer from Chicago named Noah Louis Waelchli, who went by the stage names N. Louis Clarke and Frank Scalzi. In keeping with her custom of mixing her sex life with her business life, Katy became romantically involved with him and passed herself off as his wife. She variously called herself Mrs. Catherine Waelchli, Millie Davy Clarke, and Laura Scalzi. She also wrote a new play entitled "Kate," a comedy-drama about a girl trying to break into upper-crust society in New York. In 1907 Katy and Waelchli staged the play in small theaters in Illinois and Indiana. One reviewer opined, "Millie Davy Clarke who plays the title role is an actress of wonderful magnetism, swaying her audience with alternate emotions from first to last. Too much cannot be said in favor of her work." The same year she obtained copyrights for "Kate" and her drama about Pearl, under a new title, "Arizona's Girl Bandit." And despite her unstable romantic life, she had enough business sense to copyright them under her real name, Catherine Amelia Davy. Katy's playwriting and acting were extraordinary achievements for a woman raised in poverty, illiteracy, and abuse.[21]

Meanwhile their sister Amy had met a responsible, hardworking bricklayer, Holley Dewey, and married him in 1905. They made their home in Kansas City, Missouri. Dewey gave his name to Amy's (or Pearl's) children, John and Anna Lilly, and raised them as his own. Pearl's brother Willie, however, had trouble giving up his wild life as a notorious thief and jailbreaker. After marrying and divorcing in the 1890s, he moved to Chicago where he worked as a tailor, a skill he had likely learned while locked up in the Boys Reformatory of Upper Canada. In 1906 Willie wed Helen Shirley, whose father, John Shirley, was bookkeeper for a Chicago bank. After that, Willie Davy made a half-hearted effort to go straight. Like Pearl and Katy, he had a creative streak and wrote plays and short stories in his spare time.[22]

Henry Davy, on the other hand, continued to run afoul of the law. After being released from jail in Kansas City, he returned to the family's former home in Toledo. Seven months later, in November 1904, he met an eighteen-year-old Toledo boy, Lawrence Boudrie. The two beat their way around southern Michigan until police arrested them on suspicion of counterfeiting. Henry identified himself as William Hennessey and insisted that he was innocent. But a terrified Boudrie admitted to stealing and told the officers that "Hennessey compelled him, by murderous threats, to travel around the country with him, begging from farmers and others, and that the older man abused him terribly." When the officers pressed for more details, Boudrie said that so-called Hennessey had sodomized him. His claim was certainly true, for given the widespread prejudice against homosexual relations in that era, no young man would admit to it otherwise. However, it is an open question whether or not the sex was consensual.[23]

The two were locked up in the jail at Monroe, Michigan. Henry's jury trial began a few months later, in February 1905, on the scandalous charge of what was then called *the infamous crime against nature.* Despite Henry Davy's claims of innocence, the thoroughly shocked jurors believed Lawrence Boudrie. They promptly convicted Henry and sentenced him to an indeterminate term of six to fifteen years in the Michigan state prison. Pearl Hart's time in Yuma had been brief by comparison. As he was led out of the courtroom, an enraged Henry threatened to do up Boudrie and the local sheriff. He was taken to the penitentiary in Jackson, where he settled in for a long stay. But before long, Henry's violent temper brought him even more trouble. After quarreling with a fellow inmate, he stole a knife from the prison shoe shop. One evening in October 1905, Henry lay in wait while the other cons were being locked in their cells. As his enemy passed by the front of his cell, Henry whipped out the shoe knife and slashed the convict across the chest. It was a deep and bloody wound, but fortunately for Henry Davy his victim did not die.

Henry was lodged in the prison dungeon and charged with attempted murder. But Henry—like his siblings—was both intelligent and creative. He played what was then known as the insanity dodge and managed to get transferred to the Michigan Hospital for the Criminally Insane. Some of his family—probably Pearl and Katy—then hired a local attorney to petition the governor of Michigan for a pardon. Despite the fact that he had been convicted, sentenced, and then stabbed a fellow convict, the governor commuted his sentence. On March 1, 1907, Henry was released, having served but two years of his sentence. Henry later told a reporter that "a majority of the jurors in the case had signed a petition for his acquittal and the governor had released him immediately upon reading the evidence in the case." However, on another occasion he boasted that he had feigned insanity and had "fooled them at Jackson" prison.[24]

Though Henry had made a very narrow escape, he could not stay out of trouble. He went to Chicago, where his brother Willie now lived with his new wife, Helen Shirley Davy. In early April 1907, just a month after his release, Henry visited his sister-in-law's family, who lived in Lakeside, a Chicago suburb. Helen's sixteen-year-old brother, Allen Shirley, was particularly intrigued with Henry, who loved to boast about his adventures as a hobo. Allen, enthralled with Henry's tales, obtained his father's permission to accompany him to Chicago to open a small express-delivery business. Once they got there, Henry chose instead to head west to visit Pearl, Amy, and their mother in Kansas City. The teenage Allen decided to go along. They boarded a freight train and beat their way to Kansas City. There the two moved in with Henry's sister Amy, and for the next week they worked for her husband Holley Dewey, doing carpentry and bricklaying.[25]

Just as in the Lawrence Boudrie affair, there was probably a homosexual aspect to the relationship between Henry Davy and Allen Shirley. But young Allen quickly got homesick, and Amy gave him a postcard so he could write to his father and ask for railroad fare home. John Shirley received the card a few days later and was much relieved to hear from his son, whom he believed had run away from home. He asked the Chicago police to take steps to have the boy picked up in Kansas City and returned to him. Two mounted Kansas City police officers were dispatched to Amy's home. As the policemen neared the house, they passed a wagon loaded with wood, with a man driving and a teenage boy in the back.

The youth called out, "I'm the one you're looking for!"

He jumped down and ran to the officers. "I'm Allen Shirley, and that's the man you want, there."

Henry Davy had been in so much trouble with the law over the years that his first instinct was to flee. He whipped up his team, and as the officers galloped in pursuit, Henry leaped from the wagon and ran. The patrolmen quickly overtook and arrested him, then brought the pair to police headquarters. There Allen told detectives, "Davy told me he had money and would buy a wagon and team and we'd go into the express business in Chicago. I told my father this when I left. When we got to Chicago, Davy said a friend who lived three miles in the country from Chicago would give him the money to buy the team. We started to walk to this man's home. There Davy frightened me. He told me to look him straight in the eye. He pointed his finger at me, holding it close to my eyes. He kept repeating, 'You are coming with me. You are going to do whatever I tell you.' He said he'd kill me if I didn't do as he told me. I was afraid to try to run away from him. We worked our way to Kansas City on freight trains."[26]

The officers booked Henry on a charge of vagrancy, and the next morning Allen Shirley appeared in police court to testify against him. This time he added more flourishes to his story. "He showed me a big knife and said he would cut my throat if I ever told that he had forced me to leave home," Allen told the judge. "Besides that, I could not resist the man anyway. Whenever I would speak of going home he would point his finger at me and tell me to say nothing. I had to obey. I have been in terror of him ever since he took me away from home. He made me do everything."

Henry denied the charges and insisted that young Shirley had asked to come to Kansas City with him. The police were not aware that Henry Davy had just served a prison term in Michigan under the name Hennessey. However, Henry's prior arrest record in Kansas City and the fact that he was the brother of Pearl Hart were well-known. As a result, the judge ignored his plea of innocence.

"I believe that you used threats and your influence to get this boy away from home," he declared. "The boy had a good home. There was no object in him beating his way on freight trains and roughing it around the country. Your fine is $500 and that means a long time in the work house. When you get out of there you will know enough to leave boys alone."

Because Henry had no money to pay the fine, he served the time. And the judge's final remark suggests that he suspected that Henry had a predatory sexual interest in young Shirley.[27]

Still, Allen Shirley's claim that Henry abducted him was probably not true. "I think this thing has been stretched," his father told a Chicago reporter. "I don't know that Davy used any particular force to get my boy away. Allen goes to the public school at Lakeside. On April 4, during his vacation week, he sought and received my permission to come to Chicago with Davy. Allen is a good boy, but a bit too ambitious, and I suppose Davy put it into his head to go into some small business with him. I guess he just coaxed him a bit too hard and Allen could not resist."

However, Allen was not as good a boy as his father asserted. A few days later the elder Shirley changed his mind and refused to pay for his son's train fare back to Chicago. Instead he sent a smaller sum and directed that Allen be sent to the home of an uncle in Kansas.[28]

By the time Henry was convicted, young Shirley had related another story, and this one turned out to be substantially true. Allen admitted to the prosecuting attorney that he had stolen a horse and buggy belonging to a local doctor, but he claimed that Henry Davy had forced him to do it. The police soon found the abandoned buggy and learned from its owner that in fact it had been stolen. But the prosecutor allowed Henry to serve out his term in the workhouse and did not file a case against him for horse theft. Even though Allen Shirley's stories were suspect, it had been Henry's bad record that landed him behind bars. And

Henry Davy was fortunate that the Kansas City authorities did not discover that he was an ex-con who had served a term in Michigan for sodomy, or things would have gone much worse for him.[29]

Upon his release, Henry made the foolish decision to return to Monroe, Michigan, to seek revenge against Lawrence Boudrie. He blamed Boudrie for the two years he spent in the Michigan state prison. In October 1907 he found Boudrie working at a mill there and threatened to kill him. Two law officers quickly responded and lodged Davy in jail. But as a local journalist reported, "Young Boudrie stood in great fear" of Henry Davy and "was reluctant to appear against him." The reporter explained that the sheriff released Henry "upon his promise to get out of the county and never return." Once again Henry was lucky, because threatening a witness would normally have landed any felon back in prison.[30]

Next it was Willie Davy's turn to run afoul of the law. Willie had continued his work in Chicago as a tailor and pursued his writing. In 1907 he copyrighted three plays: "The White Squaw," "Greed for Gold," and "The Mad Captive." Willie wanted his wife, Helen, to star in "The White Squaw." A reporter who met Helen called her "a beautiful young woman." Helen told the journalist that she had run away from her home in Chicago and married Willie in Ottawa, Canada. She was twenty-one, and Willie was thirty-six. Though Davy tried to settle down and reform, getting his plays produced proved a bridge too far. Whenever he and Helen found themselves short of cash, he would journey to the rural towns just west of Chicago, steal a horse and buggy, and then sell them in the city. The Chicago police later concluded that between 1906 and 1908, Willie Davy stole at least forty horses.[31]

Despite the fact that automobiles had been manufactured since the late 1890s, travel by horse and buggy was then still common. In 1907 there were a hundred and forty thousand autos in the US, a number that would explode to almost five million in the next ten years. The huge number of motor vehicles, coupled with rapid paving of roads, would change American transportation forever. But horses, not autos, were Willie Davy's game. In March 1907 he and Helen rented a horse and buggy in Wheaton, a farm town just west of Chicago. They drove into Chicago, where Willie sold the horse and rig. More thefts followed during the next year. Then, in March 1908, Willie made off with a horse and buggy in Joliet, and a few weeks later he stole another in Chicago. Two Chicago police detectives got on his trail, and the following month they picked up Willie for horse theft and arrested his wife as an accessory. Helen's banker father, John Shirley, posted her bail, but law officers took Willie to jail in Wheaton. There he was charged with stealing the livery horse a year earlier. Because Willie was unable to make bond, he languished behind bars to await trial.[32]

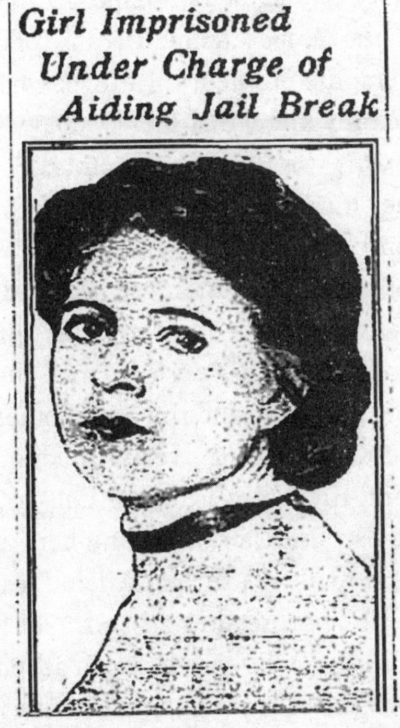
Girl Imprisoned Under Charge of Aiding Jail Break

AUTHOR'S COLLECTION.

A 1908 newspaper photograph taken of Katy Davy when she was arrested in Chicago for trying to break her brother Willie out of jail.

The Davy siblings, drawn together by their extremely rough and traumatic upbringing, always relied on each other for help. Willie wrote to his sisters, but Pearl, given her own past legal travails, was in no position to aid him. Katy, however, dutifully came to Wheaton. Just as she had done for her ex-husband Howard Allen in Stillwater, Oklahoma, Katy procured acid and hacksaw blades, hoping that Willie could use them to cut through the bars of his cell. She also bought several bars of green soap. The inside of the jail and the cell bars were painted green, and the soap was to be used to cover up the saw marks. Katy managed to bring the soap and some knives into the jail, but she was unable to slip the acid and saws past the guards. The plot was uncovered in early October when Willie's jailers noticed that a strap of iron had been loosened and rivets had been removed from his cell window. He had used the soap to fill in the empty rivet holes.[33]

Within days Katy was arrested in Chicago and jailed in Wheaton for assisting in the escape attempt. Because of the poor communications of that era, the prosecuting attorney had no knowledge of her history. He only knew that she was Davy's sister. Katy first claimed that her name was Laura Scalzi, and later identified herself as Catherine Waelchli, using the surnames of her current lover. Her trial for attempted jailbreaking began a few days later, and Noah Waelchli attended, posing as her husband. The main witness was a prisoner who testified to Katy's part in the escape plan.

A reporter described Katy's performance in the courtroom: "Mrs. Scalzi is a frail woman and the confinement in the jail told on her. She was convulsed with weeping when she entered the courtroom. Several times it was feared she would faint. When Prosecutor Hadley accused her of putting her fingers in her eyes to make her tears flow freely, she gasped and leaned on her husband for support." The prosecutor argued, "that the woman was an actress from Chicago who would laugh at the 'farmer jury' if she were acquitted." But the jurors, just like those twelve men in Kansas City, could not bring themselves to convict a beautiful, seemingly distraught, woman. Once again Katy walked free.[34]

Willie's trial began next, after the prosecutor dismissed the charges against his wife, Helen. Katy and Noah Waelchli testified on Willie's behalf, claiming that they were with him in Chicago the very day the horse and buggy were stolen in Wheaton. That was totally false, and the jury did not believe them. Willie received a term of three to twenty years in the Illinois state prison in Joliet. The prosecutor then filed charges against Katy and Waelchli for perjury. She was released on bail, but Waelchli did not have the thirty-five hundred dollars bond, and he remained in jail for several months. Waelchli's trial came up first, in March 1909. The jury promptly convicted him, and the judge sentenced him to an indeterminate term of one to fourteen years in the Joliet penitentiary. No doubt he rued the day he had met the Davy family. Katy's trial took place three months later. Despite considerable tears and borderline hysteria, this time she could not sway the jurors. They found her guilty of perjury, and she joined her brother and Noah Waelchli in Joliet. Katy received the same punishment as Waelchli: one to fourteen years.[35]

AUTHOR'S COLLECTION.

Katy's lover Noah L. Waelchli, theater producer and con man.

This was by far the most humiliating experience of Katy's adult life. And her misguided loyalty to her family had finally caught up with her. Due to her skill as a seamstress, she was put to work in the prison garment factory, sewing and repairing clothing for the inmates.

Katy and Noah Waelchli behaved themselves in Joliet, and both were released on parole in August 1910, after serving just over a year. Although they embarked on a brief theater tour in Illinois, Waelchli had had enough of the Davys. He and Katy went their separate ways, but Waelchli could not stay out of trouble. In 1920 he opened a phony tuberculosis clinic in Denver, and four years after that he was sent to the Colorado state penitentiary for raping a thirteen-year-old girl. Willie Davy was the last of the trio to leave Joliet. His conduct was good, and he earned his parole at the end of 1912.[36]

While Willie had been stealing horses near Chicago, Earl Lighthawk had fully recovered from his self-inflicted gunshot wound. He and Pearl decided to make another try at producing Katy's play about her stage-robbing exploits. They thought that the Southwest might provide their best audience, and since Pearl did not want to return to Arizona, they entrained for the village of Carlsbad, New Mexico, in June 1908. "The original Arizona bandit girl Pearl Hart is in town and will open an engagement at the Opera House next week," the Carlsbad newspaper announced. "The company is said to be the most interesting on the road." But the production was not a success, so they went eighty miles north to the larger town of Roswell. There Lighthawk obtained work with a local theater company, and he and Pearl gave up on the idea of producing "The Arizona Female Bandit."

On July 30 Pearl and Lighthawk got into a loud quarrel in their room in a Roswell rooming house. Several lodgers heard them yelling and cursing. They summoned a police officer who arrested the pair for disturbing the peace. Pearl, ever quick on her feet, claimed to a reporter, "We were rehearsing our parts in the play, 'A Family Quarrel' when a man in citizens' clothing rapped at the door. I answered the call, and when he asked what was going on inside, I remarked, 'It's only a family quarrel,' and then he explained that he was a policeman and had come to arrest us for disturbing the peace." She added, "You see the lines use the word 'damn' in two or three places, and the complaint of the neighbors was that we were using loud and profane language. That is all there is to the case." The two were charged in police court and then released. This was Pearl Hart's last arrest, and it marked an ignominious end to her budding acting career in New Mexico.[37]

This was the also the last time that she would appear publicly as Pearl Hart. For the rest of her life she would use her married names, Lillie Lighthawk and Lillie Meyers. Though she had basked in notoriety following her arrest in Arizona, all that changed. Ever after, she assiduously avoided publicity and lived anonymously. Her siblings all kept her secret. And unlike Willie, Henry, and Katy, Pearl never set foot in prison again.

12

The Final Curtain

Pearl Hart's life of lawbreaking was over—almost. She and Earl Lighthawk spent the next few years in Kansas City where they identified themselves as actors. Pearl, however, seems to have done little if any acting, while Lighthawk managed to earn enough money to support his wife and their baby daughter, Millie. Lighthawk also performed on the vaudeville stage in the Midwest as one of the Lighthawk Brothers. The identity of the other brother in his act is unknown. In 1909 a Kansas City reviewer offered them this compliment: "The Lighthawk Brothers are in a class by themselves. They are comedy acrobats and their stunt at the finish on a trapeze is not only laughable, but cleverly done."[1]

While Pearl and Lighthawk were performing in New Mexico, Anna Davy married for the third and final time. Pearl's mother had left her second husband, Daniel Perry, and in the summer of 1908 she married a reputable carpenter named Stephen Aldrich. Anna was sixty-two and Aldrich sixty-nine when they wed in Kansas City. Aldrich, a widower with numerous grandchildren, was a prominent member of the Masonic fraternity. He was also a Civil War veteran, having served with distinction in the Union Army from 1861 until he was wounded in action in 1865. He and Anna moved to his home in Ellis, a small farm town in central Kansas. Anna learned to read and write and corresponded regularly with her children. Stephen Aldrich was a far cry from Albert Davy, and Anna would live out her final years in a happy and secure marriage.[2]

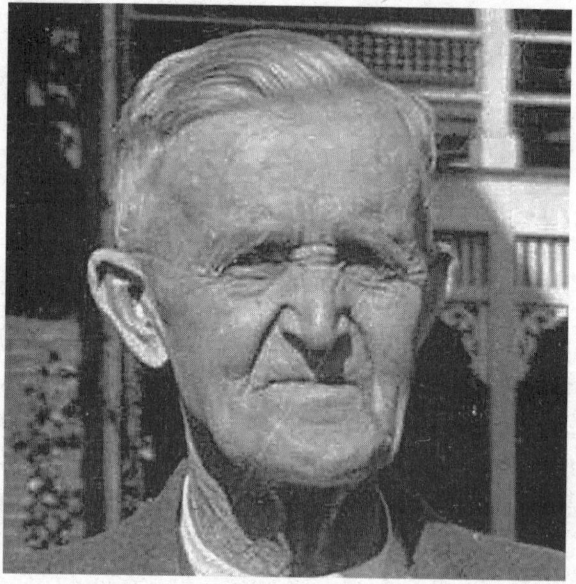

RENEE GALLAGHER COLLECTION.

Stephen Aldrich, the third and final husband of Anna Davy.

Things also began looking up for Katy. Following her release from the Illinois state prison she settled in Chicago. There Katy earned a living acting and writing theater scripts and short stories. Long afterward she recalled, "For many years I was an ingenue playing in repertoire throughout the East and Middle West, much of the time writing and producing my own plays." In Chicago she met and began living with David Lipman, a handsome Jewish salesman who, at age twenty, was a whopping nineteen years her junior.[3]

Henry Davy had also settled in Chicago and made a lukewarm effort to reform. Like Pearl, Katy, and Willie, Henry was creative and enjoyed writing songs and sheet music. He later explained, "When I was small I was injured and have never been able to work at hard labor, but have always made a living some way or another. I was editor on a small paper called the *Times* at Pewaukee, Wisconsin, for some time, and have always been writing songs and poems and some prose. I also write music for my songs, have them published, and sell them myself." Henry traveled about the Midwest, peddling his compositions door-to-door.[4]

Henry Davy may have been either bisexual or, like many gay men of that era, led a closeted life. In February 1909 he wed eighteen-year-old Ella Hillebrand in Chicago. Perhaps it was a marriage of convenience. Two months later he was back on the road in rural Michigan, west of Detroit. Selling sheet music was a hardscrabble existence, and in April he skipped out from a lodging house without paying his bill. A deputy sheriff arrested Henry and took him to jail in the county seat of Jackson, which happened to be the same town where the state penitentiary was located. In an attempt to conceal the fact that he had served a prison term as William Hennessey, he truthfully identified himself as Henry Davy. As the deputy walked him into the jail, a city policeman spotted the pair and called out "Hello there, Hennessey."

"Hello," Davy responded.

"Is your name Hennessey?" the surprised deputy sheriff asked. A glum Henry Davy acknowledged that Hennessey was his alias. He could not deny it, for the police officer who recognized him was a former guard at the state penitentiary. By coincidence, the county grand jury was then investigating numerous allegations of graft in the prison. Questions were immediately raised about Henry's early release and whether his family had paid a bribe to get him out of prison. While Henry was held in jail as a material witness, his former lawyer testified before the grand jury and denied any illegal conduct. The grand jurors concluded that no bribery had taken place in the penitentiary. Henry was released from jail, but it had been yet another close call.[5]

He returned to his bride, Ella, in Chicago, and they soon had a baby boy. Henry continued his songwriting and had some minor success in 1911 with a ballad he titled "The Heroes of the Stockyard Fire." It was a tribute to the twenty-one firemen who lost their lives in the Chicago stockyard fire of 1910, one of America's deadliest firefighting disasters. Henry claimed he sold forty thousand copies of the sheet music. Almost all middle-class homes had a piano, and sheet music remained wildly popular at a time when phonographs were new and broadcast radio was unknown. In 1912 Henry wrote another song, "Swinging," had copies published, and headed into Michigan, riding on the backs of freight trains. Davy walked door-to-door through rural towns, selling the sheet music for ten cents each. He sent his earnings to Chicago to support his now-pregnant wife and their two-year-old son. But Henry's boyhood years of poverty, abuse, neglect, and hunger had made an indelible mark. Larceny had become a lifelong habit.[6]

On August 5, 1912, Henry jumped off a boxcar in Adrian, Michigan, forty miles northwest of Toledo. While loitering in the rail yards he fell in with Arthur Yoder, a young hobo. Henry was broke, and he suggested that they steal a horse and sell it in Ohio. Yoder agreed, and late that night the pair crept into a barn and made off with one horse. However, after discovering that the animal was blind, they quietly returned it to the stable. Henry and Yoder then slipped into another barn, hitched a horse to a buggy, and headed south into Ohio. They drove all night, and in the morning raided a chicken coop on a farm near the village of Pioneer. As the pair roasted purloined poultry over a campfire, a farmer discovered them, and they leaped into the buggy and fled. Unfortunately for the fugitives, many of the farms were connected by newfangled residential telephones. Such rural phone systems, with numerous users on a single party line, had spread rapidly after the 1890s. Soon the phone lines were abuzz, and by the time Henry and Yoder got to Bryan, fourteen miles south, a sheriff was waiting for them.[7]

ARCHIVES OF MICHIGAN.

Mug shot of Henry Davy taken at the Michigan state prison in 1913.

Law officers returned the two thieves to Adrian and lodged them in the county jail. Arthur Yoder agreed to testify against Henry Davy, then pleaded guilty and received a two-year term in the state reformatory. Henry insisted that he was innocent, and his jury trial began in November. His ever-loyal sister Katy dutifully came to his aid. Henry later said that she "spent her last cent in his defense." His wife, Ella, with their two-year-old boy and three-week-old infant, was there. Katy and her new beau, David Lipman, also attended the trial. The main prosecution witness was Arthur Yoder, who testified in detail about how they had stolen the horse and rig. Other witnesses swore that they had seen Henry and Yoder in Adrian the day of the theft, and the sheriff described arresting the pair in the stolen buggy. However, communications were so primitive that the prosecutors were unaware of Henry Davy's terms in the State Industrial School in Rochester or his arrest record in Kansas City. They were also unaware that Katy had served a prison term for perjury.

Henry then testified in his own defense. He told a wild yarn in which he claimed to be "the son of wealthy parents" and that Henry Davy was not his true name. "I told you under oath that I would not reveal my real name," he declared, adding that he was protecting his father from scandal. He admitted that he had been in Adrian on the night of the theft, selling his sheet music, but claimed that he then jumped a freight train to Toledo. Henry said that he returned to Adrian the next day and found Yoder driving the buggy. He admitted riding in the rig with Yoder, but insisted that he had no idea it was stolen. Under cross-examination, Davy admitted that he had served a two-year prison term for sodomy under the name William Hennessey. Ella must have been shocked at that revelation, but she got really upset when the prosecutor asked Henry "if it was not true that his wife's parents had denounced him as a hobo and had refused to have anything to do with him."

"It's a lie!" she shrieked, and the judge had to gavel her down. At one point Henry's young son ran noisily to the witness stand, interrupting the trial. This angered the prosecutor, who exclaimed, "I object to a show for the purpose of exciting sympathy!"

Henry, seizing on the drama, clutched the youngster and shouted, "I take exception to the prosecutor's words. This child is no animal!"

The judge ordered Ella to take the boy out of the courtroom. Then, after two days of testimony, the jury retired to consider the case. A couple of the jurors proved either extraordinarily sympathetic or extraordinarily naive, for the panel hung ten to two in favor of conviction. Davy was returned to jail to await his retrial. Because Ella had no money, county officials paid her train fare back to Chicago. Before she left, Henry asked the local newspaper to report that "out of justice to his wife he wanted it stated that the evidence produced against him in the Monroe court did not prove that he was guilty of the crime [of sodomy] for which he was convicted."[8]

Ella decided to stand by her man. Henry's second trial began two months later, in January 1913, in a courtroom filled with interested onlookers. Once again his wife, their two children, his sister Katy, and David Lipman were there. This time Henry tried to establish an alibi by showing that he was in Toledo soon after the theft took place. Lipman took the stand and swore that he was a friend of Henry but failed to disclose that he was also Katy's lover. He produced a card, postmarked in Toledo the day following the crime, and said that Henry had mailed it to him in Chicago. On cross-examination, however, Lipman was unable to explain why he had not produced the postcard at Henry's first trial, even though he had been in court. Lipman was also dismissive of the prosecutor's questions and sarcastic in his responses, which did not help Henry's case. The lovestruck Lipman was willing to lie on the stand for Katy. However, it seems certain that she never told him that her previous lover, Noah Waelchli, had ended up in state prison for providing a phony alibi for her other brother.

A Michigan law allowed a defendant to make his own argument to the jury, and Henry insisted on doing so, against the advice of his lawyer. According to a reporter who attended the trial, "He closed with a well worded appeal in which he declared that he was not guilty of the crime and pointed out his wife and children to the jurors, declaring that being a husband and father to them, he could not have committed such an offense." The jurors deliberated for four hours, which gave the Davy family hope that they might issue a verdict of acquittal. But when they returned from the jury room and found him guilty, Katy and Ella broke into tears. Katy leaped from her seat and rushed toward the judge's bench, followed by Ella who screamed, "It was all a lie!"[9]

A bailiff escorted Henry's wife from the courtroom and returned him to his jail cell. Two days later he appeared in court for sentencing. When asked if he had anything to say, Henry pulled out a piece of paper and read a rambling statement, accusing the prosecutor of paying witnesses to testify falsely, the sheriff's officers of prejudicing the jury pool against him, and the town's newspapers of publishing lies about him. The judge was unmoved and sentenced Henry to a term of five to fifteen years in the state prison at Jackson. But Pearl and Katy were determined to try to help their brother. They convinced Earl Lighthawk to sign a declaration in which he swore that he had seen Henry Davy in Toledo soon after the horse had been stolen. Lighthawk signed the affidavit with his alias of Jack Earle. Then Henry's attorney used it as the basis for a motion for a new trial. Neither the prosecutor nor the judge knew that this Jack Earle was the husband of Pearl Hart, the stage robber. Nonetheless, the judge—rightly suspicious—rejected Lighthawk's declaration and denied the motion.[10]

RENEE GALLAGHER COLLECTION.

Katy Davy and David Lipman at the time of their marriage in 1915.

Pearl had not dared attend Henry's trial, no doubt because she feared that if anyone figured out who she was, her brother's case would be doomed. And though her felonious attempt to aid Henry had utterly failed, she and Katy were not ready to give up. Katy soon enlisted the aid of America's most famous trial lawyer, Clarence Darrow, whom she met in Chicago. Although Katy insisted that Henry was innocent, Darrow seems to have believed that, after two trials, his best chance was a pardon. Darrow told Davy's lawyer that the Michigan governor was "anxious do to the square thing in every case brought before him." Darrow added that he "would be glad to place the matter before him on its merits." However, Henry Davy had already duped one governor into giving him a pardon, and that was not going to happen twice. Clarence Darrow was unable to win his freedom, and Henry served out his second term in the Michigan state prison.[11]

Meanwhile in Kansas City, Earl Lighthawk struggled to support Pearl and their daughter, Millie. In 1912 the three of them moved in with her mother and Stephen Aldrich at the latter's home in Ellis, Kansas. Pearl had always been close to her mother and must have been happy to be with her. While Anna watched Millie, Pearl and Lighthawk traveled by wagon from farm to farm in the Kansas countryside. He posed as a medicine man and sold snake-oil "Indian" remedies to the countryfolk. Such salesmanship was dishonest, but in that era of lax drug and food regulation, it was not illegal.

On November 14, 1915, at the Aldrich home, the person most important to Pearl died. Anna Davy was sixty-eight and had lived a long life for that time, especially considering her history of poverty, privation, and domestic abuse. Stephen Aldrich paid for Anna's body to be shipped to his family's plot in Illinois for burial. Pearl was surely heartbroken over the loss of her mother, who had been the single stabilizing influence in her tumultuous life.[12]

Pearl Hart's marriage to Earl Lighthawk proved volatile and traumatic. In 1918 Lighthawk left her and went alone to Cape

Girardeau, Missouri. There he adopted a new alias, Doctor Earl Lighthall, and passed himself off as a supposed Indian medicine man. In February 1919, with a legitimate local doctor as his partner, he opened the Lighthall Indian Sanitarium in Cape Girardeau. He ran newspaper advertisements offering "Indian medication with the latest scientific methods for the treatment of chronic diseases of men, women and children." This was at the height of the Spanish-flu epidemic, and the public was fixated on health care. Soon after the sanitarium opened, Lighthawk found himself under arrest and charged with practicing medicine without a license. The case against him was later dismissed. In July 1919, despite the fact that he was still married to Pearl Hart, the forty-four-year-old Lighthawk wed a sixteen-year-old local girl who worked for him as a nurse. Not surprisingly, that relationship did not work out. Two months later Lighthawk sold his interest in the sanitarium and returned to Pearl and their daughter Millie.[13]

That winter Pearl made the remarkable decision to move with her husband and daughter to Phoenix. No doubt she thought that after the passage of more than twenty years she would not be recognized as the notorious ex-prostitute and stagecoach robber. In Phoenix she and Earl identified themselves as the Lighthall family. A census taker visited their rented home in January 1920 and recorded the trio as Doc and Lillie Lighthall, and thirteen-year-old Millie. Her husband worked in Phoenix as a traveling salesman—likely still peddling quack medicine. As Pearl had hoped, no one suspected her identity during the one or two years they lived in Phoenix. That was surprising, because Pearl Hart the stage robber remained a popular topic, and her name was frequently mentioned in Arizona's newspapers. In 1923, the *Tucson Citizen* ran a detailed story about her wild career and concluded, "Whether Pearl Hart is living yet no one knows."[14]

On one occasion in the early 1920s Pearl made a visit to Tucson. Several years later Lorenzo Walters, a Tucson police officer who was also an avid local historian, recorded what happened.

"One day an elderly lady walked into the Pima County jail and asked that she might look the jail over. As such a request was rather unusual without some explanation, she was asked the reason for her anxiety to look over the jail. She replied, 'I am Pearl Hart and spent some time here about twenty-five years ago and I would like to see my old cell.' Needless to say, she was accorded the privilege of inspecting her old quarters and, after thanking the officer in charge for his courtesy, departed, no one knowing where to or when." Walters was wrong about her being elderly—she was then a little more than fifty. But as a Tucson policeman, he was in a position to learn the story firsthand. Walters kept it to himself and only made the account public when he included it in his book, *Tombstone's Yesterday*, published in 1928. This was the last time that Lillie Davy would admit publicly that she was Pearl Hart.[15]

While she was living in Arizona, Pearl may have learned some of the history of her former husband, Dan Bandman. In 1901, when she was in Yuma prison, he had married a Tucson woman. Bandman and his bride then moved to the Arizona copper-mining town of Bisbee, where he taught piano. But his true colors quickly came through. After two years of marriage, his wife filed for divorce, alleging "neglect, extreme cruelty, and that defendant is addicted to the opium habit." Bandman later left Arizona, drifting around as an itinerant musician, first to the mining town of Goldfield, Nevada, then to San Francisco, and finally, Sacramento. In 1913 Bandman was arrested in Sacramento for possessing illegal narcotics. Three years later he headed north to Fairbanks, Alaska, where he became a popular and well-known piano player. In 1919 he joined an eight-member jazz band and later tried his hand at prospecting for Alaska gold and working for a railroad. Bandman returned to Sacramento in 1932, but his years of drug abuse had taken their toll. In January 1934 he became seriously ill. As a former soldier, Bandman was admitted to the Veterans Home in Yountville, California, where he died a week later, aged seventy. A number of his old friends traveled from San Francisco and Sacramento to attend the funeral. Surprisingly, the group included George Vice, the US Marshal for Northern California, who had been Bandman's friend for years in Sacramento. One can only wonder if Marshal Vice knew that his old comrade had once been the brutal and abusive husband of Pearl Hart.[16]

Early in 1922 Pearl, with her husband and daughter, moved to Southern California. Earl Lighthawk continued traveling as a medicine man and peddling dubious native remedies. Though he dropped the surname Lighthall, he still used his Lighthawk alias as a salesman. Domestically he went by his real name, Earl Meyers, and Pearl began calling herself Lillie Meyers. Lighthawk was often not at home. He traveled by automobile through rural California, selling his bogus medicines door-to-door. In April 1922 he took a room in a lodging house in Marysville in Northern California, where the local police—remarkably—issued him a permit to peddle his ostensible Indian cure-alls. Lighthawk met a fellow lodger who suffered from epilepsy and persuaded him to hand over all his money, thirty-five dollars, for a guaranteed cure. Instead, policemen soon found the epileptic prone on the sidewalk, suffering from a seizure. When he told the officers how he had been defrauded, they promptly arrested Lighthawk and confiscated the money. Then the police chief revoked his peddler's license and ordered the huckster out of town.[17]

Not long after this, Pearl Hart broke up with Earl Lighthawk for good. Their daughter, Millie, now seventeen, met Adna Gilbert, a twenty-two-year-old machinist with the US Navy. In October 1923 they married in Los Angeles and made a strong union that would last the rest of their lives. Soon afterward, Millie moved to Hawaii where Adna had been stationed at Pearl Harbor. Adna served on the USS *R-4*, one of the earliest submarines commissioned by the US Navy. Pearl soon received news from Hawaii that Millie and her husband were expecting their first child. How she got the money for her passage from Los Angeles is unknown, but in January 1925 Pearl boarded a steamer for Honolulu. Three weeks after her arrival, Millie gave birth to a daughter she named Naomi, after her mother's middle name.

In October of that year, Adna Gilbert took part in an incident that became famous in the history of naval aviation. He and his fellow submariners rescued the crew of a Navy airplane that had tried to make the first nonstop flight from the US mainland to Hawaii. The aircraft, a flying boat, ran out of fuel and landed in the Pacific. When a massive search failed, the crewmen fashioned a sail and, with little water and no food, spent nine days trying to reach Hawaii. Finally they were found and rescued by the men of submarine USS *R-4*. Pearl must have been proud of her adventurous son-in-law. She spent two happy years with Millie and Adna in Honolulu. During that time, Millie gave her a second granddaughter, Margueritte, born in 1926. Living in the island paradise and helping raise two grandchildren was one of the highlights of her life. And it was a far and incongruous cry from Pearl Hart's wild career on the Arizona frontier.[18]

Meanwhile Katy Davy married for the last time. In June 1915, after a three-year relationship, she and David Lipman boarded a train in Chicago and went to Indiana where they tied the knot. On their wedding license Katy claimed to be twenty-five. As an existing photograph of the couple shows, she looked much younger than her real age of forty-two. Lipman soon opened a motion-picture theater in Chicago, but not surprisingly, the couple's union proved a stormy one. After seventeen months of marriage, Katy filed for divorce on grounds of cruelty. However, the pair later reconciled and continued living as man and wife. Lipman then sought a more lucrative career. He studied law and in 1920 obtained his license as an Illinois attorney. David Lipman worked hard and became a successful Chicago lawyer.[19]

Katy also achieved modest success as a writer, actress, theater producer, and acting coach. In the early 1920s she and Lipman bought a spacious, three-story brick house at 208 East Superior

Street, just north of Chicago's downtown. At about the same time Katy, attracted by the burgeoning silent-film industry in Hollywood, purchased a second home in Los Angeles. It was a three-bedroom, Spanish colonial style bungalow at 2283 Glendale Boulevard in the tony Silver Lake neighborhood, situated just east of Hollywood. From her new California home, Katy wrote radio plays, taught acting, and ran ads in the *Los Angeles Times*: "Theatrical director. Experienced. Will train people of all ages for stage. Results guaranteed." Katy energetically pursued her career by traveling back and forth by train between her homes in Chicago and Los Angeles. She also tried her hand at acting on the silver screen. "I played in the silent movies with Myrtle Stedmen, Charles Clary, Tom Mix, and others," Katy once recalled. Her parts were probably minor roles, and the names of her films have been lost to history. But like Pearl's new life, it was a far cry from the grinding poverty and abuse of their youth.[20]

AUTHOR'S COLLECTION.

The home of Katy Davy and her husband David Lipman in Chicago.

The *Hollywood Filmograph*, a trade paper for the motion-picture industry, introduced Katy as "one of America's foremost short story writers and a recent arrival at the film colony, where she is now negotiating with producers to screen a number of her stage plays." The announcement was an exaggeration, for she was not widely known. Katy also joined the Photoplaywright's club of Los Angeles, a group of writers working in the film industry. "Mrs. Catherine D. Lipman will give an informal talk on 'The Man in the Editor's Chair'" announced the *Los Angeles Times* in 1923. "Mrs. Lipman is a writer of dramas, having had a number produced, and also is a short story writer. She has been for a number of years a leading member of well-known Eastern dramatic companies." Needless to say, Katy certainly did not regale her buttoned-down audience with stories of her real dramatic career. One can only imagine their shock if they knew that this petite, well-dressed, glamorous brunette had once been a notorious prostitute in Buffalo, a jailbreaker in three states, and a state-prison convict in Illinois.[21]

By this time Henry had joined Katy in Los Angeles. He had exhibited good behavior in the Michigan penitentiary and was released early in 1919 after serving five years. His wife Ella finally saw the light and divorced him while he was behind bars. Henry first went to Chicago where he lived with Katy and David Lipman and worked as a taxi driver and songwriter. He soon remarried, but that union also proved a failure and lasted less than three years. In 1923 Henry took a train to Los Angeles where he moved into Katy's Glendale Boulevard home. He lived there the rest of his life, making frequent trips to Chicago to visit friends. Instead of hitching rides on freight trains like he had in his youth, Henry bought a small motorcycle and rode cross-country.[22]

The next year, Katy's forty-four-year-old sister Jennie moved to Chicago. After her troubled upbringing and the time she spent in the State Industrial School in Rochester, Jennie had turned her life around. As a girl she reconnected with her younger sister, Mary, who had been adopted by the Apfel family in Rochester. By 1905 Jennie and Mary moved to New York City where they lived together in a Manhattan lodging house and worked as actresses. Mary had a beautiful soprano voice and became a professional singer. Jennie soon met Felix Guilleaume, a New York City jeweler. They married in 1910 and had a son. But their marriage was rocky, and the couple separated in 1924. Jennie then joined Katy in Chicago, as her sister had come from Los Angeles and was living with David Lipman in their home on East Superior Street.[23]

The sisters' extraordinarily dysfunctional upbringing had made them unstable and erratic. On May 29, 1924, the pair had an ugly quarrel in Katy's house. A distraught and suicidal Jennie stormed out with her six-year-old son and walked a quarter mile east to the shore of Lake Michigan. Picking up the boy in her arms, she started to leap into the lake when a bystander rushed in and stopped her. The police were summoned, and a hysterical Jennie told them of the fight with her sister and said that she was despondent over the death of her husband. She claimed that he had been killed fighting in France in the Great War. In fact, Felix Guilleaume was alive and well. He remarried in New York City seven months later and did not die until 1969.[24]

Meanwhile Pearl Hart avoided such Davy-family drama and enjoyed her new life as a grandmother in Hawaii. Her son-in-law was soon to be discharged from the Navy. In January 1927 Pearl returned by steamship to Los Angeles with her two-year-old granddaughter, Naomi. Pearl and little Naomi moved into Katy's home on Glendale Boulevard, while Millie stayed behind in Honolulu with her infant to await Adna's discharge. When Gilbert completed his service, he and Millie left Hawaii and settled in with Pearl and Katy in Los Angeles. The house on Glendale Boulevard would be a permanent home for several of the Davy siblings.[25]

In 1927 what would become a very popular book was released,

written by journalist Duncan Aikman and titled *Calamity Jane and the Lady Wildcats*. In addition to Calamity Jane, its author featured such noted Western wild women as Belle Starr, "Cattle Kate" Watson, and, of course, Pearl Hart. The book received a prominent review in the *Los Angeles Times*. Whether Pearl actually read the tome is unknown, but surely she knew about it. Aikman's chapter about her was both long and heavily fictionalized. He followed the 1899 *Cosmopolitan* story but filled in the missing details with his own imagination. Aikman claimed that Pearl, at sixteen, was seduced in Lindsay by "an attractive young rake about town named Hart." In Aikman's story they eloped in 1889 and drifted around Ontario while Hart worked "as a racing tout and semi-professional gambler." Pearl finally left him and went West, supporting herself "as a cook in private homes and mining camps" before becoming the noted woman bandit. In Yuma prison, she "kept her head and avoided scandal by quickly reducing the guards to the condition of harmless but emulously sympathetic boyfriends." Given that Pearl had gone from boasting of her exploits to living a secret life, she could not have been happy about her newly revived notoriety.[26]

Years later, Pearl's family recalled that she became somewhat reclusive, and perhaps Aikman's book had something to do with that. By 1930 she had moved to Victorville, located in the Mojave Desert eighty miles northeast of Los Angeles. Just like in Arizona, she seemed to like the desert, as well as the solitude it offered after her tumultuous life. Back in California, her daughter Millie and son-in-law Adna bought a home for their growing family. It was a single-story bungalow, still standing, at 940 South McDonnell Avenue in East Los Angeles. Pearl moved in with them and enjoyed the company of her young granddaughters. For Pearl, this quiet Los Angeles home was a world away from the tumbledown shack in Campbellford, the State Industrial School in Rochester, the Mercer Reformatory, and Yuma prison. And though Pearl Hart, the stage robber, continued to be featured occasionally in magazines and newspapers, her family kept her identity a closely guarded secret.[27]

In 1934 Pearl's name prominently reappeared when newspapers reported that a friend of Sheriff Truman had donated her Merwin & Hulbert revolver to the Arizona Historical Society in Tucson. By this time her decades of heavy smoking had caused heart and respiratory problems. In November of that year she became ill, and four months later her condition worsened. Millie did all she could for her mother and paid for a doctor to visit regularly. But Pearl's opium and morphine abuse in the 1890s had also taken a heavy toll, and her health steadily declined. Finally, on May 9, 1935, she died at age sixty-four in Millie's home, her devoted daughter at her side. Pearl Hart was interred in Rose Hills Memorial Park in nearby Whittier under her real name, Lillie Naomi Meyers. Her death merited but a three-line obituary in the *Los Angeles Times*. The Old West's most famous female bandit died as she wished, in total obscurity.[28]

RENEE GALLAGHER COLLECTION.

Pearl's sister Saphronia Davy Wahl, at right, with her daughter Ethel, about 1910.

She was the first of the Davy siblings to die, following ten-year-old Acle's passing in Toledo forty years earlier. Pearl's ne'er-do-well ex-husband, Earl Lighthawk, outlived her by nine years. He died in Colorado in 1944 and was buried in Los Angeles under his real name, Earl Meyers. Pearl's siblings also showed greater longevity. Jennie raised her son in Chicago, opened a small grocery store, and died there in 1947, age sixty-seven. Saphronia had divorced her saloonkeeper husband Andrew Wahl in 1904, then moved to New York and promptly remarried. After the death of her second husband in 1928, Saphronia went to California and lived in the Glendale Boulevard home with Katy and Henry.[29]

Not surprisingly, Katy's marriage to David Lipman failed. They divorced in about 1927, and a few years later she moved permanently to her Los Angeles house. During the Great Depression, Katy struggled to support herself, Saphronia, and Henry. In 1940 she wrote to the famed actor Edward G. Robinson, asking for his help in getting her short stories published. Katy did not know Robinson, but a mutual friend told her that the actor was "always ready and willing to do good." She pleaded, "I am under great financial strain, being the sole support of an elder sister and brother, and in dire need of finding a market now." Whether Robinson helped her is unknown, but Katy finally had some success in 1945 when Doubleday published a science-fiction novel that she had written, titled *After the Clouds*.[30]

In Los Angeles, Henry Davy concealed his long criminal record by using several aliases. He continued writing songs but earned little money and even sold "magical fortune-telling calendars" through newspaper advertisements. Henry was still living with Katy and Saphronia in Los Angeles when he died in 1950, age seventy-three. His sisters paid for an obituary to be published in the *Los Angeles Times*. It extolled his songwriting and creative abilities, but, of course, said not a word about the many dark episodes of his past nor of his connection to the notorious Pearl Hart.[31]

Mary Davy, because of her adoption by the Apfel family, led a more stable life than her siblings. She received a much better education and enjoyed a career as an opera singer under the name Clara Miceli. Mary performed in Italy and Germany, as well as on transatlantic ocean liners and radio stations in New York. But she had no better success with men than did Pearl or Katy. After being married and divorced twice, she moved to Katy's Los Angeles home in 1944. Because Mary had grown up in a secure and stable family, she developed into an even-tempered woman. But after living for a time with Katy, Saphronia, and Henry, she found them to be highly emotional, erratic, and eccentric. Mary could not get along with them. She moved to a building one block down Glendale Boulevard, where she became an apartment manager.[32]

Pearl's sister Amy lived a long and productive life. She and her husband, Holley Dewey, moved from Kansas City to St. Joseph, Missouri, where he established a successful brick-contracting business. In addition to raising John and Anna Lilly, she and Holley had four of their own. Holley died following a truck accident in 1932, but Amy was tough and resilient, just like Pearl and her other sisters. She hired a lawyer and sued the company that owned the vehicle that caused the collision. The jury awarded Amy ten thousand dollars—a fortune during the Depression. She then lived for decades, active in her church until her death in 1965, age ninety. Amy was survived by four children, twelve grandchildren, and twenty-four great-grandchildren. It was an enduring and tangible legacy.[33]

Pearl's possible son and daughter each led productive and law-abiding lives. John Dewey spent most of his adult years in Kansas City. He served in the US Army in World War I, married, had a son, and later divorced. He worked as a printer and automobile painter but saw hard times during the Great Depression and lost his home. He then became a laborer for the Work Projects Administration. The WPA was an essential element of President Franklin Delano Roosevelt's New Deal and provided jobs to millions of unemployed men. John Dewey died in Wichita, Kansas, in 1973.[34]

Anna Lilly Dewey also lived in Kansas City, where she married James Wilson, a teamster. The couple had two sons and three daughters, one of whom they also named Lilly. They divorced in 1937. She remarried in 1948, but that union lasted only five years. She then married for a third and final time and died in Kansas City in 1962, leaving behind her adult children and twelve grandchildren. Anna rarely, if ever, discussed her family's connection with Pearl Hart. As a result, the current generation grew up knowing nothing about their relationship to the noted female bandit. However, once, in an unguarded moment, Anna's daughter Lilly exclaimed, "I can't believe my mother named me after a stagecoach robber!"[35]

In 1950, after Henry had died, Amy's granddaughter, Rovilla Dewey, drove from Missouri to Los Angeles to visit her great-aunts. She moved in with Katy and Saphronia and stayed for several weeks. Rovilla learned that Mary had moved down the street due to friction with her sisters. She later recalled that Katy and Saphronia were very eccentric and lived on the brink of poverty. They had several small dogs, and each pet sat in a chair and ate at the dinner table. Katy owned trunks filled with beautiful gowns and fancy gloves from her acting career, but she never wore them or allowed anyone to touch them. In later years Rovilla enjoyed telling stories about her great-aunts, saying "One was an actress, one was an opera singer, and one was a stage robber. They were all a little crazy."[36]

Pearl's daughter Millie was devoted to her aunts and provided care for Katy, Saphronia, and Mary during their final years. In the early 1950s, Katy's health began failing. It was made worse by the bullet she still carried, fifty years after she had been shot in the back by Thad Brookings in Omaha. When Katy suffered a heart attack on May 17, 1957, Millie took her to a hospital in Hollywood. She died there later that day, age eighty-three. Katy's death may have been too much for Saphronia. Millie tended to her, but just three months later Saphronia died at the age of ninety. Their younger sister Mary lived another year, passing away in Los Angeles in the fall of 1958, aged seventy-six. Katy, Henry, Mary, and Saphronia all rest today in Forest Lawn Memorial Park in Glendale, just north of Los Angeles.[37]

Katy Davy had led a wild and frequently traumatic life, exceeded only by that of her sister Pearl. At age eleven Katy witnessed the gang rape of her mother. At thirteen she rode with her sister on freight trains across the Midwest, dressed like a boy, and escaped from the Erring Women's Refuge in Chicago. At sixteen she ran a brothel in Buffalo and stabbed a patron in the eye. At twenty-three she was a pioneer balloonist and skydiver. At twenty-four she twice broke her husband out of jail in Oklahoma and Texas. At thirty she was shot and almost killed. At thirty-six she served time in the Illinois state prison. In between, she followed a career as a glamorous actress in theater and film. Katy would have had far more success as an author had she written a factual autobiography of her incredible life. But few would have believed it, and today she is completely forgotten. Even her house is gone. In true Los Angeles fashion, it was demolished in 1990 and an eight-unit condominium building erected in its place.

And what became of Willie Davy? Just like his sisters, he went straight. After being paroled from prison in 1912, Willie settled in Wichita, Kansas, where he worked as a tailor and amateur writer. He got divorced, then married for a third and last time in 1920. Willie returned with his new wife to Chicago, where they raised two children. Following World War II, he moved his family to Joplin, Missouri. In 1954 Willie decided to write the story of Pearl Hart. He sent a letter to the Arizona Historical Society in Tucson asking for information about her stage-robbing career, but in typical Davy-family custom, he concealed the fact that she was his sister.

"This will surprise you, but in fact I knew Pearl Hart in her school days, back in the late Eighties," Willie wrote. "She was born in 1871, in the town of Peterborough. Sometime later her parents moved to Toronto, where I met her as we attended the same school." He promised to send a copy of his story when it was completed, but that never happened. A year later eighty-six-year-old Willie Davy died in Joplin.[38]

In the end, every one of Pearl Hart's siblings took her secret to the grave. That was exactly the way she wanted it. But now, this book will hopefully raise the final curtain on an extraordinary Canadian–American drama.

Epilogue

Falsehoods and Folklore

In 1935 Niven Busch was a rising star among Hollywood screenwriters. He would soon author best-selling novels as well as the screenplays for such classic films as *The Westerner* (1940), *The Postman Always Rings Twice* (1946), and *The Furies* (1950). His studio office in Hollywood was but fifteen miles from the humble bungalow in East Los Angeles where Pearl Hart spent her final years. But Busch, a recent arrival in California from New York City, had never heard of Pearl Hart. Then, one day in February 1941, he was on a trip through West Texas when he picked up an El Paso newspaper and read about the death of James Morrison, a ninety-year-old pioneer. The news report mentioned that Morrison, as an Arizona lawyer, had once defended a woman stage robber named Pearl Hart.

Niven Busch was thunderstruck. He had never heard of a woman bandit in the Old West. Busch recalled that he had a brainstorm. "The Western formula had worked since the earliest movies, so why change it? If the leading man wanted to kiss anybody, he could kiss his horse. The problem was to get a woman in it. That was absurd. Women in the actual West were present in considerable numbers. Instead of wondering how to work a woman into the plot, I decided to build the entire plot around a woman." He spent the next few months interviewing old-timers and searching through faded newspaper files for information about Pearl Hart. The result was his best-selling 1944 novel, *Duel in the Sun*, which two years later became the critically acclaimed blockbuster film of the same name, directed by King Vidor and starring Jennifer Jones and Gregory Peck.

"The story is about a lady stagecoach robber named Pearl Hart. She operated in Arizona," Busch explained. "She had slept out in the sagebrush with her lovers, held up stagecoaches. Such behavior bore little resemblance to the shy schoolteachers who had previously been a Western's notion of femininity." Busch wanted an independent, nonconformist woman like Pearl Hart as his protagonist. "She's my heroine," he said. "I changed her name to Pearl Chavez." But like most Hollywood adaptations of history, Busch's final story bore no resemblance to reality. Nonetheless, Pearl Hart—at least in her younger years—would have loved the fact that she inspired one of Hollywood's most popular films. And she would have been delighted that its overheated sex scenes gave the film its time-honored nickname, "Lust in the Dust."[1]

In the fall of 1950, Universal Pictures announced that it was producing a big-budget Technicolor film, *The Yuma Story*, based on the career of Pearl Hart. The heavily fictionalized plot had the stage-robbing Pearl entering Yuma prison, only to discover that the warden was her former lover. The motion picture was to be filmed on location at Yuma, with Shelley Winters starring as Pearl Hart. The screenwriters intended their script to be a prison-reform story, but once studio hacks got their hands on it, the screenplay devolved into a typical horse opera. As Hollywood columnist Hedda Hopper described the plot, "She's jailed, became a trusty, falls in love with the warden, is rebuffed, joins a gang, breaks jail, and in a fight with a posse led by the warden, is killed." A few months later Universal announced that Shelley Winters "is out of the picture." Newspapers reported, "The studio decided the part wasn't big enough for her." Universal then dropped the project, and *The Yuma Story* was never made.[2] Pearl Hart finally appeared on screen in 1960, when she was featured as a stage robber in an episode of the popular television series *Tales of Wells Fargo*. But like most Hollywood Westerns, the final product contained barely a particle of truth. Somewhat more accurate was a 1964 episode of *Death Valley Days*, which featured Anne Francis as Pearl Hart. This television program was largely responsible for spreading the widely believed myth that Pearl pulled the last stagecoach robbery of the Old West.

Western outlaws tend to attract fables and folklore, and few have had so many falsehoods written about them as Pearl Hart. Because the Davy family so successfully concealed Pearl's identity, that void was filled in by countless fictitious stories about her background. In 1899 a writer for the *New York Sun*, a very popular newspaper of the era, created one of the earliest myths about Pearl Hart. He rewrote her account in *Cosmopolitan* magazine and then added this gem: "At the age of sixteen she eloped from boarding school with a man named Hart." In 1927 this yarn reached an even-wider audience in Duncan Aikman's book, *Calamity Jane and the Lady Wildcats*. Based on such flimsy sources, subsequent writers invented a variety of names for Pearl's husband: Brett Hart, Frederick Hart, Frank Hart, and William Hart.[3]

Aikman's book was also responsible for spreading the fable that Pearl Hart's maiden name was Pearl Taylor. That story had its origins in news reports of the 1899 letter written from Toledo by Amy's husband, James Taylor, to the sheriff in Phoenix. When Arizona newspapers first published the letter, they correctly quoted Taylor as stating that he was Pearl Hart's brother-in-law. However, subsequent wire-service accounts paraphrased the letter and reported that Taylor was Pearl's brother. Based on that mistake, the author of a popular history of Arizona, published in 1916, concluded that her real name was Pearl Taylor. His erroneous conclusion was followed by Aikman and most other writers ever since.[4]

Just a week after Pearl was released from Yuma, the *Chicago Inter Ocean*, a widely read newspaper, published more fabricated background material. Its lengthy account claimed that her real name was Caroline Hartwell, the daughter of a respectable family in Toledo, Ohio. The writer claimed to have interviewed one of her high-school classmates, who said that Caroline had once been insulted by the school principal. She ostensibly slapped him and declared, "You insult me again and I'll brain you. I'm here to learn, not to be treated like a cur on the street." Eventually she eloped with Dick Baldwin, a railroad surveyor, and finally drifted into Arizona where she became Pearl Hart. The yarn seems to have been spun out of whole cloth by the *Inter Ocean* reporter, for there is no record of anyone named Caroline Hartwell living in Toledo at that time.[5]

Not to be outdone, three weeks later the *Detroit Free Press* concocted its own contribution to folklore: "Pearl Hart, as a mere girl, lived in Phoenix a few years ago. She was a slender, dark-eyed maiden, unassuming and quiet of demeanor and modest of speech. She did not distinguish herself from any of her school companions, and did not develop any of those traits which afterward made her famous, until she was about eighteen years of age. Then, it is said, she showed a surprising fondness for reading of the adventures of Dick Turpin, Jack Sheppard and other luminaries who have figured so extensively in criminal history as stage robbers. The modern imitators of these notorious criminals, especially Billy the Kid and other desperadoes with whose deeds Arizona has not yet ceased ringing, seemed to fire the imagination of the young girl, and she often expressed herself as admiring a bandit above all other men."[6]

As early as 1899, newspapers reported that Pearl was the West's first woman stage robber. That was not true. In 1874, teenaged Lizzie Keith, with her lover Fred Wilson, held up a stagecoach in the Coast Range south of Hollister, California. They were promptly captured, and Lizzie agreed to testify against Wilson. She was freed, and he was sent to San Quentin prison. Another persistent myth is that Pearl Hart committed the last stage robbery in America. That claim is wildly inaccurate. Pearl did not even pull the last stagecoach holdup in Arizona. The territory saw one in 1901, two the following year, one in 1903, and one more in 1906. Dozens of stage robberies took place in the American West after 1899. For example, horse-drawn coaches bringing tourists into the national parks of Yosemite and Yellowstone proved favorite targets of highwaymen. California robbers stood up stagecoaches to Yosemite on multiple occasions after 1900, the last in 1907. And Yellowstone stages were held up in 1908, 1914, and 1915; in one incident, bandits stopped and robbed fifteen coaches. The final holdup of a horse-drawn stagecoach in the West took place near Jarbidge, Nevada, in 1916.[7]

Pearl was the subject of many more outlandish tales: she came from a wealthy family in Canada; her father was a civil engineer; she worked in carnivals in Chicago; she was virtuous and made her living in Arizona as a cook; when her husband joined the US Army at the outbreak of the Spanish–American War, she told her friends that she "hoped the Spaniards would get him." One of the most persistent fables holds that Pearl, after serving her time in Yuma, toured with Buffalo Bill's Wild West show. That seems to be a relatively recent invention, dating from 1966 when an Arizona old-timer told a Phoenix newspaper that Pearl had returned to Yuma in 1908, "appearing with Buffalo Bill's Wild West show as a woman rough rider."[8]

Of all the bogus stories told about Pearl Hart, the most inane was that she returned to Globe, married a local miner named Calvin Bywater, and lived out her life as Pearl Bywater. This story was publicized in the 1960s by Clara Woody, a Globe resident and amateur historian. Mrs. Woody claimed that she had been a census taker in 1940 and had enumerated Pearl Bywater at her ranch in the Dripping Springs Mountains. She recalled, "Mrs. Bywater had grown stout and was dressed in well-worn jeans, as one might expect of a woman living on a working ranch, and the room was littered with cigar butts." When Mrs. Woody asked her where she was born, Mrs. Bywater replied, "I wasn't born anywhere." But Clara Woody's account was false, for she did not enumerate Pearl Bywater for the 1940 census. And the male census taker who did visit the ranch listed her husband, Calvin Bywater, as living in the household. Any cigar butts were undoubtedly his.[9]

Pearl Bywater was no criminal. She was born Pearl Kibbey in Arkansas in 1876 and at age sixteen married a cowboy in Arizona. They later divorced, and she then wed Calvin Bywater, a widower with a young son. In 1913 the Bywaters moved to the Dripping Springs Mountains. They were respectable citizens and raised a family at their remote ranch. Pearl Bywater had no connection whatsoever with Pearl Hart. Clara Woody seems to have based her speculation on the fact that both women were named Pearl, and the Bywaters lived not far from the scene of the stage robbery. Mrs. Woody claimed that she last saw Pearl Bywater "on the streets of Globe in 1957." That would have been a remarkable feat, given that Mrs. Bywater died in 1955. In the end, Clara Woody's conclusion was the worst sort of back-fence gossip. Nonetheless, almost every subsequent chronicler of Pearl Hart has repeated it as gospel.[10]

The phony tales about Pearl have become ubiquitous, repeated in hundreds of magazine articles, books, and web pages. As recently as 2016, *Time* magazine published an error-laden account of Pearl Hart. Its story, part of an "ongoing series on the unsung women of history," claimed that she "was born to an affluent family in Canada." Pearl left boarding school and then "associated with gamblers, pimps and drug dealers." She married in Canada and moved to Chicago where her husband "worked as a carnival barker." Pearl and Joe Boot robbed a stage in "Cage Springs Canyon" and then "were incarcerated in federal prison." Finally, upon her release, she joined Buffalo Bill's Wild West show.[11]

Despite the myths, Pearl Hart, unlike almost every notorious woman of the Old West, was a real frontier bandit. Ill-informed modern writers often feature a plethora of purported women Western desperadoes. The problem is that few of these so-called wild women were outlaws. Annie Oakley was a sharpshooter and performer, not a criminal. Calamity Jane (true name Martha Jane Canary) claimed to have been a US Army scout, but in fact she was a frontier prostitute and camp follower. Eleanor Dumont, better known as Madame Moustache, was a Western gambler, not a desperado. Many have claimed that Belle Starr (1848–1889) was a frontier robber, and she is known today as the Bandit Queen of Oklahoma. In fact, Belle Starr was primarily a consort of outlaws. Although she was once convicted of horse theft, she never robbed anyone.

There were a number of other women outlaws of the Old West, but few were bandits. Cattle Kate (Ellen Watson) was a homesteader in Wyoming; in 1889 vigilantes accused her of cattle theft and strung her up. She was one of a handful of women who were lynched on the frontier. In 1895 the teenagers Cattle Annie and Little Britches (Anna McDoulet and Jennie Midkiff) donned men's clothing, rode horseback, and associated with the notorious Bill Doolin gang in Oklahoma. Neither was a robber; both ended up behind bars for selling liquor to the American Indians. Rose Dunn, notorious as Rose of Cimarron, was also a consort of the Doolin gang and not a bandit. Much more obscure is Cora Hubbard. She was a real Western robber who, armed and dressed like a man, took part in a Missouri bank holdup in 1897. Cora was quickly captured and spent seven years in prison for that escapade. Though her story made newspaper headlines, she garnered far less attention than did Pearl Hart.

Pearl was unique in the history of the Wild West. No "wild woman" of that era had a life anything like hers nor a story that has been so long buried. So how did the author uncover her true history? I started by doing online newspaper and genealogical research. The first clue came from reading the Kansas City newspaper reports from 1903 and 1904 which showed that Pearl ran a cigar store and had been arrested for receiving stolen property under the name Lillie Keele. That seemed to show that her correct first name might have been Lillie. The newspapers also reported that a man named Henry Davy was arrested in Kansas City and he was the brother of Pearl. More online research showed that a woman named Pearl Hart had married one Earl Lighthawk in Kansas City in 1905. Digital newspaper searches for the name Earl Lighthawk revealed his connection with Millie Allen when she was shot in Omaha while rehearsing the play "The Arizona Female Bandit." Reports of the shooting revealed that Millie's maiden name was also Davy. Further research indicated that Millie Allen was Pearl's sister who wrote a play about her and visited her in Yuma prison. Finally, a check of the 1881 census for Lindsay, Canada, revealed only one Davy family, and among the children were Lillie, Catherine Amelia (the nickname for Millie), and Henry.

After months of reading hundreds of digitized newspapers and genealogical records, I concluded that Pearl Hart was actually Lillie Davy. I was feeling quite proud of myself when it occurred to me that the local library in Lindsay, Ontario, might have some information about the Davy family. I wrote to the library and was flabbergasted when I promptly received numerous genealogical documents showing that Pearl Hart's full name was Lillie Naomi Davy. The files also included background material and newspaper accounts about the Davy family in Canada. The dedicated librarians at the Kawartha Lakes Library had discovered Pearl Hart's identity several years earlier. I was chagrined when I realized how much time I could have saved by simply writing to the Lindsay library in the first place.

Once I had obtained all the names of the Davy family members, I conducted extensive, often mind-numbing, searches of digital historical newspapers and uncovered the life of the real Pearl Hart. This would not have been possible but for the wonders of the internet. Just twenty years ago—before the advent of online newspaper and genealogical websites—such a result would have been inconceivable. So in these pages appears for the first time the true and untold story of Pearl Hart, minus the falsehoods and folklore.

Her true story surpasses the wild imaginings of the fictional accounts, and Pearl would have liked that just fine.

★★★★★

Acknowledgments

Outlaws by their very nature are shadowy and secretive. They don't leave correspondence, diaries, and detailed records of their lives. Researching them is more than difficult. In the case of Pearl Hart, the efforts she and her family made to hide her identity made the job even harder.

This book could not have been written without the generous assistance of several people. First and foremost, I must acknowledge the help and cooperation of Renee Gallagher, great-grandniece of Lillie N. Davy, alias Pearl Hart. Renee is the daughter of Rovilla Dewey Hartmann, who in turn was the granddaughter of Amy Davy, younger sister of Pearl Hart. She generously provided me with family photos, documents, genealogical records, and recollections which helped greatly in fleshing out the story.

Jean Smith, an accomplished Arizona historian, researcher,

and writer, unselfishly shared with me her files and findings on Pearl Hart. I am fortunate to count Jean and her husband, Chuck, as longtime friends and colleagues. I could not have written this book without Jean's help.

This book is dedicated to my wife Marta S. Diaz, who has always been my biggest supporter and my best critic. She served almost forty years as a juvenile attorney and California juvenile-court judge. During that career she developed great insight into the lives of troubled youth, especially abused girls and young women. Her practical experiences and advice have helped me understand Pearl Hart and her siblings, and her suggestions and input have been indispensable contributions to this book.

A number of other people graciously assisted me. Especially helpful was Letitia J. Plate, great-granddaughter of either Amy Davy or Lillie Davy (Pearl Hart), who graciously provided valuable family information. The staff of the Kawartha Lakes Library in Lindsay, Ontario, provided me with copies of their research on the Davy family, which proved crucial to uncovering the real life of Pearl Hart. Sara Walker-Howe of the Olde Gaol Museum in Lindsay, Ontario, gave me jail-register information for Albert Davy. My friend Ron Woggon of Tucson generously visited the Arizona Historical Society to obtain information about Pearl Hart. Catheryne Popovitch of the Illinois State Archives and Donna Freymark of the Wheaton (IL) Public Library kindly tracked down obscure information about the Davy family. Thanks are also due to the helpful staffs of the Archives of Ontario in Toronto and the Arizona State Archives in Phoenix.

I would also like to express my gratitude to the members of the Wild West History Association for their fellowship and support. Its bimonthly journal and annual rendezvous are highly recommended. Anyone interested in the history of the Old West is encouraged to join this organization.

Last, to my agent, Claire Gerus, and my editor, Peter Joseph, go my heartfelt thanks for all their work on this book.

Notes

Introduction

1. John Boessenecker, *Gold Dust and Gunsmoke: Tales of Gold Rush Outlaws, Gunfighters, Lawmen, and Vigilantes*. New York: John Wiley & Sons (1999), p. 134.

2. John Boessenecker, *Ride the Devil's Herd: Wyatt Earp's Epic Battle Against the West's Biggest Outlaw Gang*. New York: Hanover Square Press (2020), pp. 53–54, 219–220.

Chapter 1

1. Lindsay (ON) *Canadian Post*, August 31, September 7, 21, 1877.

2. Andrew C. Isenberg, *Wyatt Earp: A Vigilante Life*. New York: Hill and Wang (2013), pp. 26–27.

3. Anglican Parish Records, Diocese of Ontario, Kingston, ON; J. R. McNeillie, "Town of Lindsay, Facts and Suggestions, 1912," at www.ontariogenealogy.com.

4. Michigan Divorce Records, Anna Davy v. Albert Davy, Monroe County, September 12, 1898, showing date of marriage August 29, 1864, on www.ancestry.com; California Death Index, Saphronia Ratan Newton, date of birth April 1, 1867; Certificate of death, William B. Davy, Joplin, MO, showing date of birth May 15, 1869.

5. Data from Lindsay jail register, Olde Gaol Museum, Lindsay, ON; Wesleyan Methodist Baptismal Registers, Catherine Amelia Davy, Lindsay Public Library. The Canadian and American newspapers, cited in the notes that follow, used numerous variations in spelling the first names of the sisters Saphronia, Lillie, and Katy, and they also spelled the surname both Davy and Davey. For ease of reading, and to avoid confusion, I have employed consistent spellings throughout the narrative. I have also corrected various misspellings and misidentifications in the newspaper quotes in this book.

6. Ontario Birth Registrations, Amy Nancy Davy, October 11, 1875, on www.rootsweb.com; California Death Index, Henry Esau Daney [Davy], showing date of birth March 4, 1877; Lindsay (ON) *Canadian Post*, August 31, 1877; *Lindsay Directory*. Brantford: William W. Evans (1877), p. 69.

7. Lindsay (ON) *Canadian Post*, August 31, September 7, 21, 1877; Whitby (ON) *Chronicle*, September 6, 1877; Wilmington (DE) *Morning Herald*, November 7, 1877.

8. Lindsay (ON) *Canadian Post*, September 21, 1877; Ted McCoy, *Hard Time: Reforming the Penitentiary in Nineteenth-Century Canada*. Edmonton: AU Press (2012), p. 47.

9. Death record, Anora Jane Davy Guilleaume, showing date of birth March 27, 1880, on www.familysearch.org; Lindsay (ON) *Canadian Post*, May 27, 1881.

10. Canada Census, 1881, Orillia, Ontario; Social Security Applications and Claims Index, Mary A. Davy, 1952, and Petition for Naturalization, Mary A. Davy, 1952, showing date of birth May 13, 1882, both on www.ancestry.com; Toronto (ON) *Daily Mail*, October 20, 1884; Kingston (ON) *Daily British Whig*, November 13, 1884.

11. Lindsay (ON) *Canadian Post*, May 18, 1888.

12. William B. Davy to Eleanor Sloan, May 26, 1954, Arizona Historical Society, Tucson.

13. Canada Census, 1881, Village of Campbellford, Northumberland, Ontario; Barrie (ON) *Northern Advance*, November 13, 1884.

14. Deposition of James Anderson, October 24, 1884, *Dominion of Canada v. William Keating, Narcisse Fauchier, Alexander Armour, and Philip Hearn*, Criminal Assize Clerk files, Archives of Ontario.

15. Depositions of James Anderson, October 4, 24, 1884; Depositions of Anna Davy, October 4, 24, 1884; Deposition of John McCoy, October 4, 1884; all in *Dominion of Canada v. William Keating, Narcisse Fauchier, Alexander Armour, and Philip Hearn*, Criminal Assize Clerk files, Archives of Ontario; Toronto (ON) *Daily Mail*, October 20, 1884; Orillia (ON) *Packet*, November 14, 1884.

16. Toronto (ON) *Daily Mail*, October 20, 1884; Kingston (ON) *Daily British Whig*, November 13, 1884; Orillia (ON) *Packet*, November 14, 1884.

17. New York (NY) *Times*, October 20, 1884; Kingston (ON) *Daily British Whig*, November 13, 1884; Barrie (ON) *Northern Advance*, November 13, 20, 1884; John Wilson Murray, *Memoirs of a Great Detective*. New York: Baker & Taylor Co. (1905), pp. 219–220. In Murray's account he calls Anna Davy *Mrs. Bennett* to protect her privacy.

18. Orillia (ON) *Packet*, November 14, 1884.

19. Ottawa (ON) *Journal*, January 18, 1887.

20. Chicago (IL) *Inter Ocean*, April 17, 1904.

21. Acle Davey family tree, showing date of birth January 10, 1885, on www.ancestry.com.

Chapter 2

1. *Rochester Directory*. Rochester: Drew, Allis & Co. (1886), p. 140.

2. Minneapolis (MN) *Star Tribune*, March 13, 1887; *Rochester Directory* (1886), p. 104.

3. Rochester (NY) *Democrat and Chronicle*, May 5, 6, August 15, 1886; Saint Paul (MN) *Daily Globe*, March 13, April 13, 1887.

4. Rochester (NY) *Democrat and Chronicle*, August 15, 1886.

5. Winnipeg (MB) *Manitoba Free Press*, March 26, 1887; Chicago (IL) *Daily News*, April 27, 1887.

6. Saint Paul (MN) *Daily Globe*, April 13, 1887; Washington (DC) *Evening Star*, April 15, 1887.

7. Rochester (NY) *Democrat and Chronicle*, August 15, 1886; St. Louis (MO) *Post-Dispatch*, April 12, 1887.

8. Chicago (IL) *Daily News*, April, 27, 1887.

9. Allan M. Brandt, *The Cigarette Century: The Rise, Fall, and Deadly Persistence of the Product That Defined America*. New York: Basic Books (2007), pp. 26–31; Cassandra Tate, *Cigarette Wars: The Triumph of "The Little White Slaver."* New York: Oxford University Press (1998), pp. 10–14.

10. Cleveland (OH), April 13, 1887; Brooklyn (NY) *Times Union*, April 9, 1887; Oil City (PA) *Derrick*, April 16, 1887.

11. Buffalo (NY) *Commercial*, August 27, 1886; Buffalo (NY) *Times*, August 28, 1886; Rochester (NY) *Democrat and Chronicle*, August 28, 1886; City of Rochester Municipal Archives Historic Marriage Records.

12. Rochester (NY) *Democrat and Chronicle*, February 15, 16, 1887; Springfield (IL) *State Register*, March 26, 1887.

13. Saint Paul (MN) *Daily Globe*, March 25, 1887; Chicago (IL) *Inter Ocean*, April 27, 1887, April 17, 1904; Salt Lake City (UT) *Tribune*, May 23, 1909.

14. Windom (MN) *Reporter*, March 17, 1887; Saint Paul (MN) *Daily Globe*, March 16, 25, 1887; New York (NY) *Herald*, March 16, 1887; Minneapolis (MN) *Star Tribune*, March 24, 1887; Chicago (IL) *Daily News*, April 27, 1887; Chicago (IL) *Inter Ocean*, April 27,

1887; Chicago (IL) *Times*, quoted in Wisconsin Rapids (WI) *Wood County Reporter*, May 19, 1887.

15. St. Louis (MO) *Post-Dispatch*, March 16, 1887; Cleveland (OH) *Plain Dealer*, March 17, 1887; Minneapolis (MN) *Star Tribune*, March 24, 1887; Decatur (IL) *Herald*, March 26, 1887; Springfield (IL) *State Register*, March 26, 1887.

16. Windom (MN) *Reporter*, March 24, 1887; Minneapolis (MN) *Star Tribune*, March 24, 1887; Saint Paul (MN) *Daily Globe*, March 25, 1887.

17. Saint Paul (MN) *Daily Globe*, March 25, April 13, 1887; Rochester (NY) *Democrat and Chronicle*, April 28, 1887.

18. New York (NY) *Times*, April 10, 1887; Rochester (NY) *Democrat and Chronicle*, April 10, 1887; Saint Paul (MN) *Daily Globe*, April 10, 1887; New York (NY) *World*, reprinted in St. Louis (MO) *Post-Dispatch*, April 12, 1887; Olean (NY) *Democrat*, April 14, 1887; Washington (DC) *Evening Star*, April 15, 1887.

19. New York (NY) *Herald*, April 14, 1887.

20. Saint Paul (MN) *Daily Globe*, April 13, 1887.

21. Saint Paul (MN) *Daily Globe*, April 13, 27, 1887; New York (NY) *Herald*, April 14, 1887; New York (NY) *Times*, April 14, 1887.

22. Chicago (IL) *Daily News*, April 27, 1887.

23. Saint Paul (MN) *Daily Globe*, March 25, 1887; Cleveland (OH) *Leader*, April 13, 1887; Chicago (IL) *Times*, quoted in Wisconsin Rapids (WI) *Wood County Reporter*, May 19, 1887; Chicago *Inter Ocean*, April 27, 1887.

24. Rochester (NY) *Democrat and Chronicle*, April 28, 1887; Chicago (IL) *Daily News*, April 28, 1887. The Erring Women's Refuge was located at 3111 South Indiana Avenue.

25. Chicago (IL) *Inter Ocean*, February 3, 1888; Chicago (IL) *Tribune*, December 15, 1889.

26. Chicago (IL) *Inter Ocean*, May 21, 23, 1887, April 17, 1904; Rochester (NY) *Democrat and Chronicle*, May 24, 1887.

27. Rochester (NY) *Democrat and Chronicle*, June 7, 1887.

Chapter 3

1. Rochester (NY) *Democrat and Chronicle*, June 7, 8, 1887.

2. Rochester (NY) *Democrat and Chronicle*, June 9, 1887; Kathleen Barry, *Susan B. Anthony: A Biography*. New York: New York University Press (1988), p. 271.

3. Rochester (NY) *Democrat and Chronicle*, June 9, 18, 1887.

4. Rochester (NY) *Democrat and Chronicle*, July 15, 16, 1887, March 31, 1893.

5. Monroe County Penitentiary register, 1887, Lillie Dean, on www.ancestry.com; Rochester (NY) *Democrat and Chronicle*, October 8, November 26, 1887.

6. Rochester (NY) *Democrat and Chronicle*, June 21, 1885, February 13, 1888.

7. Rochester (NY) *Democrat and Chronicle*, October 11, 1887.

8. Rochester (NY) *Democrat and Chronicle*, October 30, November 26, 1887.

9. Rochester (NY) *Democrat and Chronicle*, November 23, 24, 26, 27, 1887.

10. Rochester (NY) *Democrat and Chronicle*, January 9, 1888.

11. Rochester (NY) *Democrat and Chronicle*, February 19, March 2, 17, 20, May 9, 1888.

12. Rochester (NY) *Democrat and Chronicle*, April 25, 1888; Hamilton (ON) *Spectator*, quoted in the Lindsay (ON) *Canadian Post*, May 18, 1888.

13. Hamilton (ON) *Spectator*, quoted in the Lindsay (ON) *Canadian Post*, May 18, 1888. No record of Katy's marriage appears in the City of Rochester Municipal Archives Historic Marriage Records.

14. Montreal (QC) *Gazette*, May 8, 1888; Toronto (ON) *Daily Mail*, May 8, 1888; Hamilton (ON) *Spectator*, quoted in the Lindsay (ON) *Canadian Post*, May 18, 1888; Whitby (ON) *Chronicle*, May 25, 1888.

15. "An Arizona Episode," *Cosmopolitan*, vol. XXVII, no. 6 (October 1899), p. 673.

16. Bowmanville (ON) *Canadian Statesman*, December 19, 1888.

17. Rochester (NY) *Democrat and Chronicle*, August 1, 2, 1888; Oswego (NY) *Daily Palladium*, August 3, 1888.

18. Rochester (NY) *Democrat and Chronicle*, August 24, 1888, January 25, 1889.

19. Oswego (NY) *Daily Palladium*, March 15, 1889.

20. Rochester (NY) *Democrat and Chronicle*, October 28, 1888, June 18, 1889.

21. Bowmanville (ON) *Canadian Statesman*, December 19, 1888.

Chapter 4

1. Buffalo (NY) *Times*, May 14, 1890.

2. New York (NY) *Ledger*, January 26, 1867; also in Fanny Fern, *Folly as It Flies*. New York: G. W. Carleton & Co. (1868), p. 223. Fanny Fern was the pen name of Sara Willis Parton (1811–1872).

3. Quoted in Mark Goldman, *High Hopes: The Rise and Decline of Buffalo, New York*. Albany: State University of New York Press (1983), p. 166.

4. Buffalo (NY) *Morning Express*, November 28, 1894; Buffalo (NY) *Courier*, November 28, 1894; Buffalo (NY) *Evening News*, July 19, 1895, July 31, 1900.

5. Buffalo (NY) *Times*, May 14, 1890.

6. Buffalo (NY) *Times*, May 14, 1890. On Michigan Street brothels, see Buffalo (NY) *Times*, January 16, February 11, June 7, 1889; Buffalo (NY) *Weekly Express*, April 25, 1889; Buffalo (NY) *Morning Express*, February 18, 1890; Buffalo (NY) *Evening News*, January 30, 1891.

7. Buffalo (NY) *Courier*, May 8, 1890.

8. Buffalo (NY) *Morning Express*, March 24, 25, 1890; Buffalo (NY) *Evening News*, March 24, 1890; Buffalo (NY) *Commercial*, March 24, 1890; Buffalo (NY) *Courier*, March 24, 25, 1890.

9. Buffalo (NY) *Times*, May 14, 1890.

10. Buffalo (NY) *Courier*, May 8, 9, 1890; Buffalo (NY) *Times*, May 8, 14, 1890; Buffalo (NY) *Morning Express*, May 9, 1890; St. Lawrence (NY) *Herald*, June 27, 1890.

11. Los Angeles (CA) *Times*, June 11, 1899; "An Arizona Episode," *Cosmopolitan*, p. 673.

12. Daniel E. Bandman, Veterans Administration Master Index, on www.familysearch.org; US Census Population Schedules, Union, New Jersey, 1870; *Hand-book Almanac for the Pacific States*. San Francisco: H. H. Bancroft & Co. (1864), p. 157; *Papers Relating to the Foreign Relations of the United States*. Washington, DC: Government Printing Office (1880), pp. 1036–1037; New York (NY) *Real Estate Record and Builder's Guide*, August 13, 1870; San Francisco (CA) *Chronicle*, August 28, 1892, September 23, 1893.

13. New York, Passenger and Crew Lists, 1880, on www.ancestry.com; US Census Population Schedules, New York, NY, 1880; *Langley's San Francisco Directory*. San Francisco: Francis, Valentine & Co. (1891), p. 209.

14. Daniel E. Bandman to Commissioner of Immigration, October 3, 1905, Immigration and Naturalization Service, Record Group 85, National Archives, Washington, DC.

15. Los Angeles (CA) *Times*, June 11, 1899; Chicago (IL) *Inter Ocean*, April 17, 1904; "An Arizona Episode," p. 674.

16. Thomas P. Kelley, Jr, "The Incredible 'Doc' Kelley," *Canadian Weekly*, June 5, 1965, p. 4; Thomas P. Kelley, Jr, "My Dad Was King of the Medicine Men," *Macleans*, March 14, 1959, p. 45.

17. New York State Census, 1892, Rochester, Ward 2; *The Rochester Directory*. Rochester: Drew, Allis & Co. (1892), p. 658; Rochester (NY) *Democrat and Chronicle*, March 5, 21, April 2, 20, 26, 1892.

18. Rochester (NY) *Democrat and Chronicle*, October 25, 26, 1892; Case Files from State Institutions for Youth, Series 10706, New York State Archives, Albany, NY.

19. Rochester (NY) *Union and Advertiser*, July 27, 1893; Rochester (NY) *Democrat and Chronicle*, March 7, July 28, 1893.

20. Rochester (NY) *Democrat and Chronicle*, April 12, May 31, 1893; Buffalo (NY) *Enquirer*, May 31, 1893; Buffalo (NY) *Evening News*, April 1, 1893.

21. San Antonio (TX) *Daily Light*, July 28, 1898.

22. Council Bluffs (IA) *Daily Nonpareil*, August 26, 1901; *Rochester Directory*. Rochester: Drew, Allis & Co. (1893), p. 171.

23. Cincinnati (OH) *Gazette*, November 24, 1881.

24. Cincinnati (OH) *Enquirer*, June 21, 22, July 25, 1894; Cincinnati (OH) *Post*, July 25, 1894; Cincinnati (OH) *Commercial Gazette*, June 21, July 25, 1894.

25. Cincinnati (OH) *Enquirer*, August 1, 2, 3, 1894; Cincinnati (OH) *Commercial Gazette*, August 1, 2, 3, 1894.

Chapter 5

1. Philadelphia (PA) *Inquirer*, July 7, 1901; "An Arizona Episode," p. 674; Jan MacKell, *Brothels, Bordellos, and Bad Girls: Prostitution in Colorado, 1860–1930*. Albuquerque: University of New Mexico Press (2004), pp. 112–113.

2. "An Arizona Episode," p. 674.

3. Boessenecker, *Ride the Devil's Herd*, pp. 108–109; Clare V. McKanna, *Homicide, Race, and Justice in the American West*. Tucson: University of Arizona Press (1997), pp. 41–42.

4. Phoenix (AZ) *Weekly Republican*, June 4, 25, 1879, August 4, 1882; Tucson (AZ) *Daily Star*, August 3, 1882.

5. "An Arizona Episode," p. 674; Phoenix (AZ) *Republican*, October 25, 1893.

6. Phoenix (AZ) *Republican*, June 23, 1894; Phoenix (AZ) *Weekly Herald*, June 8, 1899.

7. Daniel E. Bandman, Great Register of Maricopa County, May 16, 1894, on www.ancestry.com; "An Arizona Episode," p. 674.

8. Phoenix (AZ) *Weekly Herald*, June 8, 1899; Los Angeles (CA) *Times*, June 11, 1899.

9. Los Angeles (CA) *Times*, June 11, 1899.

10. Phoenix (AZ) *Republican*, August 11, 1894; Phoenix (AZ) *Weekly Herald*, June 8, 1899; "An Arizona Episode," p. 674.

11. Phoenix (AZ) *Republican*, August 21, 1894.

12. Marriage record of James Taylor and Amy Davy, Toledo, OH, December 16, 1895, on www.familysearch.org; *Toledo City Directory*. Toledo: Toledo Directory Co. (1896), p. 387; "An Arizona Episode," p. 674.

13. Census Population Schedules, Toledo, Ohio, 1900; World War I Draft Registration Cards, John Andrew Dewey, on www.ancestry.com; Chicago (IL) *Inter Ocean*, April 17, 1904; "An Arizona Episode," p. 674; Renee Gallagher to author, September 20, 2020.

14. US Census Population Schedules, 1910, Islip, New York, household of Saphronia Newton; San Antonio (TX) *Daily Light*, August 8, 1898; Tampa (FL) *Tribune*, August 5, 1913.

15. San Antonio (TX) *Daily Light*, July 28, 1898.

16. Ava (MO) *Douglas County Herald*, November 5, 1896; Austin (TX) *Daily Statesman*, July 23, 1897.

17. Austin (TX) *Daily Statesman*, July 24, 25, 26, 1897.

18. Austin (TX) *Daily Statesman*, August 1, 2, 1897; Shiner (TX) *Gazette*, August 4, 1897.

19. Austin (TX) *Daily Statesman*, August 7, 8, 9, 1897.

20. Austin (TX) *Daily Statesman*, August 15, 16, 19, 23, 1897; Tampa (FL) *Tribune*, August 5, 1913, March 30, 1915; Tampa (FL) *Times*, March 29, 1915.

21. Oklahoma City (OK) *Daily Oklahoman*, December 16, 1897; Oklahoma City (OK) *Champion*, December 17, 1897; Cincinnati (OH) *Enquirer*, July 28, 1898.

22. Stillwater (OK) *Gazette*, December 9, 1897, January 20, 1898; Stillwater (OK) *Daily Oklahoma State*, March 15, 1898; Oklahoma City (OK) *Daily Oklahoman*, December 21, February 2, 1897.

23. Stillwater (OK) *Daily Oklahoma State*, March 15, 16, 1898.

24. Stillwater (OK) *Daily Oklahoma State*, March 17, April 26, 1898; Stillwater (OK) *Gazette*, April 28, 1898.

25. Marriage record of H. W. Allen and C. A. Davy, May 19, 1898, on www.familysearch.org; Stillwater (OK) *Gazette*, July 28, 1898; San Antonio (TX) *Daily Light*, July 28, 1898.

26. San Antonio (TX) *Express*, July 25, 1898; Stillwater (OK) *Gazette*, July 28, 1898; St. Louis (MO) *Republic*, July 27, 1898; San Antonio (TX) *Daily Light*, July 24, 25, 1898.

27. San Antonio (TX) *Daily Light*, July 28, 1898.

28. San Antonio (TX) *Daily Light*, August 3, 6, 7, 8, 1898.

29. Kansas State Prison Register, Howard Allen, inmate no. 463, Kansas State Archives; Stillwater (OK) *Gazette*, August 18, November 3, 1898; Lansing (KS) *News*, November 4, 1898.

30. San Antonio (TX) *Daily Light*, September 11, 12, November 6, 1898.

31. Great Register of Yavapai County, Voter Registrations, Jerome, AZ, October 7, 1896, p. 143, on www.ancestry.com; Tucson (AZ) *Daily Star*, October 31, 1897; Tucson (AZ) *Citizen*, October 21, 1899; "An Arizona Episode," p. 674.

32. Phoenix (AZ) *Republican*, May 23, 1896; Phoenix (AZ) *Weekly Herald*, June 8, 1899; "An Arizona Episode," p. 674.

33. Phoenix (AZ) *Republican*, June 11, July 1, 18, 20, December 9, 1898; Phoenix (AZ) *Weekly Republican*, September 22, 1898; US Veterans Administration Master Index, Daniel E. Bandman, on www.familysearch.org.

34. Phoenix (AZ) *Republican*, October 15, 1898.

35. Phoenix (AZ) *Republican*, November 24, 26, December 9, 1898; *Revised Statutes of Arizona* (1887), sections 508, 509, 510.

Chapter 6

1. "An Arizona Episode," p. 674; Florence (AZ) *Tribune*, June 10, 1899; Bernard W. Muffley, "The History of the Lower San Pedro Valley in Arizona," master's thesis (1938), University of Arizona Library, Tucson, AZ, pp. 35–36.

2. St. Johns (AZ) *Herald*, May 24, 1894; Tucson (AZ) *Daily Star*, October 1, 1936, January 5, 1953; Muffley, "The History of the Lower San Pedro Valley," pp. 36, 45, 50–51, 63–65.

3. Salt Lake City (UT) *Tribune*, May 23, 1909.

4. Yuma Prison Register, Joe Boot, inmate no. 1558; Salt Lake (UT) *Tribune*, May 23, 1909; Los Angeles (CA) *Times*, June 5, 1899; Phoenix (AZ) *Republican*, June 6, 1899.

5. Eugene W. Childs, "Pearl Hart Story," unpublished manuscript, Arizona Historical Society, Tucson, AZ.

6. Salt Lake (UT) *Tribune*, May 23, 1909; "An Arizona Episode," p. 674.

7. Salt Lake (UT) *Tribune*, May 23, 1909.

8. US Veterans Administration records, Daniel E Bandman, on www.familysearch.org; Phoenix (AZ) *Republican*, February 25, 1899; Globe (AZ) *Silver Belt*, June 8, 1899; "An Arizona Episode," p. 674.

9. Phoenix (AZ) *Republican*, November 25, 1899; "An Arizona Episode," pp. 674–675.

10. San Francisco (CA) *Chronicle*, June 5, 1899.

11. John Boessenecker, *When Law Was in the Holster: The Frontier Life of Bob Paul*. Norman: University of Oklahoma Press (2012), pp. 128, 160, 238–255.

12. St. Louis (MO) *Post-Dispatch*, December 13, 1903; "An Arizona Episode," p. 675.

13. Salt Lake City (UT) *Tribune*, May 23, 1909.

14. St. Louis (MO) *Post-Dispatch*, December 13, 1903.

15. Phoenix (AZ) *Republican*, February 15, 1902; John Boessenecker, *Shotguns and Stagecoaches: The Brave Men Who Rode for Wells Fargo in the Wild West*. New York: Thomas Dunne Books (2018), pp. xiv–xix.

16. Florence (AZ) *Tribune*, May 27, 1899; Phoenix (AZ) *Republican*, May 31, 1899; San Francisco (CA) *Examiner*, June 11, 1899; Kansas City (MO) *Journal*, June 18, 1899.

17. "An Arizona Episode," p. 675.

18. St. Louis (MO) *Post-Dispatch*, December 13, 1903.

19. Salt Lake City (UT) *Tribune*, May 23, 1909.

20. *Territory of Arizona v. Joe Boot and Pearl Hart*, Indictment for Robbery, November 7, 1889, case no. 207, District Court, County of Pinal, Arizona State Library Archives, Phoenix, AZ; Phoenix

(AZ) *Republican*, May 31, June 8, 1899; Globe (AZ) *Silver Belt*, June 1, 1899; Florence (AZ) *Tribune*, June 3, 1899; Los Angeles (CA) *Times*, June 11, 1899. Harry "Hank" Barton later served twenty years as a constable and deputy sheriff. Phoenix (AZ) *Republican*, March 20, 1940.

21. Los Angeles (CA) *Times*, June 11, 1899.

Chapter 7

1. "An Arizona Episode," p. 676.

2. Salt Lake City (UT) *Tribune*, May 23, 1909.

3. "An Arizona Episode," p. 676.

4. *Territory of Arizona v. Joe Boot and Pearl Hart*, Criminal Complaint, May 30, 1899, Arizona State Archives; Phoenix (AZ) *Republican*, June 8, 1899.

5. Florence (AZ) *Tribune*, June 3, 1899; Phoenix (AZ) *Republican*, December 3, 1928; Boessenecker, *When Law Was in the Holster*, pp. 32, 34, 114, 384–385; R. Michael Wilson, *Encyclopedia of Stagecoach Robbery in Arizona*. Las Vegas: RaMa Press (2003), pp. 147–150.

6. Los Angeles (CA) *Times*, June 11, 1899; San Francisco (CA) *Examiner*, June 11, 1899.

7. "An Arizona Episode," p. 676.

8. St. Louis (MO) *Post-Dispatch*, December 13, 1903.

9. Florence (AZ) *Tribune*, June 10, 1899.

10. Florence (AZ) *Tribune*, June 10, 1899; St. Louis (MO) *Post-Dispatch*, December 13, 1903.

11. "An Arizona Episode," pp. 676–677.

12. St. Louis (MO) *Post-Dispatch*, December 13, 1903.

13. Tucson (AZ) *Daily Citizen*, June 18, 1891; Phoenix (AZ) *Republi-*

can, September 7, 1893; Tucson (AZ) *Daily Star*, July 22, 1936; US Census Population Schedules, Benson, Arizona, 1900.

14. Phoenix (AZ) *Republican*, June 5, 1899; Los Angeles (CA) *Times*, June 11, 1899.

15. St. Louis (MO) *Post-Dispatch*, December 13, 1903; "An Arizona Episode," p. 677.

16. Florence (AZ) *Tribune*, June 10, 1899; Los Angeles (CA) *Times*, June 11, 1899.

17. Phoenix (AZ) *Republican*, June 5, 1899; "An Arizona Episode," p. 677.

18. Los Angeles (CA) *Times*, June 5, 1899; Arizola (AZ) *Oasis*, June 10, 1899. The 1891 Pinal County courthouse is still standing and has been fully restored.

19. Tucson (AZ) *Weekly Star*, June 1, 1899; St. Louis (MO) *Post-Dispatch*, June 5, 1899; Ottawa (ON) *Journal*, June 5, 1899; Phoenix (AZ) *Republican*, June 6, 1899; Washington (DC) *Evening Times*, June 13, 1899; Buffalo (NY) *Evening News*, June 20, 1899.

20. San Francisco (CA) *Chronicle*, June 5, 1899; Phoenix (AZ) *Republican*, June 6, 1899; Florence (AZ) *Tribune*, June 10, 1899.

21. Los Angeles (CA) *Times*, June, 11, 1899; Florence (AZ) *Tribune*, June 10, 1899; San Francisco (CA) *Examiner*, June 11, 1899; Phoenix (AZ) *Weekly Herald*, June 8, 1899.

22. Los Angeles (CA) *Times*, 5, June 11, 1899; Tucson (AZ) *Daily Citizen*, June 6, 1899; San Francisco (CA) *Examiner*, June 11, 1899.

23. Los Angeles (CA) *Times*, June 11, 1899.

24. Los Angeles (CA) *Times*, June 11, 1899; Washington (DC) *Evening Times*, June 13, 1899.

25. Los Angeles (CA) *Times*, June 11, 24, 1899.

26. Phoenix (AZ) *Republican*, June 13, 1899.

27. *Territory of Arizona v. Joe Boot and Pearl Hart*, order, June 16, 1899; Phoenix (AZ) *Republican*, June 13, 1899; Los Angeles (CA) *Times*, June 24, 1899; Tucson (AZ) *Daily Star*, June 27, 1899.

28. "An Arizona Episode," p. 677.

Chapter 8

1. On the life of Bob Paul, see Boessenecker, *When Law Was in the Holster.*

2. Tucson (AZ) *Citizen*, June 20, 1899; Florence (AZ) *Tribune*, June 24, 1899.

3. Tucson (AZ) *Citizen*, June 21, 23, July 15, October 12, 1899; Tucson (AZ) *Star*, September 14, 1899; Los Angeles (CA) *Times*, July 12, 1899.

4. Tucson (AZ) *Citizen*, September 28, October 2, 1899; Phoenix (AZ) *Republican*, September 30, 1899; Chicago (IL) *Inter Ocean*, April 17, 1904.

5. Tucson (AZ) *Star*, July 21, 1899; Phoenix (AZ) *Republican*, October 17, 1899.

6. Tombstone (AZ) *Prospector*, October 17, 1899; Boessenecker, *When Law Was in the Holster*, pp. 132–133, 393–394, 423n5.

7. Tucson (AZ) *Citizen*, August 5, 1899; Chicago (IL) *Inter Ocean*, April 17, 1904.

8. Tucson (AZ) *Citizen*, September 28, 1899; Denver (CO) *Post*, October 15, 1899; Tucson (AZ) *Daily Star*, May 19, 1904.

9. Phoenix (AZ) *Republican*, January 5, 6, June 6, 8, 9, 23, August 22, 1899; Tucson (AZ) *Daily Star*, January 6, October 13, 1899; Tucson (AZ) *Citizen*, October 12, 1899.

10. Chicago (IL) *Inter Ocean*, April 17, 1904.

11. Tucson (AZ) *Daily Citizen*, October 12, 21, 1899; Tucson (AZ)

Daily Star, October 13, 1899; Tombstone (AZ) *Prospector*, October 13, 1899; San Francisco (CA) *Chronicle*, October 13, 1899.

12. Tucson (AZ) *Citizen*, October 21, 1899.

13. Phoenix (AZ) *Republican*, October 13, 14, 17, 19, 1899; Tucson (AZ) *Daily Star*, October 21, 1899; Nogales (AZ) *Border Vidette*, October 14, 1899; San Francisco (CA) *Examiner*, October 13, 1899; New York (NY) *Sun*, October 15, 1899.

14. Tucson (AZ) *Daily Star*, October 13, 1899.

15. Phoenix (AZ) *Republican*, October 14, 1899.

16. Tucson (AZ) *Daily Star*, October 21, 22, 1899; Tucson (AZ) *Citizen*, October 21, 1899.

17. Fort Worth (TX) *Daily Gazette*, October 20, 1887; Robert K. DeArment, *George Scarborough: The Life and Death of a Lawman on the Closing Frontier*. Norman: University of Oklahoma Press (1992), pp. 36–38.

18. DeArment, *George Scarborough*, pp. 103–112, 144–150.

19. DeArment, *George Scarborough*, pp. 57–59, 151–153; Boessenecker, *Shotguns and Stagecoaches*, pp. 274–282.

20. Deming (NM) *Headlight*, October 21, 28, 1899; Tucson (AZ) *Citizen*, October 21, 1899; San Francisco (CA) *Examiner*, October 21, 1899.

21. San Francisco (CA) *Chronicle*, October 21, 1899; Lordsburg (NM) *Western Liberal*, October 27, 1899.

22. Tucson (AZ) *Daily Star*, May 19, 1904.

Chapter 9

1. Los Angeles (CA) *Times*, October 24, 1899; Tucson (AZ) *Citizen*, May 19, 1904.

2. Tucson (AZ) *Citizen*, October 21, 1899.

3. Los Angeles (CA) *Times*, October 24, 1899; Deming (NM) *Headlight*, October 28, 1899.

4. *Territory of Arizona v. Joe Boot and Pearl Hart*, Indictment, November 7, 1899; Los Angeles (CA) *Times*, October 24, 1899; Tucson (AZ) *Daily Star*, November 7, 8, 1899.

5. Nashville (TN) *Tennessean*, November 13, 1899.

6. Florence (AZ) *Tribune*, November 18, 1899; Los Angeles (CA) *Times*, November 16, 1899; Marshalltown (IA) *Evening Times-Republican*, November 18, 1899; Phoenix (AZ) *Republican*, September 23, 1956.

7. Los Angeles (CA) *Times*, November 16, 1899; Florence (AZ) *Tribune*, November 18, 1899; Phoenix (AZ) *Republican*, November 20, 1949.

8. *Territory of Arizona v. Joe Boot and Pearl Hart*, court minutes, November 14, 15, 17, 1899; Florence (AZ) *Tribune*, November 18, 1899.

9. Yuma Prison Register, Pearl Hart, inmate no. 1559; Yuma (AZ) *Sentinel*, November 18, 1899; Tucson (AZ) *Daily Star*, November 24, 1899; Don G. Malone, "History of the Arizona Territorial Prison," master's thesis (1969), Texas Tech University, Lubbock, TX, p. 72.

10. San Antonio (TX) *Daily Light*, July 28, 1898; St. Joseph (MO) *Gazette-Herald*, August 5, 1901; Kansas City (MO) *Times*, August 6, 1901.

11. San Antonio (TX) *Daily Light*, July 28, 1898; Houston (TX) *Post*, April 23, 24, 1899; Kansas City (MO) *Star*, September 21, 1899; Kansas City (MO) *Journal*, September 21, 1899; Kansas City (MO) *Times*, September 21, 1899; St. Joseph (MO) *News-Press*, August 5, 1901.

12. Phoenix (AZ) *Republican*, November 25, 1899.

13. St. Louis (MO) *Republic*, August 5, 1901; St. Joseph (MO) *Gazette-Herald*, August 5, 1901; Kansas City (MO) *Times*, August 6, 1901;

Omaha (NE) *Daily Bee*, August 25, 1901; Ellis (KS) *Review-Headlight*, November 11, 1910; US Census Population Schedules, Blue Township, Jackson County, MO, 1900; Michigan Divorce Records, Anna Davy v. Albert Davy, Monroe County, September 12, 1898, on www.ancestry.com.

14. Kansas City (MO) *Star*, September 21, 1899, August 18, 1900; St. Louis (MO) *Post-Dispatch*, August 11, 1900; Sedalia (MO) *Evening Democrat*, August 13, 1900; St. Louis (MO) *Republic*, August 19, 1900.

15. St. Louis (MO) *Republic*, August 19, 1900.

16. Sedalia (MO) *Evening Sentinel*, November 13, 1900; St. Joseph (MO) *Gazette-Herald*, August 5, 1901; Omaha (NE) *World-Herald*, August 5, 1901; Missouri State Penitentiary Database, H. W. Allen, inmate no. 3640, Missouri State Archives.

17. Kansas City (MO) *Times*, August 6, 1901.

18. On Thad Brookings see Cedar Rapids (IA) *Gazette*, April 29, 1892; Des Moines (IA) *Register*, August 19, 1896; Council Bluffs (IA) *Daily Nonpareil*, March 26, 1897; Des Moines (IA) *Leader*, October 18, 1901.

19. On Burt Adams see Omaha (NE) *Daily Bee*, October 3, 1896, January 1, February 5, 1897, October 31, November 26, 1898, May 27, 1903; US Census Population Schedules, Omaha, NE, 1900.

20. Omaha (NE) *World-Herald*, August 5, 1901; St. Joseph (MO) *Gazette-Herald*, August 5, 1901.

21. Omaha (NE) *Daily Bee*, August 5, 1901.

22. St. Joseph (MO) *Gazette-Herald*, August 5, 1901; Omaha (NE) *World-Herald*, August 5, 1901.

23. Omaha (NE) *Daily Bee*, August 5, 1901; Omaha (NE) *World-Herald*, August 5, 1901.

24. Omaha (NE) *Daily Bee*, August 5, 1901; Omaha (NE) *World-Herald*, August 5, 1901; St. Joseph (MO) *Gazette-Herald*, August 5, 1901.

25. Omaha (NE) *Daily Bee*, August 5, 1901; Omaha (NE) *World-Herald*, August 5, 6, 1901; New York (NY) *Times*, August 5, 1901. An account of Katy's shooting appears in Michelle Morgan, *The Battered Body Beneath the Flagstones, and Other Victorian Scandals*. London: Little, Brown (2018). The author confuses Katy Davy, a.k.a. Millie Allen, with a popular actress of the era, Minnie Allen. They were two different women; at the same time Katy was shot in Omaha, Minnie Allen was performing in Washington, DC. See Washington (DC) *Times*, August 4, 1901.

26. Omaha (NE) *World-Herald*, August 6, 8, 1901; Omaha (NE) *Daily Bee*, August 7, 8, 9, 1901; Lincoln (NE) *Nebraska State Journal*, August 7, 1901; Kansas City (MO) *Times*, August 6, 1901.

27. Omaha (NE) *World-Herald*, August 6, 1901.

28. Omaha (NE) *Daily Bee*, August 25, 1901.

29. Omaha (NE) *World-Herald*, August 30, 1901.

Chapter 10

1. Phoenix (AZ) *Republican*, November 16, 1901.

2. San Francisco (CA) *Chronicle*, June 14, 1896; Los Angeles (CA) *Times*, February 1, 1901; Paul G. Hubbard, "Life in the Arizona Territorial Prison, 1876–1910," *Arizona and the West*, vol. 1, no. 4 (Winter, 1959), p. 324.

3. Tucson (AZ) *Daily Star*, November 26, 1899, June 2, 1900; Tucson (AZ) *Citizen*, November 27, 1899; Los Angeles (CA) *Times*, February 4, 1900.

4. Phoenix (AZ) *Arizona Graphic*, January 27, 1900.

5. Phoenix (AZ) *Arizona Graphic*, January 27, 1900.

6. Tucson (AZ) *Daily Star*, October 4, 1900; Boessenecker, *When Law Was in the Holster*, pp. 401–404.

7. Tombstone (AZ) *Weekly Epitaph*, December 3, 1899.

8. Yuma (AZ) *Sentinel*, July 27, 1872; Malone, "History of the Arizona Territorial Prison," p. 81.

9. Los Angeles (CA) *Herald*, August 23, 1891; Malone, "History of the Arizona Territorial Prison," p. 95; John Boessenecker, *Bandido: The Life and Times of Tiburcio Vasquez*. Norman: University of Oklahoma Press (2010), pp. 311–315.

10. Yuma (AZ) *Sentinel*, March 21, 1900.

11. Tucson (AZ) *Daily Star*, June 2, 1900; Yuma (AZ) *Weekly Sun*, July 31, 1903; Hubbard, "Life in the Arizona Territorial Prison, 1876–1910," pp. 328–330.

12. DeArment, *George Scarborough*, pp. 222–229; Jeff Burton, *The Deadliest Outlaws: The Ketchum Gang and the Wild Bunch*. Denton: University of North Texas Press (2009), pp. 256–270.

13. Tucson (AZ) *Daily Star*, November 13, 1949; Tucson (AZ) *Daily Citizen*, April 13, 1956; Michael Howard, *Billy Stiles: Chasing the Wind*. Tucson: Santa Cruz Valley Press (2009), pp. 97–99.

14. Los Angeles (CA) *Times*, March 2, 1930.

15. Yuma Prison Register, Elena Estrada, inmate no. 1137; Phoenix (AZ) *Republican*, November 2, 1890, July 11, 1900; Tucson (AZ) *Citizen*, July 6, 1900; Tucson (AZ) *Star*, July 7, 12, October 4, 1900.

16. Yuma (AZ) *Sentinel*, December 5, 1900.

17. Yuma (AZ) *Sun*, reprinted in Florence (AZ) *Tribune*, February 16, 1901; San Francisco (CA) *Chronicle*, February 13, 1901; Grass Valley (CA) *Union*, February 14, 1901.

18. William Brent and Milarde Brent, *The Hell Hole: The Yuma Prison Story*. Yuma: Hell Hole Publishing (1962), pp. 52–54.

19. Yuma Prison Register, Alfreda Mercer, inmate no. 1816, and Rosa Duran, inmate no. 1818; Phoenix (AZ) *Republican*, November 11, 1900, December 5, 22, 1900, November 15, 17, 1901; Prescott (AZ) *Weekly Journal-Miner*, November 13, 1901. The Yuma Prison Register gives Fred Crosley's age as eighteen. In 1926 he entered Folsom

prison in California; its register shows his date of birth as January 16, 1887, which would make him thirteen in 1900.

20. Phoenix (AZ) *Republican*, May 24, November 15, 16, 1901; Yuma Prison Register, Alfrida [sic] Mercer, inmate no. 1816.

21. Yuma Prison Register, Alfreda Mercer, inmate no. 1816, and Rosa Duran, inmate no. 1818; Yuma (AZ) *Sentinel*, December 17, 1902.

22. Tucson (AZ) *Citizen*, May 13, 1902; Yuma (AZ) *Sun*, quoted in Tombstone (AZ) *Weekly Epitaph*, May 25, 1902.

23. Safford (AZ) *Graham Guardian*, March 21, October 31, 1902; Clifton (AZ) *Copper Era and Morenci Leader*, February 27, 1902, October 26, November 9, 1905; Phoenix (AZ) *Republican*, June 22, 1903, October 8, 1905; *Trimble v. Territory* (1903), *Pacific Reporter*, vol. 75, pp. 932–935.

24. *Report of the Governor of Arizona to the Secretary of the Interior.* Washington, DC: Government Printing Office (1902), p. 33.

25. Tucson (AZ) *Daily Star*, November 13, 1949; Tucson (AZ) *Daily Citizen*, April 13, 1955.

26. Phoenix (AZ) *Republican*, October 8, 1967.

27. Donna Crail-Rugotzke, "The Treatment of Minorities and Women by Southwestern Courts and Prisons," PhD dissertation, University of Nevada, Las Vegas (2008), p. 38; *Report of the Governor of Arizona to the Secretary of the Interior.* Washington, DC: Government Printing Office (1902), p. 33.

28. Phoenix (AZ) *Republican*, December 14, 1902; Tucson (AZ) *Citizen*, December 15, 1902; Yuma (AZ) *Sun*, December 19, 1902.

Chapter 11

1. Yuma (AZ) *Sentinel*, December 17, 1902.

2. El Paso (TX) *Times*, December 17, 1902; El Paso (TX) *Herald*, December 17, 1902.

3. Oakland (CA) *Tribune*, December 2, 1928.

4. Albuquerque (NM) *Journal*, December 19, 1902.

5. Kansas City (MO) *Star*, November 29, 1903; Independence (KS) *Daily Reporter*, May 14, 1904.

6. Kansas Marriages, 1840–1935, on www.familysearch.org; Kansas City (MO) *Star*, November 29, 1903; Topeka (KS) *State Journal*, May 14, 1904; Independence (KS) *Daily Reporter*, May 14, 1904.

7. Lindsay (ON) *Watchman Warder*, September 21, 1899, July 4, 1901, October 15, 1903; Lindsay (ON) *Weekly Post*, October 9, 1903; Fenelon Falls (ON) *Gazette*, October 9, 1903.

8. Kansas City (KS) *Times*, January 14, 1904; Leavenworth (KS) *Times*, January 20, 1904; Kansas City (KS) *Republic*, January 21, 1904; Independence (KS) *Daily Reporter*, May 14, 1904; Kansas City (KS) *Star*, March 13, 1905.

9. Kansas City (MO) *Times*, March 18, 1904.

10. Kansas City (KS) *Star*, April 6, 1904.

11. Chicago (IL) *Inter Ocean*, April 17, 1904.

12. Kansas City (KS) *Star*, May 13, 1904; Kansas City (MO) *Times*, May 13, 1904; Topeka (KS) *State Journal*, May 14, 1904.

13. Independence (KS) *Daily Reporter*, May 14, 1904; Tucson (AZ) *Daily Star*, May 19, 1904.

14. Kansas City (MO) *Star* May 14, 16, 17, 1904; Kansas City (MO) *Times*, May 14, 1904.

15. Kansas City (MO) *Star*, June 22, 1904; Kansas City (MO) *Times*, June 23, 1904; Yuma (AZ) *Examiner*, May 5, 1910. On Augustus C. Durham (1872–1933), see Lumberton (NC) *Robesonian*, January 26, 1933.

16. Registers of Enlistments in the US Army, Elihu Keele, October 6, 1904, on www.familysearch.org.

17. Jackson County, Missouri, marriage records, October 27, 1904, on www.ancestry.com.

18. Kansas City (KS) *Star*, June 22, 1904, March 13, 1905; Paola (KS) *Miami Republican*, May 5, 1905; *Dramatic Compositions Copyrighted in the United States, 1870 to 1916, Volume 1*. Washington, DC: Government Printing Office (1918), p. 1290.

19. US Census Population Schedules, Manhattan, NY, 1900; Quincy (IL) *Daily Journal*, May 30, 1905.

20. Quincy (IL) *Daily Journal*, May 30, 1905; Marshalltown (IA) *Evening Times-Republican*, May 31, 1905; Catholic Church baptismal records, McGregor, Ontario, Canada, October 2, 1910, on www.ancestry.com; California Death Index, Mildred Saphronia Meyers Gilbert.

21. Joliet Prison Register, Noah Louis Waelchli, inmate no. 1237, Catherine Waelchli, inmate no. 1347, Illinois State Archives; Crystal Lake (IL) *Herald*, July 5, 1906; Joliet (IL) *News*, January 7, 11, 1907; Angola (IN) *Steuben Republican*, February 20, 1907; New York (NY) *Clipper*, November 23, 1907; *Dramatic Compositions Copyrighted in the United States, 1870 to 1916, Volume 1*, pp. 88, 1166.

22. Leavenworth (KS) *Times*, June 25, 1905; Streator (IL) *Times*, May 2, 1908; Marriage record of Holley A. Dewey, June 24, 1905, on www.familysearch.org; US Census Population Schedules, Jackson County, Missouri, 1910, and Joliet, Illinois, 1910; Marriage record of William B. Davy, Toronto, Ontario, Canada, February 25, 1891, on www.familysearch.org.

23. Grand Rapids (MI) *Press*, November 11, 1904; Marshall (MI) *Daily Chronicle*, November 12, 1904; Adrian (MI) *Daily Telegram*, January 17, 1913.

24. Prisoner Index Card, Henry Davy, inmate no. 8155, Michigan State Archives; Bay City (MI) *Times*, February 8, 1905; Marshall (MI) *Expounder*, November 10, 1905; Grand Rapids (MI) *Press*, November 1, 29, 1905; Detroit (MI) *Free Press*, October 11, 1907; Detroit (MI) *Times*, March 31, 1909; Adrian (MI) *Daily Telegram*, November 13, 1912, January 16, 1913.

25. Adrian (MI) *Daily Telegram*, November 14, 1912.

26. Chicago (IL) *Tribune*, April 13, 1907; Kansas City (MO) *Times*, April 13, 1907.

27. Kansas City (MO) *Star*, April 13, 1907.

28. Chicago (IL) *Tribune*, April 13, 1907; Kansas City (MO) *Star*, April 18, 1907.

29. Kansas City (MO) *Star*, April 14, 1907.

30. Detroit (MI) *Free Press*, October 11, 12, 1907.

31. Streator (IL) *Times*, May 2, 1908; Rockford (IL) *Daily Register-Gazette*, December 7, 1907; Wheaton (IL) *Illinoian*, May 1, July 10, 1908; *Dramatic Compositions Copyrighted in the United States, 1870 to 1916.* Washington, DC: Government Printing Office (1918), pp. 864, 1353, 2559.

32. Chicago (IL) *Inter Ocean*, April 17, 1908; Chicago (IL) *Tribune*, April 17, 1908; Joliet (IL) *News*, April 18, 1908; Springfield (IL) *Daily State Register*, February 16, 1911.

33. Wheaton (IL) *Illinoian*, October 9, 1908; *People v. Olson* (1913) *Northeastern Reporter*, vol. 101, p. 521.

34. Chicago (IL) *Inter Ocean*, October 17, 1908; Springfield (IL) *Daily State Register*, February 16, 1911. On Catherine Davy and Frank D. Scalzi, see New York (NY) *Clipper*, November 23, 1907.

35. Joliet Prison Register, Noah Louis Waelchli, inmate no. 1237, Catherine Waelchli, inmate no. 1347, and William Davy, inmate no. 968; Chicago (IL) *Examiner*, December 31, 1908; Wheaton (IL) *Illinoian*, May 21, July 2, 1909; Joliet (IL) *News*, August 4, 1911; Sycamore (IL) *True Republican*, July 29, 1911; *People v. Olson*, pp. 521–522.

36. Joliet Prison Register; US Census Population Schedules, Joliet, IL, 1910; Denver (CO) *Post*, December 1, 1920, February 22, 1924, June 30, 1928.

37. Carlsbad (NM) *Current*, July 3, 1908; Roswell (NM) *Daily Record*, July 27, August 1, 6, 1908; Santa Fe (NM) *New Mexican*, August 5, 1908.

Chapter 12

1. Kansas City (KS) *Globe*, July 6, 1909; Concordia (KS) *Blade-Empire*, June 28, 29, 1909; Hammond (IN) *Lake County Times*, September 16, 1909; Decatur (IN) *Daily Democrat*, June 23, 1910; *Gould's Kansas City Directory*. St. Louis: Gould Directory Co. (1909), p. 832.

2. US Census Population Schedules, Ellis, Kansas, 1910. Anna Davy married Stephen Aldrich on August 16, 1908. See Kansas City (MO) *Star*, August 16, 1908. On Stephen M. Aldrich (1837–1922) see Ellis (KS) *Review-Headlight*, February 24, 1922.

3. Catherine Davy Lipman to Edward G. Robinson, June 15, 1940, Renee Gallagher collection.

4. Springfield (IL) *Daily Illinois State Register*, August 10, 1912; Adrian (MI) *Daily Telegram*, August 30, 1912.

5. Cook County, IL, Marriage Index, February 16, 1909, on www.ancestry.com; US Census Population Schedules, Chicago, IL, 1910; Detroit (MI) *Free Press*, February 10, March 31, April 2, May 2, 1909; Saline (MI) *Observer*, April 8, 1909.

6. Adrian (MI) *Daily Telegram*, October 12, November 11, 1912; John F. Hogan and Alex A. Burkholder, *Fire Strikes the Chicago Stock Yards: A History of Flame and Folly in the Jungle*. Charleston: The History Press (2013), p. 120.

7. Adrian (MI) *Daily Telegram*, August 6, 7, 8, 16, 26, 30, October 12, November 12, 1912, January 15, 1913.

8. Adrian (MI) *Daily Telegram*, November 11, 12, 13, 14, 1912, January 17, 1913.

9. Adrian (MI) *Daily Telegram*, January 14, 15, 16, 17, 1913.

10. Adrian (MI) *Daily Telegram*, February 10, 1913.

11. Adrian (MI) *Daily Telegram*, January 6, 1914.

12. Wakeeney (KS) *Daily News*, December 27, 1912; Hays (KS) *Ellis County News*, November 20, 1915; Davy family genealogical notes of Rovilla Dewey, Renee Gallagher collection.

13. Draft Registration Card, Doc Earle Lighthall, September 12, 1918, on www.familysearch.org; Application for License to Marry, Earl Lighthall, July 7, 1919, on www.familysearch.org; Sharon K. Sanders, "The Lighthall Indian Sanitarium," Cape Girardeau (MO) *Southeast Missourian*, June 7, 2012.

14. US Census Population Schedules, Phoenix, AZ, 1920; Tucson (AZ) *Citizen*, March 4, 1923.

15. Lorenzo D. Walters, *Tombstone's Yesterday*. Tucson: Acme Printing Co. (1928), p. 243.

16. Marriage license of Daniel E. Bandman and Annie Reed, Tucson, AZ, September 30, 1901, on www.ancestry.com; US Census Population Schedules, Goldfield, Nevada, 1910, and Fairbanks, Alaska, 1930; Tucson (AZ) *Daily Star*, June 14, 1902; Bisbee (AZ) *Daily Review*, September 20, 1902; Tucson (AZ) *Citizen*, January 20, 1904; San Francisco (CA) *Call*, March 12, 1911; Sacramento (CA) *Union*, March 19, 1913; Cordova (AK) *Daily Times*, April 18, 1916; Fairbanks (AK) *Daily Alaska Citizen*, December 27, 1919; Anchorage (AK) *Daily Times*, November 20, 1924, November 13, 1926; Napa (CA) *Napa Valley Register*, January 25, 27, 1934.

17. Marriage certificate of Millie Saphronia Meyers and Adna A. Gilbert, Jr, Los Angeles, CA, October 11, 1923, on www.familysearch.org; Sacramento (CA) *Bee*, April 17, 1922.

18. Passenger and Crew Lists, Honolulu, Hawaii, September 27, 1924, January 24, 1925, on www.ancestry.com; Social Security Applications and Claims Index, Margueritte Gilbert, born April 22, 1926, on www.ancestry.com; Honolulu (HI) *Star-Bulletin*, February 25, 1925 (birth of Naomi Louise Gilbert on February 19, 1925); Chanute (KS) *Weekly Tribune*, October 2, 1925.

19. Indiana Marriages, Porter, IN, June 28, 1915, on www.familysearch.org; US Census Population Schedules, Chicago, IL, 1920;

Illinois State Bar Records, David I. Lipman, October 13, 1920; Chicago (IL) *Day Book*, November 21, 1916; Muncie (IN) *Evening Press*, March 23, 1920; Chicago (IL) *Tribune*, May 26, 1949.

20. Los Angeles (CA) *Times*, February 7, May 9, 1927, October 23, 1949, February 22, 1990; Catherine Davy Lipman to Edward G. Robinson, June 15, 1940.

21. Los Angeles (CA) *Times*, March 18, 1923; *Hollywood Filmograph*, n.d., Renee Gallagher collection.

22. Prisoner Index Card, Henry Davy, inmate no. 9753, Michigan State Archives; Los Angeles (CA) *Times*, October 23, 1949; World War I Draft Registration Card, Henry E. Davy, September 1, 1918; Marriage license of Henry E. Davy and Oma Roubenall, Miami, IN, April 16, 1919, on www.familysearch.org. They were divorced in September 1922, and Oma remarried. See marriage license of Oma Davy, Miami, IN, October 30, 1922, on www.familysearch.org.

23. State Census, Manhattan, NY, 1905; New York City Marriage Records, Julius Felix Guilleaume and Jane Davy, April 28, 1910, on www.ancestry.com; US Census Population Schedules, Manhattan Ward 12, New York, NY, 1910.

24. Social Security Death Index, Felix Guilleaume, 1969, on www.familysearch.org; New York City Marriage Records, Julius Felix Guilleaume, April 28, 1910, January 19, 1925, on www.familysearch.org; Chicago (IL) *Tribune*, May 30, 1924.

25. Passenger and Crew Lists, Honolulu, Hawaii, February 5, 1927, on www.ancestry.com.

26. Los Angeles (CA) *Times*, February 5, 1928; Duncan Aikman, *Calamity Jane and the Lady Wildcats*. New York: Henry Holt and Co. (1927), pp. 253–279.

27. US Census Population Schedules, Victorville, CA, 1903; Adna Gilbert, Index to Register of Voters, Laguna Precinct No. 24, Los Angeles, 1934, on www.ancestry.com.

28. Death certificate of Lillie Davy Meyers, Los Angeles, CA, May 11, 1935, on www.familysearch.org; Tucson (AZ) *Daily Star*, June 6, 1934; Los Angeles (CA) *Times*, May 10, 1935.

29. Illinois Death Index, Anora Jane Guilleaume, May 24, 1947, on www.ancestry.com; US Census Population Schedules, Suffolk, NY, 1910, and Los Angeles, CA, 1930, 1940; Kansas City (MO) *Star*, April 23, 1904; Greeley (CO) *Daily Tribune*, September 27, 1944.

30. Catherine Davy Lipman to Edward G. Robinson, June 15, 1940.

31. Death certificate of Henry Esau Davy, Los Angeles, CA, June 29, 1950, on www.familysearch.org; Long Beach (CA) *Independent*, December 29, 30, 31, 1948; Los Angeles (CA) *Times*, July 1, 1950.

32. US Census Population Schedules, Islip, NY, 1920; US Naturalization Records, Mary Alena Davy Sander, February 6, 1952, on www.ancestry.com; New York (NY) *Daily News*, May 23, 1924; Rochester (NY) *Democrat and Chronicle*, August 10, 1924; author interview with Renee Gallagher, April 8, 2020.

33. St. Joseph (MO) *News-Press*, February 1, 1922, February 6, 1932, November 22, 1932; St. Joseph (MO) *Gazette*, December 8, 1965.

34. US Army Transport Service, Passenger Lists, John A. Dewey; US Census Population Schedules, Kansas City, MO, 1920, 1930, 1940; Social Security Death Index, John A. Dewey; all on www.ancestry.com.

35. Kansas City, MO, Marriage Records, Anna L. Wilson, 1948, on www.ancestry.com; Independence (MO) *Examiner*, September 4, 2003; Kansas City (MO) *Times*, September 18, 1937, November 25, 1953, January 23, 1954, January 16, 1960, June 19, 1962; author interview with Letitia J. Plate, granddaughter of Amy Lilly Dewey, October 8, 2020.

36. Author interview with Renee Gallagher, April 8, 2020.

37. Adolph Hartung, MD, Medical report on Catherine Davy Lipman, January 24, 1924, Renee Gallagher collection; certificate of death, Catherine Davy Lipman, May 17, 1957; California Death Index, Saphronia Ratan Newton, August 21, 1957, and Mary Alena Davy, October 14, 1958, on www.familysearch.org.

38. US Census Population Schedules, Chicago, IL, 1930, 1940; William B. Davy to Eleanor Sloan, May 26, 1954, Arizona Historical

Society, Tucson; Death certificate of William B. Davy, July 1, 1955, on www.familysearch.org; Fort Scott (KS) *Daily Tribune-Monitor*, February 26, 1920; Joplin (MO) *Globe*, July 24, 1953.

Epilogue

1. Phoenix (AZ) *Republic*, February 6, 1941; El Paso (TX) *Times*, January 2, 1944; Orangeburg (SC) *Times and Democrat*, May 28, 1980.

2. Los Angeles (CA) *Times*, October 13, 1950; Yuma (AZ) *Daily Sun*, November 10, 1950; Tucson (AZ) *Daily Citizen*, November 13, 1950; New York (NY) *Daily News*, January 7, 23, 1951.

3. New York (NY) *Sun*, October 15, 1899; Aikman, *Calamity Jane and the Lady Wildcats*, p. 256.

4. James H. McClintock, *Arizona, the Youngest State*. Chicago: S. J. Clarke (1916), vol. 2, p. 475.

5. Chicago (IL) *Inter Ocean*, December 21, 1902. The story also fooled this author, who included it in his 2012 book, *When Law Was in the Holster: The Frontier Life of Bob Paul.*

6. Detroit (MI) *Free Press*, January 11, 1903.

7. Hollister (CA) *Enterprise*, July 18, 1874; San Benito (CA) *Advance*, September 5, 1874; Globe (AZ) *Silver Belt*, December 9, 1906; R. Michael Wilson, *Encyclopedia of Stagecoach Robbery in Arizona*. Las Vegas: RaMa Press (2003), p. 219; Jack Ellis Haynes, *Yellowstone Stage Holdups*. Bozeman: Haynes Studios, Inc. (1959), pp. 15–28; William B. Secrest, *The Great Yosemite Holdups*. Fresno: Saga-West Publishing Co. (1968), pp. 6–14, 27–37; Boessenecker, *Shotguns and Stagecoaches*, p. xvii.

8. Phoenix (AZ) *Arizona Republic*, August 7, 1966.

9. US Census Population Schedules, Dripping Spring, AZ, 1930 and 1940; Tucson (AZ) *Daily Star*, September 22, 1974; Clara T. Woody and Milton L. Schwartz, *Globe, Arizona*. Tucson: Arizona Historical Society (1977), pp. 236–238.

10. Death certificate of Pearl Bywater, December 28, 1955, on www.ancestry.com; Prescott (AZ) *Weekly Journal-Miner,* December 28, 1892, March 30, 1898; Phoenix (AZ) *Arizona Republic,* August 19, December 30, 1955.

11. "The Surprising Story of America's Most Famous Female Stagecoach Robber," *Time,* November 21, 2016.

Index

Page numbers in *italics* indicate illustrations.

Y